The Fear & Anxiety Solution

Friedemann Schaub, MD, PhD

The Fear & Anxiety Solution

A Breakthrough Process for Healing and Empowerment with Your Subconscious Mind

Sounds True, Inc.
Boulder, CO 80306

Published 2012

Book design by Karen Polaski
Cover by Dean Olson

Printed in Canada

Library of Congress Cataloging-in-Publication Data

Schaub, Friedemann.
The fear and anxiety solution : a breakthrough process for healing and empowerment with your subconscious mind / Friedemann Schaub.
p. cm.
Includes bibliographical references and index.
ISBN 978-1-60407-856-5
1. Self-actualization (Psychology) 2. Fear. 3. Anxiety. I. Title.
BF637.S4S3423 2012
152.4'6—dc23
2012007172

eBook ISBN 978-1-60407-916-6

10 9 8 7 6 5 4 3

This book is dedicated to my parents,
Drs. Eva and Kurt Schaub.

Contents

Introduction

WHILE I WAS finishing this book, both my parents passed away—my mother less than four months after my father. One night, a few days after my mom's funeral, I woke up drenched in a cold sweat, gasping for air, and completely overwhelmed by a flood of emotions. My mind was spinning, and it took me a while to comprehend that I was having a panic attack. Although the loss of my parents had certainly taken an emotional toll on me, I hadn't expected to tumble into a state of uncontrollable anxiety. As I gradually slowed my breathing, I noticed from deep within a small but undeniable voice asking, "What am I going to do? Who will take care of me? Who will make sure I'm safe?"

I knew these fearful thoughts didn't come from my conscious adult mind. Logically, there was no reason for me to be worried. I'd been independent of my parents' support for the past twenty years. But I also knew that logic and reasoning weren't nearly enough to address this panic attack, because the source of this fearful voice came from a deeper place: my subconscious mind. So I applied some of the principles and methods of this book to consciously work with my subconscious mind, and within a matter of minutes, I felt much calmer and more at ease. Although I miss my parents and still grieve the loss, the panic I felt that night never returned.

THE POWER OF THE MIND

You may wonder what this conscious-subconscious approach to working through fear and anxiety is all about and why or how I developed it. Well, it actually *did* start with my parents. Both were family doctors in the small town of Lauterbach, located in the middle of the beautiful Black Forest in Germany. I always admired my parents' dedication to their patients, many of whom they'd known since birth. They took the time to listen to their patients and then carefully considered their entire story—including their living situations, mental and emotional states, and histories—when evaluating the diagnosis and treatment plans. My parents taught me to view every person as a whole human being and not just as his or her symptoms or illness.

Of all my parents' routine treatments, one fascinated me the most. Whenever children came to their practice with multiple warts on their hands or feet, my mother or father would pull out a massive bottle that contained some mysterious, colorful fluid. With great care, they'd fill a small vial with that potion and give it to the children, telling them to use a little brush to apply this medicine to their warts three times a day. "If you do this every day," they said, "at exactly the same time, your warts will disappear in a few weeks." The success rate of this treatment was astonishing.

However, when it was my turn to have my warts treated, my father didn't pull out the magic bottle. Instead he revealed to me that the liquid was only water with food coloring. "All you need is to believe that the warts will disappear, and they will," he explained. And so they did. The fact that we can make warts, which are caused by a virus, quickly disappear by simply believing they will, was for me the first compelling and influential demonstration of the power of the mind.

Yet it was a completely different demonstration of the power of our minds that motivated me years later to develop the breakthrough process for fear and anxiety described in this book. During a practicum in the local hospital, which was a part of my first year in medical school, I met an elderly farmer who'd been admitted with a broken leg. Despite a lifetime of hard physical labor, he had the constitution and vigor of a much younger man and was proud that this was the first time he had seen a hospital from the inside. One afternoon he confided to me that he was extremely worried about the upcoming surgery to set his leg. "Somehow I just know that if the doctors operate on me, I will die," he said. I reassured him that this was a simple routine procedure, that there was nothing to worry about, and that everything would go as planned, without any complications. And it did.

The next morning the farmer was found dead in his hospital bed. Since there was no autopsy done, it remains unclear what caused his death. I often wondered whether his anxiety played a part in his unexpected death. Could his system have shut down because the physical stress of the operation and the emotional stress of his fears were too much for him to bear?

THE WISDOM OF THE CELLS

After I became a physician, I worked in a huge cardiology unit at the University of Munich, Germany. Most of the patients I dealt with were suffering from strokes or heart attacks. Although an increasing number of studies have demonstrated how stress and anxiety could promote cardiovascular diseases, the emotional challenges of our patients were neither investigated nor addressed in the treatment plans. The focus was on treating the physical symptoms and controlling the common risk factors, such as high blood pressure, nicotine consumption, excessive weight, and elevated cholesterol levels—all of which can result from chronic stress. I often wanted to sit down with my patients and talk about their lives and how their illnesses were impacting them both mentally and emotionally. However, as is common in big hospitals, we could spend only ten to fifteen minutes per day with each patient—obviously not enough time to really get to know the people who faithfully put their lives in our hands.

After several years, the stress of my high-powered job and my growing dissatisfaction with the rather "mechanical" healing approach of allopathic medicine started to drain me. I decided to take a break and accepted a scholarship for a postdoctoral research position at the University of Washington in Seattle, which, after four years, gave me a PhD in molecular biology. My research focused on *apoptosis,* or programmed cell death, which describes the phenomenon in which cells sacrifice themselves for the greater good of the whole organism. This is not a rare event. Every day, about 50 billion cells in our body "decide" to terminate their existence so that the balance of the system remains stable.[1, 2]

Being immersed in the world of basic research significantly changed my perspective on human potential. As a physician, I was trained to view the body as rather fragile and prone to failure. Science, however, illuminated a simple fact that I hadn't fully realized until then: each and every cell of our bodies has an intelligence and sheer unlimited potential to grow, adapt, and heal in ways that are still far too complex for us to fully comprehend. The ability of our body to maintain trillions of cells in a delicate equilibrium of growth, healing, and death is truly ingenious and suggests that there is a regulating consciousness that connects and directs all of our cells. For me, the next logical questions were what is this regulating consciousness, and how can we access and work with it to utilize our innate healing potential as effectively as possible?

A NEW PERSPECTIVE ON HEALTH AND HEALING

By then, I knew I wouldn't find the answers to these questions in test tubes or the red-eyed Fischer rats that had been my research patients. At the same time, two occurrences significantly influenced my life.

First, I stumbled into a yoga and meditation class, which focused on the subconscious mind. Soon I noticed how the meditations and exercises relaxed and recharged my mind and my body more quickly than anything I had done before. As I deepened my yoga practice, I realized that during the classes I was able to somehow avert oncoming colds or hay-fever outbreaks by simply focusing my mind on the meaning of yoga—the union of mind, body, and spirit.

Second, I discovered Dr. Paul Tournier's book *Zu Hoeren Koennen (A Listening Ear)* on my bookshelf, where it had been collecting dust since it had been given to me by a close friend fifteen years earlier. As early as the 1940s, Tournier, a Swiss physician, claimed that allopathic medicine failed to consider the wholeness of the human being, which, he said, consists of body, mind, and spirit. Much ahead of his time, Tournier combined medicine and counseling in his practice and frequently invited his patients to his home to sit with him by the fireplace. In this book, he described how his patients, when given the time and space to share the thoughts, feelings, and stories behind their physical challenges, started to relax, open up, and enter into a healing state. Tournier found that these conversations often seemed to accomplish more than the medicine he had prescribed to them.

Having had the privilege of witnessing many similar healing openings in my own practice over the years, I believe that when people have the opportunity to realize and speak their truths, their minds, bodies, and spirits start to realign, enabling them to access their true healing potential.

The longer I studied the mind-body-spirit connection, the more I realized my traditional perspective on health and healing was undergoing a serious transformation. Healing isn't supposed to be a battle between good and evil or health and disease, where we doctors sweep in like knights in shining armor equipped with powerful and often deadly weapons, determined to "win" at any cost. And the patient isn't meant to be the battlefield, staying passive and "patient," still until the war is over.

I certainly appreciate how medicine has benefitted and improved our lives in so many ways. And I have gratefully taken my share of pain medication or antibiotics and will continue to do so when necessary. However, the current paradigm of allopathic medicine doesn't encourage us to trust or utilize our own innate wisdom and healing potential. Instead it fosters a sense of dependency, disempowerment, and fear of illness. In new mind-body-spirit healing perspectives, illness is not the enemy of health, but an integral component of a powerful organic system, which has evolved throughout hundreds of thousands of years. The primary purpose of illness is to alert us that we are, on some level, distressed and out of balance. To heal and regain our natural state of wholeness—the alignment of mind, body, and spirit—we need to identify and address the deeper root causes of this stress and imbalance. Even more important, we must learn how to take advantage of our innate healing powers.

HEALING EMOTIONS

What is the connecting force—the nexus where mind, body, and spirit meet? And how can we consciously access and leverage this force to promote health and accelerate the healing process?

The key is our subconscious mind—and in particular our emotions, which have the potential to reach every cell of our bodies. How? Emotions prompt the release of neurotransmitters, small peptides that flow through our bodies until they land and dock on the surface of a cell. Like keys opening locks, they can activate certain genes, trigger protein production, stimulate the release of endocrines and hormones, and much more. Studies have shown that positive emotions can boost the immune system, decrease the symptoms of diabetes, and improve heart conditions.[3, 4] On the other hand, negative emotions, such as stress, anxiety, and depression, have the opposite effects and can cause serious health problems.[5, 6]

So to promote health and healing, we need to work with our subconscious minds and stay in charge of our emotions, right? Well, here lies the issue. How many of us have felt overwhelmed by our emotions, especially by fear and anxiety, which can make us feel anything else but in charge? How many of us would rather avoid our emotions than become all worked up by them? And truthfully, how many of us trust our subconscious mind or know how to better understand it?

On the one hand, our subconscious minds are the keys to accessing our innate healing potential. On the other hand, that same subconscious creates emotions, such as fear and anxiety, that damage our health and well-being. Is there a disconnect within the subconscious? No, but there is a disconnect between our conscious and subconscious minds. We usually interpret emotions, especially those such as fear and anxiety that we deem "negative," as flaws and weaknesses that need to be overcome, managed, or suppressed rather than understanding them to be the subconscious mind's means of communicating with us. Consequently "negative" emotions don't get adequately addressed; instead, they accumulate in our subconscious and eventually cause greater emotional and physical challenges. In other words, the real problem is that we don't know how to listen or relate to our subconscious, let alone consciously guide and work with it.

Realizing the powerful healing opportunities a conscious-subconscious collaboration could provide, I extensively studied mind-activating modalities such as Neuro-Linguistic Programming (NLP), Time Line Therapy®, and clinical hypnotherapy. In my practice, I developed a "breakthrough and empowerment program" that blends these methods with my knowledge of medicine and science to help people learn to understand, overcome, and utilize the most challenging of all emotions—fear and anxiety.

This book, which is based on my program, approaches fear and anxiety not as problems or disorders, but as symptoms of and information from your subconscious mind when you're out of balance and alignment with yourself. As you embark on this journey of healing, empowerment, and self-awareness, the processes and tools of each chapter will show you how to bridge the gap between your conscious and your subconscious mind. They allow you to pinpoint and understand the root causes and deeper meanings of your fear and anxiety, provide you with the leverage needed to release emotional blocks from the past, and help you turn up your inner light, so that you can shine more of who you truly are out into the world.

Even more important than the processes and tools you will learn to use is what you discover about yourself and your untapped potential. Harnessing this potential is not about suppressing strong forces such as fear and anxiety, but transforming them into powerful allies, messengers, and healing catalysts that lead to greater confidence, self-worth, and wholeness. The true healer is within you.

PART I

Awareness

CHAPTER I

An Overview of Fear and Anxiety

I'M SITTING AT the desk, and my heart is pounding. My chest is tight, and I have a hard time breathing. My mind races so fast that my thoughts appear as a blur. I know if I don't calm down now, I'll look terrible at our weekly work meeting. What if I freeze again in front of my peers? Why do I feel so stressed about that? Why do I care so much what others think of me? Nobody else seems to have this problem. What's wrong with me?" Finally Steve, my client, takes a breath and says, "I think I have an anxiety problem. How can I get rid of it and be my normal self again?"

Anxiety is the epidemic of the twenty-first century. According to the National Institute of Mental Health, about 20 percent of American adults eighteen years and older are diagnosed with anxiety disorder, which translates to more than fifty million adults.[1]

In this book, I use the terms *fear* and *anxiety* interchangeably and often simultaneously, even though these terms have slightly different meanings. Fear is commonly associated with specific situations and concrete known (or, often, imagined) threats, whereas anxiety is a vague sense that something dangerous might occur in the future. In my experience, people are often more comfortable with calling themselves anxious rather than fearful and vice versa, largely due to the personal associations they have with one word or the other. Because of the similarities in the ways fear and anxiety are created, the responses they produce, and the principles they follow, it seems appropriate to address them together.

WHAT DO FEAR AND ANXIETY FEEL LIKE?

Fear and anxiety are primarily perceived as unpleasant internal sensations that signal potential danger: your heart beats faster, your breath shortens, your muscles tighten, your hands sweat, the hairs on your body may stand up, and you might start shaking from head to toe. Reactions can range from apprehension to a full-blown panic attack. Fear and anxiety can appear very abruptly and are often overwhelming.

For example, you may be feeling perfectly peaceful on your way to work, when suddenly you wonder whether you've forgotten to turn off the iron at home. The fear hits when you start thinking of all the awful consequences this situation might create. Or, one week before a big presentation at work, the vague undercurrent of anxiety you've been feeling noticeably increases. Or, you wake in the morning and anxiety immediately appears, seemingly out of nowhere, ready to take control of your day. It's as if these emotions happen *to* you, leaving you feeling powerless and out of control.

Commonly, it is not the direct, immediate threat most people worry about, but instead it is the possibility that something awful might happen in the future. You may ask yourself, "What if the iron sets my home on fire and I lose all of my possessions?" What if you draw a blank and forget your lines during your speech? Or, in regard to the free-floating anxiety that appears seemingly out of the blue, what if you fall prey to something that you aren't even able to foresee right now?

When you stop and think about it, you may be able to rationally address the reasons for your anxiety. If you've left the iron on, it's highly unlikely that it will set anything on fire—and you can always call your neighbors to check that your house isn't ablaze. If you're afraid of forgetting your lines while delivering your presentation, you know you can consult your notes as you're speaking. In the case of the unknown fear, you can tell yourself that, logically, there's nothing you can do if you don't know what the fear is about. However, for most people this analytical approach provides only brief relief; soon the next wave of anxiety "attacks," which shows that anxiety isn't a rational problem.

WHEN DO FEAR AND ANXIETY BECOME A PROBLEM?

The point where fear and anxiety start to interfere with our abilities to function in our lives certainly varies from person to person; however, there are clear indications when these emotions are becoming serious challenges and need to be addressed. Some of these are:

- Frequently feeling overwhelmed and worried
- Obsessive thinking, overanalyzing, and ruminating about the worst-case scenario
- Overplanning and trying to control others and/or outside circumstances
- Growing difficulties with work and relationships due to insecurity, doubt, and self-sabotaging behavior
- Feeling paralyzed and stuck because of an inability to make decisions or move forward
- Seeking distraction and instant gratification in addictive behaviors such as gambling, eating, sex, or work
- Obsessive-compulsive behavior
- Self-medication with alcohol, nicotine, or other drugs
- Physical symptoms such as insomnia, high blood pressure, irregular heartbeat, chronic pain, and weight fluctuation

What can you do? You've all seen the commercials. The setting: a lively party with many happy, good-looking people. The problem: a young man standing alone—his face tense, his expression worried—and isolated from all the others, who are having such a good time. A narrator's comforting voice says that you've probably felt that way before, too. And you think, "Of course I have—whenever I'm about to meet new people, or when I need to talk to my in-laws, or when I try to make a good impression at my boss's party." The soothing voice then says that a newly developed antianxiety medication can take care of your fear, depression, and isolation. The change is clearly demonstrated by the young man, who is now engaging in conversations, laughing, and seems very comfortable with himself. If a little pill can so easily solve your anxiety problem, doesn't it make sense to take it?

Designed to relieve the symptoms of fear and anxiety, antianxiety medications are some of the most prescribed drugs in the United States.[2] Every year people spend billions of dollars to escape these "unproductive and unacceptable" feelings with the help of pharmaceutical products. These drugs are so widely used that residues have even been detected in our drinking water.[3]

On our path through life, fear and anxiety can appear as a wall, and all our efforts to overcome these emotions can feel as though we're trying to tear down that wall with a toothpick. Antianxiety drugs can then feel like the sledgehammer that is able to break down the wall. But are we treating the cause or the symptoms? In other words, is anxiety a physiological/biochemical problem that needs to be resolved medically, or does it have deeper root causes and meanings that need to be addressed and understood in order for us to heal and grow?

THE PURPOSE OF EMOTIONS

You may have experienced your emotions, in particular fear and anxiety, as random, overwhelming, even paralyzing and utterly uncontrollable. Maybe you've felt stuck, discouraged, or frustrated with yourself, because, unlike you, all the people around you seem to have it together. Wouldn't your life be much better if you could run it by logic and reason? And wouldn't it be best if you could just turn your emotions off?

Generally speaking, our modern society has little room and patience for feelings. Reason and logic are far more accepted and valued than sensitivity and emotions. However, we need emotions for guidance and to bring meaning to our lives. They provide us with important information about our likes and dislikes, our strengths and weaknesses, and the value of our actions and choices. Every day, emotions have a significantly larger impact than facts and reasoning on the choices we make and how we experience our world. Isn't it true that the moments we remember and cherish the most are those we associate with the strongest feelings?

Filmmaker Rick Ray noticed a paradox while traveling through India and other parts of the world to produce his documentary *10 Questions for the Dalai Lama.* The poorest people were frequently happier than those who seemed to be very prosperous. Ray encountered more smiles from those living in the slums than from the people who were privileged with a rather lavish lifestyle. Logically, it would seem that those suffering from poverty face the immediate danger of being without food and shelter; therefore, they have more reason to be anxious and fearful. But in reality, having very little can also mean that someone has very little to lose and more appreciation for the small joys in life.

Conversely, people who have spent most of their time and energy accumulating wealth or reaching certain external goals might identify too much with these aspects of their lives. As a result, their attachment to these possessions and achievements increases—as does the fear of losing them, which would also mean losing themselves. I am not suggesting that disposing of your goods and practicing an ascetic lifestyle will resolve your fear and anxiety and bring everlasting happiness. These observations simply underline that emotions, not facts or outer circumstances, determine our life experience.

The natural reaction to so-called negative emotions such as fear and anxiety is to try to get rid of them quickly because they feel uncomfortable and disempowering. But true healing is not about fixing or getting rid of a problem. Healing is about remembering and reinstating our wholeness. In this sense, negative emotions provide us with the opportunity to find and regain our wholeness. When we discover and understand their deeper meaning, they become powerful catalysts that lead us to our greater, self-empowered, authentic selves. After all, if fear and anxiety didn't have an important function, wouldn't evolution have eliminated them by now?

HOW DO YOU GET STUCK IN THE FIRST PLACE?

As you probably know firsthand, fear and anxiety can easily make you feel trapped and disempowered. However, it is not really the emotions that keep us stuck, but the ways we respond to them. Usually we don't know what to do, we resist change, or we identify with the problem. Let's look at these three issues further.

We don't know what to do. When we feel hungry, we know it's time to eat. When we feel thirsty, we know it's time to drink. When we feel tired, we know it's time to rest. We understand the meaning of these sensations, and we know how to address them so they disappear. But what do we do when we feel anxious? We look for potential danger or go into the "what if" mind-set, preparing to fight, flee, or hide. We switch to fight-flight-or-freeze mode, because we often interpret anxiety as a sign that there is either something threatening outside of us or something wrong with us internally. By interpreting anxiety this way, we give greater validation to the feeling and freak ourselves out, which further fuels the emotion rather than helping us to understand its real meaning and address it appropriately.

We resist change. One of the most common fears is the fear of change, which makes *changing* fear and anxiety appear even more challenging. Change usually entails leaving our comfort zone, which is why we perceive it as a somewhat uncomfortable risk. Comfort zones are created by our mind so that we can experience and engage with different aspects of our lives from a place of safety, familiarity, and control. The internal boundaries of a comfort zone are established by mental, emotional, and behavioral patterns and can be defined by the radius of our personal space, the emotional distance we keep, or by the degree to which we interact with our environment.

Our comfort zones differ greatly. Each one depends on how we feel about ourselves within the context of each aspect of our lives. For example, our work-related comfort zone may appear small and rigid in comparison to the wider and more flexible comfort zone we share with our loved ones or establish during a vacation. Comfort zones are meant to be temporary and their boundaries flexible. As we're growing and expanding and our beliefs and mental programs are shifting, we extend the boundaries of our comfort zones to adjust to whom we're becoming.

In contrast with a healthy comfort zone, an anxiety-driven one tends to work in the opposite way. Its size decreases, and its boundaries become rigid walls. Anxiety morphs comfort zones into protection zones that shield us from that which makes us fearful and anxious. Our lives shrink as we perceive an increasing number of situations and people as unsafe and, therefore, something we must avoid.

At some point, we feel as though we're no longer choosing the size of our comfort zones. Instead, our comfort zones control us and the size of our lives. A constricted comfort zone can be one of the greatest obstacles between us and positive change. The longer we stay in that constricted zone, the more we avoid and resist leaving it, even if we aren't at all comfortable in it anymore.

We identify with the problem. Fear and anxiety are especially problematic when they become a part of our identity. The moment we refer to ourselves as an anxious person or a worrier, we know that we've started to identify ourselves with these emotions. Anxiety becomes our emotional default setting, gradually restricting our choices and actions. This identification with the problem limits our self-awareness, which can diminish our ability to access our true potential to change, grow, and succeed. Eventually, we may even find it impossible to imagine life without anxiety. As a result, we believe that the best we can hope for—besides making it through the day alive and possibly unharmed—is to reduce the intensity of the feeling.

Sound familiar? The question is, what can we do to end our struggles with fear and anxiety?

HOW AND WHERE TO BEGIN

This book is designed to be a personal guide to inner peace and self-empowerment. All you need for this process to work is the willingness to accept that fear and anxiety are not happening to you; you're creating them inside yourself. Believe it or not, that's good news, because if you create your emotions, you can also uncreate them.

To help you on your healing journey, you have the most powerful tool at your disposal—your mind. After all, it was your mind that created your emotions in the first place. Your mind has the capacity to transform the wall of anxiety or fear into an open gate that leads to a place of new opportunities and unlimited possibilities. When you use your mind, getting better is no longer just about getting rid of these fears and anxieties. Instead, you can find and attend to their root causes, appreciate their true purpose, and embrace the wisdom and the power at their core.

As you go through this book's highly experiential step-by-step process, you will gain the insights, flexibility, and strength you need to break through fear and anxiety. Each chapter provides you with practical and effective tools and methods to help you access your untapped potential and to create greater confidence, inner peace, and success. Since the chapters build on each other and form a cohesive program, I recommend working through this book sequentially to get the maximum benefit. However, you won't have to wait until the end of this program to experience significant changes; they will occur along the way. Choose your own pace for this healing journey. Perhaps you'll want to move rather quickly through the book to keep your positive momentum going. Or you may find some of the chapters especially valuable and want to take more time to practice the tools and solidify the results you have gained before moving on to the next step. Just keep in mind that the benefits of this book increase exponentially as you move further along in the program, and by the time you've completed it, the changes you've made will have transformed your life. So make a commitment to yourself today: commit to taking advantage of this program and changing your life.

Exciting, right? OK, you may feel some apprehension and even anxiety after reading this introduction. You may wonder, "What if I'm not ready? Or what if I'm ready but still fail? What if this is my last chance and I'm unable to use it? If I let go of fear or anxiety, what if I don't like the person I become? Or what if I'm nothing—what if I'm empty without my fear?"

These are all valid questions that either will be answered in the course of this book or will feel completely irrelevant by the time you finish this process. Keep these questions somewhere in a corner of your mind, but remember: if our dreams and aspirations don't scare us at least a little, they're not big enough.

CHAPTER 2

The Principles of Change

MANY BOOKS HAVE been written about releasing fear and anxiety, finding more inner peace, and increasing confidence. So what's unique about this one?

The insights and processes I share in this book address fear and anxiety from all the aspects and perspectives of your mind: the conscious mind (your intellectual and analytical capabilities), the subconscious mind (your emotions, memories, beliefs), and your higher consciousness, which represents the core of your being and goes beyond your thoughts, your emotions, or your body. Your higher consciousness is strongly linked to your true essence, which some may refer to as your spirit or your soul. To work with this part of your mind, you don't need to be spiritual or subscribe to any religious belief. And even if you've never contemplated the existence of a higher consciousness, you'll find that it's quite easy and natural to connect with this part of yourself.

In my experience, all three aspects of our mind need to be addressed to break through fear and anxiety, get unstuck, and create profound and permanent change on the mental, emotional, energetic, and physical levels. The good news is that when you're working with all these aspects, you move forward and change much faster than if you work with just one or two levels of your mind—and your healing is more complete. You gain a new foundation of confidence and trust in yourself to live and express who you truly are—a self-empowered, self-reliant individual.

Sounds great, but how do you leverage the powers of your conscious mind, subconscious mind, and higher consciousness to achieve optimal results?

This is where the five principles of change come in. Following these principles enables you to utilize the powers of your entire mind and consciousness to address and heal the deeper root causes of your anxiety-related challenges. The principles are *awareness, flexibility, choice, actualization,* and *readjustment.* They are all incorporated into the exercises, tools, and processes throughout the book and provide you with a structured, logical pathway into the wisdom and healing power of fear and anxiety and help you reclaim your innate potential to change, heal, grow, and thrive.

AWARENESS

Have you ever become lost on a hike or while visiting a new city? If so, you can probably appreciate how useful a map is. A map shows you how you became lost and how you can get yourself back on track. Fear and anxiety can appear as unfriendly territories in which you somehow became lost and are unable to find your way out of. These emotions can seem so irrational and erratic that you experience them as something outside of you, your understanding, and your control.

Bill, a client of mine, is a good example of someone who got lost in these emotions. He was a very successful executive who had extremely high expectations of himself. As soon as he'd succeeded at one challenge, he was already focusing on the next, larger one. While he considered taking a lucrative offer from another company, he received a promotion from his current employer that went beyond his wildest expectations. Bill truly felt he'd arrived. He was in his early forties and had reached all the goals he'd set out for himself.

Then something happened that he didn't expect. At one of Bill's first business presentations in his new role, he completely blanked out in front of his peers and employees. At first he blamed his lapse on lack of sleep or something he'd eaten. However, after experiencing two similar embarrassing episodes during other talks, he became seriously concerned. Something was not right. His physical check-up turned out to be completely normal, and his doctor suggested that he probably had suffered panic attacks.

This diagnosis came as a shock to Bill. "Anxiety? Me? Why now?" he thought. It didn't make any sense because just a few months earlier he had single-handedly taken on and solved the biggest challenge his company ever faced. And during that demanding time, he had felt completely calm and confident. So what had changed, and why now? Not knowing made him feel even more stressed and insecure. Not knowing when the next panic attack might happen or how much worse this anxiety could get was as difficult to endure as not knowing what to do about it.

One of the first steps I worked on with Bill was helping him become aware of how his mind worked and how he created fear and anxiety. He quickly realized that his new position and the way he acquired it had triggered his anxiety. In the past, he'd always rightfully earned any success or promotion through hard work and 120-percent commitment. But this time he felt he had been ushered into the new position by his boss, the CEO, who didn't want to lose him to another company. A part of Bill subconsciously had started to feel insecure and to believe that he now was at the mercy of his boss and could no longer rely solely on his own efforts and contributions. What if he should fall from grace one day? Without consciously noticing he'd done so, he'd given his power to someone else.

Bill became aware of a deep-seated belief of not being good enough, which was rooted in his childhood. This insecurity was a life-long subconscious driving force for him. By overachieving, he'd been constantly trying to outrun the part of himself that suffered from feeling unworthy. He'd hoped through his great accomplishments to eventually establish a new, confident identity. But no matter how impressive his successes, none of them was ever good enough. When Bill felt championed by his CEO, the fear of being found out as a fraud surged from the depth of his subconscious to the surface and created these seemingly irrational panic attacks.

After Bill became aware of the inner map of his emotions and beliefs and how certain people and events of the past had led to limiting subconscious programs and patterns, he felt immensely relieved. The anxiety no longer appeared like an ominous beast that could jump him at any time. After all, we can solve a problem only if we're aware that we have one and how it became one. Knowing the deeper reasons and root causes of his fears gave Bill the comforting awareness that, from then on, he could proactively take steps to overcome these anxieties and insecurities, build real confidence based on who he was as a person, and reclaim his power.

A word of caution: becoming aware of how and why you've been dealing with patterns of fear and anxiety is not about blaming yourself for having created or held onto such negative emotions. Nor is it about blaming others, including your parents, siblings, or teachers. Many situations and events in your past might explain why you're prone to feeling fear and anxiety. Although you may have seen yourself as a victim of past circumstances, you do not need to identify yourself as a victim for the rest of your life. Instead, you have an opportunity to have more understanding and compassion for yourself, while at the same time owning your emotions and your beliefs.

As you continue your healing journey with this book as your guide, you will become aware of your inner map and recognize how and why you create fear and anxiety and how to move and evolve beyond these perceived blocks.

FLEXIBILITY

Flexibility is one of the most important qualities any being possesses to ensure its survival. Evolution is based on the principle of "the survival of the fittest," meaning the survival of those who can adapt to the demands of an ever-changing environment. This principle could just as well be called "the survival of the most flexible." Flexibility is an innate ability that we all make use of from the earliest stages of our development. At the time when we were the most physically flexible, as infants and toddlers, our mental and emotional fluidity was one of our strongest attributes, one we depended on every day. This flexibility allowed us to adjust from comfortably floating inside the womb to dealing with gravity, feeding schedules, day and night, and having to communicate our needs to those giants around us.

Someone once said that from the time of birth to the time we take the first unsteady steps, we pass through a million years of evolution. That's adaptability, don't you think? Not that we didn't complain about it, but we never gave up. We tried to walk until we fell, then we got up and tried again, with some adjustments. But no matter how far we got, we didn't become discouraged or defeated. When and why do we lose or forget the power of this amazing flexibility?

One reason is the ongoing conflict between exploring who we are and complying with the demands of society to integrate and fit into its structure. As we grow up, meeting expectations and conforming to various rules and regulations appear increasingly important to ensuring success and our rightful place in society. Many of us eventually stop wondering whether our decisions and opinions are still based upon who we are and what we really want or believe in. We can gradually become entangled in a rather rigid internal and external framework of pressures, obligations, and conditional acceptance of ourselves. This imposed reality can become *our* reality and leave us little room to think or act in a flexible, self-empowered manner. At some point, it may simply feel more comfortable and familiar to tread in the old grooves, stay in a rut, and tell ourselves that it's too late to change and make a difference in our lives. Complacency destroys flexibility. But by the mere fact that you're holding this book in your hands, you've proven to yourself that your desire to change and grow is greater than the need to remain in a continuously shrinking comfort zone. In other words, your ability to be flexible is still alive and well.

When I was five years old, I felt the dire consequences of others being inflexible. My parents took me shopping in Stuttgart, the big city in our region of Germany. It felt light years away from the small town where I grew up. At that age, my enthusiasm for shopping was nonexistent, and while my parents became more and more excited by the fascinating variety of treasures that was available, I roamed the aisles, scouring the shelves to find anything that might spark my interest.

All of a sudden I realized I was alone. My parents were nowhere in sight. I ran through the maze of aisles trying to remember where I'd started, but everything looked completely unfamiliar and more and more daunting. I was lost. I panicked and started to cry. What if I never found my parents again? What if I never got back home?

Finally a friendly store employee noticed me. She came up to me and asked, "Are you lost?"

I could only nod my little head.

"What's your name?"

Sniffling and sobbing at the same time, I exploded, "I am Friedemann Julius Walter Schaub."

All my savior could understand was *Walter*, because *Friedemann* is a very unusual name even in Germany.

She went to her microphone and announced, "Little Walter, wearing a gray poncho, is looking for his parents." Then she reassured me that my parents would come to pick me up any minute.

A minute or two passed, and many more followed, without my parents showing up. I don't really remember what I was thinking at that point, but I'm sure it wasn't uplifting.

In the meantime, my mom and my dad had separated to pursue their own shopping agendas. For some reason, each of them believed that I was with the other one (or at least that's what they told me later). So when they heard the announcement for the third time, they both thought that poor Walter must be really scared. They wondered what was wrong with his parents and why they weren't looking for him. Then at some point, my mom realized that "little Walter" was her son and that she and my father were those "terrible" parents who didn't pick him up. With a bit more flexibility in their thinking, they would have remembered my middle name and that I was wearing a gray poncho.

But who am I to talk? I have vast experience with my own lack of flexibility. I have remained stuck in comfortable relationships partly because I didn't believe that I was good enough to find real love. For many years, I held onto the belief that taking a day off during the working week meant that people were lazy, unemployed, or both. When I actually had a day off, I often felt uncomfortable leaving the house because I thought I might be seen by somebody who knew me and who naturally (I assumed) would believe that I had lost my job or that I was slacking off. So instead of doing something fun, I preferred to stay at home and work in my office. While I told myself that this belief was just a good dose of the German work ethic, I was simply too inflexible to realize that I was stuck in my own insecurities.

Lack of flexibility is one of the biggest obstacles you face when dealing with fear and anxiety, because it limits your options for perceiving and responding to internal or external stimuli and thus keeps you stuck. For example, whenever you see your boss in the hallway, you become nervous. As soon as you think about a specific event in the past or future, anxiety overwhelms you. Or when you face a new task, you immediately feel defeated and that you're not good enough. Even at times when everything is calm and stable, you wonder, "Do I still have anxiety? Do I still worry?" Once your mind becomes rigid, you react automatically, seemingly without choice and power.

When you believe that you're an anxious and insecure person or that the world is a scary and unfriendly place, you subconsciously look for evidence to corroborate these limiting ideas. This is why limiting beliefs eventually become self-fulfilling prophecies; sooner or later, your reality will match your beliefs. You feel trapped. But all you need is a greater degree of flexibility in your thinking and feeling to reclaim your power and freedom.

In yoga there is a saying: "The age of a person is not determined by his years but by his flexibility." This saying applies to more than just physical agility; it applies to emotional and mental agility, as well. With a flexible mind, you can unmask and look beyond the assumptions and projections you've (mis)taken as reality. You're open to seeing yourself and the situations you're dealing with from various angles, analyzing the details, and then taking another look at the bigger picture or from a higher perspective. Flexibility increases your range of emotional and mental responses, allows you to move more quickly through feelings that are not supportive, and empowers you to consciously see and take advantage of the opportunities in every situation. You can find answers in problems, understanding in confusion, and possibilities in limitations. Thus, flexibility is crucial not only to survival but to thriving and experiencing happiness.

It's never too late to start improving your mental and emotional flexibility. So let's start rewinding the clock to those early years when you were extremely flexible!

CHOICE

On your journey from fear and anxiety to internal peace and self-empowerment, awareness provides the map of your inner territory. Flexibility allows you to analyze your position from various angles and points of view and to identify alternative routes. However, increased awareness and flexibility are not enough to gain the momentum to move forward. You can stare at a map for a long time and examine all the different options and possibilities, but you don't get anywhere unless you choose your destination—and which route you want to take to reach it. Only the act of choosing enables you to be truly free and self-empowered.

Making a choice can be one of the greatest yet most difficult steps to take. It is a great step because the moment you consciously choose, you're moving from the passenger's seat to the driver's seat, from the "effect" side of the equation to the "cause" side. You're reclaiming your right to create your own reality. Making a choice can be difficult because it often leads to change, and as you know, change can be scary. What if you make the wrong choice? What if you don't have what it takes to change?

Every choice is also a statement about who you are and makes you take responsibility for your actions and their outcome. You can no longer blame others. Although making a choice appears like a big step, the truth is, you always choose. Even when you're remaining stuck, continuing as a passenger in your life, you're making a choice, although it may appear to you that you're powerless.

You might be thinking, "Easy for him to say. I'm really stuck and trapped here, and I'm certainly not choosing it." I completely understand what you're feeling, because I was there myself. I felt trapped during my residency at a high-powered cardiology department, mainly because I let the expectations and pressures from my superiors get to me. I often woke up at night wondering how I could endure the next thirty years of working under conditions I really had started to dislike. But because I'd already invested so much time and energy in that career and couldn't imagine any alternatives, I was afraid to let it all go.

"Nobody is really happy" was the philosophy of some of my fellow colleagues and "inmates." My favorite uncle once told me that he couldn't wait to retire. At that time, he was only in his mid-forties. He died of a massive heart attack right after he reached retirement age. For quite some time, I saw myself and those around me entangled in limiting beliefs of "I can't" and "I have to." Gradually my hopes and dreams of freedom and fulfillment were replaced with feelings of being imprisoned by a never-ending string of obligations and external expectations.

Over the years, I've come to understand and appreciate that we all have the power of choice inside of us; we just don't always know how to access it. We may feel obliged or forced to behave in ways that are determined by others; however, we can still choose our thoughts, our perspectives, and even our emotions. Although our external circumstances may not immediately change, our experience of life can dramatically improve if we choose more resourceful, supportive internal responses. In my case, I finally chose to worry less about getting approval from my superiors and instead to focus more on myself and on building trust in myself as a doctor. Interestingly, this shift in attitude brought me more positive recognition and support from my bosses, which, as I look back, was instrumental to my receiving the research stipend that brought me to the United States and ultimately set me on the path of my life's work, which includes writing this book. Just like small hinges that swing open big doors, small choices like this one can make a big difference.

A friend of mine who volunteers at a school and codirects its annual theatre production, which could rival many professionally produced shows, told me about a little girl who was born without legs and with only one arm. This little girl made the choice to be a star—so she thinks, feels, and acts like one. When she dances in her wheelchair—or dances without her chair, propelling herself with one hand across the floor—she exhibits amazing skills and agility. Her radiance and pizzazz are so bright that everyone around her feels inspired to be their best. This girl understands that there are no limitations and that people can make a choice to be either the victim or the star of their lives.

As you go through this book considering and incorporating the insights and tools that I describe, look at every chapter as an opportunity to make a choice—a choice to say yes to yourself and yes to empowering yourself to create the life you choose.

ACTUALIZATION

This principle of change can be summarized with three words that Nike made famous: *just do it.* If you don't take action when you discover the keys to unlocking yourself, moments of awareness, times of flexibility, and important choices remain just thoughts or nice dreams. How many self-help books ended up as *shelf*-help books, looking quite impressive in your library but never really having a true impact on your life? The fear of change, which is the fear of the unknown, may have kept those books sitting on the shelf and you on the fence. As someone once pointed out to me, "All I got from sitting on the fence was a sore butt."

Making that jump off the fence and taking the first step down the path of change are often easier than staying on the path. The pain of being stuck in fear and anxiety can be the catalyst that propels you forward, because anything seems to be better than that pain. But what happens if you don't reach the promised land as quickly as you'd hoped?

The saying "It often gets worse, before it gets better" describes a fascinating phenomenon, one I've observed to be true with both physical and emotional challenges. It appears that sometimes the resistance is the strongest just before the actual breakthrough. During these times, you believe you're spinning your wheels or sliding backward despite your best efforts and good intentions. This is when it's valuable to remember the self-empowering sequence of awareness, flexibility, choice, and actualization.

Actualization means to move forward with the focus on and conscious commitment to your path of growth, self-discovery, and empowerment without letting yourself become sidetracked by old patterns and habits. Actualization means staying centered and focused and continuing to commit to *you.* This does not mean that you have to dedicate most of your time and energy to your self-improvement. In fact, just as it is with reshaping your body, working consistently on yourself for a relatively short amount of time each day is more effective than pushing yourself hard only once a week.

Another common challenge can present itself after you've made progress toward your goals of emotional freedom and self-empowerment. Let's say you've been feeling good about yourself for quite some time, when suddenly you seem to fall back into old patterns and habits. Old grooves can be deep, familiar, and slippery—especially when you forget to practice and use what got you out of them in the first place. Eventually you believe that you never changed and that all your past efforts were in vain, which is one of the biggest misconceptions of life.

You can't live without changing. My friend Chris says life is a circle that continually expands, whether you're aware of it or not. After his first, and probably last, bungee jump, still a bit pale and shaken, he said to me, "I didn't really enjoy the experience, but my circle is wider now, and nothing can ever make it smaller again."

It's in our nature to expand and grow; all that varies is the speed of that expansion. This means there is no real endpoint to this journey of emotional freedom and self-empowerment, which makes it important to continuously invest focus, time, and energy. Use your awareness to determine whether you're still on track; your flexibility to define new and more resourceful ways of being, thinking, and acting; and your power of choice to decide what is truly important to you. Then put everything into action. Just do it—again and again.

INTEGRATION

This principle is all about solidifying and implementing, in a balanced and sustainable manner, the changes you have achieved. This book is designed to take you effectively *and* gently through the various stages of breaking through fear and anxiety. For some, however, taking steps on this journey may feel like walking on a tightrope. At the beginning, you may have to deal with your high expectations, which are usually coupled with impatience. You know what happens. At first you are all excited and motivated to make that big breakthrough happen. If others can do it, so can you. But rather than focusing on the journey and appreciating the progress you have made, you are so invested in your desired outcome that you force yourself to do more and push harder—until eventually you run out of steam. Or you drop the ball and give up too quickly because you haven't yet achieved the amazing results you expected. Both options only lead to more anxiety, frustration, and disappointment with yourself.

For others, the opposite may happen. Your changes and growth might be so profound and rapid that you start to feel a bit ungrounded and untethered, which might make you more susceptible to falling back into old, familiar patterns of anxiety.

To stay motivated and committed to this journey of healing and empowerment, you need to find that fine line between consistently making progress and taking time to adjust to the progress you've made. Through the process of integration, you can bring your thoughts, actions, and emotions into ever-increasing alignment with who you really are. In this regard, integration is the most important of these principles, because it allows you to own and embody your changes and, therefore, give meaning and purpose to them.

As you consciously work your way through this book and employ the principles of change, you'll notice that with increasing awareness you can see where you've been and what's waiting on the other side of your perceived limitations. With flexibility and choice, you can learn to stretch your mind beyond what you regarded as your reality. By taking action, you can step out of your comfort zone and create momentum that allows you to continue to expand your consciousness and your life. And through integration you will gain the strength and stability to solidify your new, true, and limitless identity.

Every step you take, even the smallest one, carries you forward and changes you. No matter how much time and effort you invest in the processes of this book, by the time you finish it, you'll be a different person than the one who opened the cover.

CHAPTER 3

Facts and Fiction about Fear and Anxiety

FEAR AND ANXIETY can envelop your mind like a dark, persistent cloud, or they can appear so suddenly that you feel attacked or ambushed. In either case, fear and anxiety feel more like foreign entities than something you created. Understanding some important facts about fear and anxiety is the first step to demystifying them and regaining control. After all, with awareness comes knowledge, with knowledge comes responsibility, and with taking responsibility comes true empowerment.

WHERE DOES ANXIETY COME FROM?

Although you may often feel overcome, attacked, or trapped by anxiety, it's still just a basic feeling that you've chosen to create, albeit subconsciously. A feeling is a message from the subconscious part of your mind to the conscious part. It lets you know that your subconscious has perceived something either pleasurable or dangerous. Physiologically, the intensity of physical pain indicates how much your body needs your attention; in the same way, the greater the intensity of an emotional sensation, the more closely and urgently your subconscious mind wants you to consciously pay attention to its message.

Fear and anxiety are created with a positive intention: to keep you safe. The resourceful and adaptive aspect of anxiety is that it places you on high alert, causing you to notice and anticipate danger and either take precautions or appropriately address the situation. A low-grade anxiety can keep you on your toes and prevent you from putting yourself into situations that could potentially harm you. A slightly more intense form of anxiety can help you to be fully alert and mobilize additional energy and resources so that you're mentally and physically ready to either fight the perceived source of danger or run from it.

Researchers believe that some fears, such as the fear of snakes or of anger, have been preserved during human evolution and passed down to us. Studies have shown that children, even infants, can recognize and respond to pictures of snakes and angry faces more rapidly than to neutral pictures.[1] Our relatives from the Stone Age certainly faced life-threatening situations daily, whether they had to struggle with the elements or fend off huge predators. Fear and anxiety provided them with crucial information and led them to come up with adaptive responses. For example, the development of weapons and shelter ensured the safety and survival of our prehistoric ancestors and helped them overcome their physical weaknesses and the challenges of their environment. So it makes sense that the ability to create these emotions was preserved during evolution.

WHAT ARE WE AFRAID OF NOW?

The world has changed significantly since caves were our castles. When we humans discovered how to overcome our limitations, outsmart our enemies, and emerge as the dominating species on the planet, we wasted no time extinguishing our natural predators or forcing them to retreat to small vestiges of nature, away from civilization.

Now we're the most powerful species on Earth. At the same time, we're the most dangerous threat to all living beings, including ourselves. That sounds rather bleak, and the truth is *most* humans don't pose a physical threat to each other but live according to the "don't harm and don't get harmed" creed. Thus, the vast majority of people, especially in the industrialized nations, don't face life-threatening situations on a daily basis. Yet around 17 percent of the world's population has been diagnosed with anxiety disorder.[2] What are we still afraid of today?

According to a 2001 Gallup survey, the fear of public speaking, which is the fear of public humiliation, is the second most common fear in the United States, exceeded only by the "ancient" fear of snakes.[3] In addition to the fear of losing health, face, and respect, other common modern fears are losing a job, money, security, relationships, and love. At first glance, these fears could be summarized as: the fear of losing something of value. However, underneath the fear of losing something that's important to us often lingers a greater fear, which might be also anchored in evolution: the fear of losing control and being powerless. This deep-seated fear can lead to a vicious cycle, causing us to believe that hypervigilance, micromanaging, and even obsessive behaviors are the only way to maintain some sense of power and control when, in actuality, it is fear and anxiety that control our lives more and more.

ANXIETY KEEPS US SAFE—OR DOES IT?

Many people believe that without fear and anxiety their lives would be less safe. You could argue that you need a level of anxiety to stay productive and avoid failure. Or you might be convinced that the less worried and vigilant you are, the more likely it is that you will make mistakes, disappoint others, and face criticism or failure. Some of these fears are learned during your upbringing and rooted in old proverbs and beliefs, such as, "You can't count on anybody but yourself," "You gotta watch your back," "You can't make the same mistake twice," and "Life is not fair." These beliefs have been handed down from one generation to the next and became part of your subconscious programming, conveying the notion that fear and anxiety are necessary for staying safe and well.

However, considering your current day-to-day life, how much anxiety do you really need to be OK? Do you need the worry of losing your job to persuade you to go to work and do your best every day? Do you need the fear of causing an accident to motivate you to drive responsibly? Do you treat your spouse and others with courtesy and respect just because you're afraid of what they might think about you otherwise?

Usually it's not fear and anxiety but experience, common sense, and wise choices that keep us safe. This is also true for our productivity, which may initially spike because of anxiety, but eventually decreases as ongoing stress and worry drain our energy and wear us down. Aren't joy, purpose, and fulfillment much better motivators for improving our performance and helping us sustain a highly productive level?

How much fear is actually safe? Chronic fear and anxiety exhaust you mentally and emotionally, cloud your judgment, and eventually make you feel insecure and powerless. Physiologically, even low-grade fear, experienced continuously, causes great strain on your body that can lead to severe health challenges such as high blood pressure, chronic pain, obesity, heart disease, diabetes, autoimmune disease, and even cancer. These stress-related illnesses are the most common causes of death in our modern society. Even in situations where fear may appear completely appropriate, it can paralyze you, leaving you like a deer in headlights: unable to make a decision or even physically move, which is obviously not a very safe position to be in.

When I was nineteen years old, a friend and I bicycled on our own Tour de France to the south of France. On a warm but rather stormy day, we decided to swim and body surf on the large waves of the Atlantic Ocean. We enjoyed the thrill of being tossed around by the surf so much that we didn't realize that the current was pulling us farther and farther out to the open sea. We tried to swim back to shore, but soon noticed that despite our greatest efforts, we couldn't make any progress. I was getting concerned. I didn't want to alarm my friend, but I couldn't help asking, "What if we can't make it back? There's nobody out here and nobody on the beach to help us."

My friend appeared calm, which in turn calmed me down, and I figured there was probably nothing to worry about. But then I looked at him and saw the panic in his eyes. Either my fear was contagious or he'd realized our dire situation on his own. All of a sudden, he started waving his arms wildly and screaming, "Help! Help!"

That did it for me. My sense of safety was gone because if he was scared, we must be in deep trouble. I felt the heat of fear rising inside, almost taking my breath away, as I joined my buddy in desperate shouts for help. After only a few moments, the panic had completely overtaken me. My heart was pounding. I couldn't focus my eyes; it was as if a dark curtain had been pulled in front of them. I started frantically paddling with my arms and legs, desperately trying to keep my head above water. Then two gigantic waves rolled over me in short sequence, pushing me with all their force deep underwater. After what had seemed an eternity, I came back to the surface, coughing, gagging, and spitting out saltwater. Gasping for air, I felt completely helpless and paralyzed by fear.

It's interesting what strange thoughts pop up in those moments of despair. As I struggled for my life, I contemplated how my obituary in my hometown newspaper would read and wondered how many people would show up to my funeral. Somehow, surrendering to the fact that my obituary was as good as in press, I became very calm. Then a clear message rose from somewhere deep inside: "Remember, panic is just a waste of your energy."

Good advice. I stopped shouting and fighting the elements and began instead focusing on working my way toward the shore, inch by inch. Calmer, I could access a mental and physical strength that I'm certain saved my life—and possibly that of my friend, as well, as he picked up on the shift in my energy. When we both finally crashed onto some sharp rocks, badly cutting our legs and hands, the enormous relief of recognizing that we were back on land made this one of our happiest moments ever.

This experience taught me the paralyzing limitations of fear and anxiety. While these feelings may be effective in alerting us to potential danger, when their intensity escalates, the consequences can be devastating.

THE REALITY OF ANXIETY

You are awakened in the middle of the night by a muffled noise, and you just know that somebody has broken into your house. You hear about burglaries every day on the news, so you know it can happen to you. The phone is downstairs, so you can't call the police. Your heart is pounding, and your mind is racing as you envision the possible horrific outcomes of a robbery. Holding your breath, you slip out of bed and grab a lamp, a fire poker, a baseball bat—whatever is heavy and nearby. You're determined to fend off the intruder if he or she should dare to enter your bedroom. After what seems like hours of agonizing anxiety, you tiptoe downstairs—and discover that the intruder turns out to be your cat, which has knocked over a vase.

Like most medical students who immerse themselves in the study of diseases, I went through a phase of suffering from devastating afflictions, all of which had two things in common: I'd just learned about their specific symptoms, and they all mysteriously disappeared as quickly as they came. Because of the Internet, this phenomenon seems to be no longer limited to medical schools. Many of my clients report having sleepless nights after consulting "Dr. Google" and "finding out" they have an incurable disease.

Mark Twain said, "I have experienced many catastrophes in my life—most of which never happened." It is our active imagination that turns cats into burglars and an upset stomach into cancer. If just a tiny fraction of people's anxieties were to come true, Planet Earth would have ceased to exist a long time ago.

Remember, fear is supposed to function as the inner alarm signal, a little red warning light that gives you a heads up if there is something you need to be aware of. However, if you've been dealing with fear and anxiety for an extended period of time, this warning system often becomes too sensitive and is then set off by even the slightest detail. For example, you might interpret a frown on your boss's forehead as a sign that you're one step away from being fired. Or you might believe your spouse's purchase of a new pair of sunglasses means you're doomed to financial ruin. If friends don't call you over the weekend, it's a sure sign they've stopped caring about you or that you've done something terrible to upset them. Over time, you may become so used to these constant warnings that they feel completely normal to you.

You may be thinking, "But how do I decide if a situation is truly dangerous or just a frightening interpretation of my mind? How can I know whether my *what ifs* are founded in reality or in fantasy?" In other words, how can you know if the alarm is real or not?

You can't tell—at least not right away. At first you need to reset your internal alarm system so it will respond appropriately. And then you need to do a bit of relearning and build a new inner foundation of confidence and true self-empowerment. While this may sound like a long and complicated process, it isn't if you know how to work directly with the source of fear and anxiety: your subconscious mind.

Before we probe deeper into working with the subconscious, let's have a look inside your brain to give your intellectual side something to chew on.

WHAT HAPPENS IN OUR BRAIN?

Although anxiety is often based on nothing but our imagination, the feeling of anxiety is always real to our minds and bodies. To better understand why, we need to delve a little bit into the neuro-physiological pathway of fear and anxiety.

Imagine you're walking in the forest on a warm summer day. Suddenly you spot a long, thin object hanging from a branch that stretches right above the trail. Your eyes direct this visual information to the optic nerve, which sends it to the thalamus region, one of the most important relay stations of the brain (see figure 1). The thalamus sends signals to the amygdalae, almond-shaped groups of cells that are part of the brain's limbic system and play a significant role in emotional responses and long-term memory.

The amygdalae evaluate the input by determining whether the image of the long, thin object has any emotional relevance. Could this object mean danger or pleasure? Another part of the limbic system, the hippocampus region, becomes involved. It helps scan the cortex, or outer part of your brain, for memories that may provide further information about what this long, thin thing might be. The resulting thought: it could be a snake!

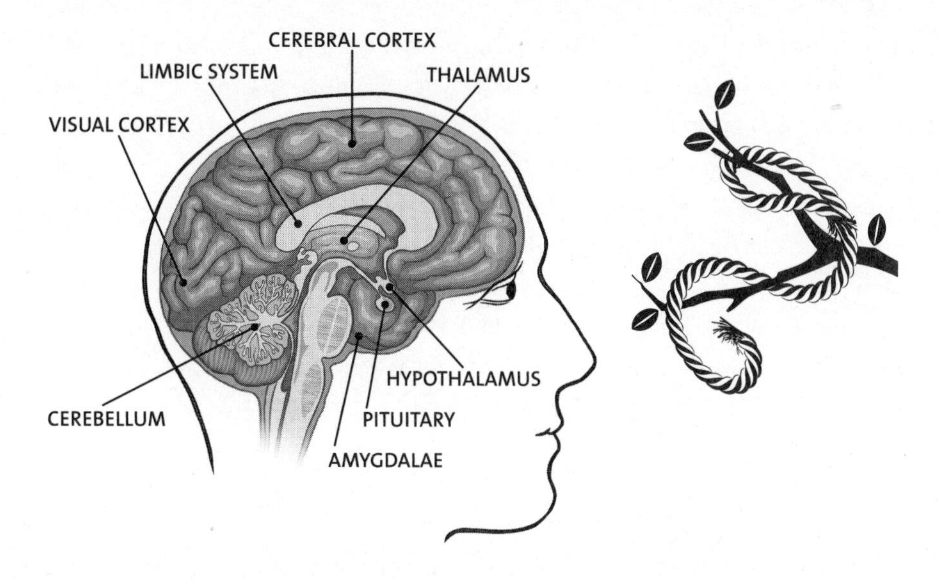

FIGURE 1 Brain pathways associated with fear and anxiety

Now your brain considers the situation potentially dangerous. The hypothalamus and the pituitary gland stimulate the release of stress hormones, such as adrenaline and cortisol, which increase your heart rate, breathing, perspiration, and blood circulation to the peripheral muscles—all of which prepare your body for an appropriate flight-flight-or-freeze response. At the same time, the cortex tries to develop a master plan for dealing with this potential threat.[4]

What is especially fascinating about this fear pathway is that only after the stress responses have been set in motion does the visual information finally reach the occipital part of the brain. This visual processing center provides an accurate analysis of the object: It's only an old rope hanging from a branch. All systems can return to normal.

Why does the fear come faster than the awareness? Why does our nervous system cry wolf rather than wait for the facts? From a survival point of view, it makes sense that evolution has favored this better-safe-than-sorry response. It was a matter of survival to be able to spot and instantly react to any potential threat—and as I mentioned before, our ancestors had to face plenty of threats on a daily basis.

The problem with this system is that the more often you activate this stress-response loop, the more likely you will react anxiously to changes in your environment and unexpected circumstances. The amygdalae function like an anxiety switch: when they are turned on, we feel anxious; when they are turned off, we don't. If you've been dealing with stress and anxiety for a long period of time, this anxiety switch can be triggered very easily or even become stuck in the "on" position, and it can activate the fight-flight-or-freeze response in situations (such as driving, flying, or spotting an elongated object hanging from a branch) where most people would experience moderate nervousness at the most.

So what can you do about this anxiety switch? How can you gain access or control over it without just getting rid of the amygdalae (which you can't and shouldn't want to do)? Does pharmacology have the answers?

IS ANXIETY A BIOCHEMICAL PROBLEM REQUIRING A BIOCHEMICAL SOLUTION?

Medical research has focused largely on a physiological solution to emotional problems such as anxiety and depression. The most prescribed antianxiety drugs are either benzodiazepines (such as Valium and Xanax), which are often used for anxiety, or selective serotonin reuptake inhibitors (SSRIs, such as Zoloft and Prozac), which are more commonly used for depression. While benzodiazepines directly affect the amygdalae by reducing their activity, SSRIs increase the level of serotonin in the brain, which is associated with mood improvement.

The good news is that using prescription drugs to alter the brain's physiology and chemistry can indeed successfully dampen fear and anxiety and make these emotions more manageable. However, this improvement often comes with a price. One of the challenges with antianxiety medications—besides their common side effects, such as drowsiness, nausea, constipation, and lower sex drive—is that they potentially lead to physical addiction, and you must wean yourself carefully when you want to stop taking them.

Many of the clients I have worked with complained that their medication not only reduced their anxiety, it also dulled or even turned off their emotions in general. It appeared to my clients as if their minds had been wrapped in cotton or a lid had been placed on their ability to feel anything. But what still hadn't vanished were their deep-seated insecurities and the limiting core beliefs they had struggled with for a long time. Beliefs such as "I'm not good enough" or "The world is not a safe place" still remained a part of their mindset, even though they didn't have the same emotional impact. As a client put it, "I basically still have the same issues, but I don't feel them as intensely. They seem to be further out of reach. It's a relief, but not really a resolution."

Unfortunately, the development of effective pharmaceutical treatments fostered the belief that emotional challenges are mainly caused by neurotransmitter imbalances in the brain and are therefore more a biochemical than a psychological problem. More and more people subscribe to a "let's get it fixed" attitude, which has been reflected in the fact that the use of antidepressant drugs in the United States doubled between 1996 and 2005. At the same time, the number of people who visited psychotherapists declined.[5]

There is no doubt that changes in the brain chemistry are connected to different emotional states. There is also no doubt that antianxiety medications have helped countless people disrupt the downward spiral of fear and anxiety and escape a state of emotional paralysis and entrapment. But what came first—the chicken or the egg? Are neurotransmitter imbalances in the brain the root cause of fear and anxiety, or are they a consequence, a biochemical symptom of our emotions? If the latter is true, does restoring the biochemical balance really address the root causes of fear and anxiety?

It boils down to a very fundamental question: what is a human being actually? Are we just an accumulation of cells controlled by neurotransmitters and hormones? Are our emotions, thoughts, and beliefs nothing but random biochemical and electrophysiological signals? Or are our minds and bodies, with all their connections and interactions, much more complex than that? And does what we call "consciousness" transcend far beyond our current scientific understanding? I believe the answer to both of the last questions is yes and that the human mind is simply unable to wrap itself consciously around its own complexity and vastness. To quote Albert Einstein, "Do you remember how electrical currents and 'unseen waves' were laughed at? The knowledge about man is still in its infancy."

I like to look at antianxiety drugs as a form of emotional painkiller. The purpose of pain medication is not to mend the fracture or close the wound that causes the pain, but to make the time it takes to heal more tolerable. It would be denial or plain ignorance if you would drown out the pain without tending to its root causes. If fear and anxiety are like physical pain, then their natural purpose must be to call your attention to the deeper emotional and mental wounds they are caused by. What if tending to these inner wounds—whether they are unresolved traumas, self-sabotaging patterns, or limiting beliefs—could lead to greater peace, wholeness, and self-empowerment? Would it still be enough for you to just fix and get rid of fear and anxiety? Or would you want to take advantage of their true meaning, heal yourself from the inside out, and gain access to your true potential? This is what I call the healing power of fear and anxiety. As you're moving step by step through this book, bridging the conscious with the subconscious and higher consciousness, you will learn how to address fear and anxiety and take advantage of their healing power.

Now don't get me wrong. I'm not saying that you shouldn't take antianxiety medication or can't work on the deeper root causes of fear and anxiety while you're on it. Taking medication can be a first empowering step. Just don't let it be the entire journey.

One final note on this subject—something taught to me by my father, who was a truly amazing physician. To paraphrase him: "Remember, it's the patient who does the healing, not the doctor or the drugs." Our potential to heal is much greater than we believe or have been led to believe. In fact, the power of belief is a major key. Clinical studies have shown that placebos, sugar pills without medicinal value, can significantly reduce moderate depression and anxiety.[6] So just believing that you will feel better can be as effective as using a drug that is designed to alter your brain chemistry. Imagine what is possible when you apply the same trust and belief in your own power to heal, change, and thrive.

PART II

Flexibility

CHAPTER 4

The Subconscious Mind and the Root Causes of Anxiety

IT HAPPENS QUITE often: clients come to me with one specific problem they want to overcome and soon realize that their real issue is something more profound and fundamental. Judy, a successful graphic designer in her midfifties, wanted to let go of the growing anger she'd harbored toward her father for many years. Throughout her life, he'd been neglectful, unavailable, and selfish. After he retired, he entertained himself mainly with drinking and gambling, which enraged Judy even more. Because nothing that she did or said to her father seemed to make a difference, her frustration and resentment increasingly occupied her thoughts and drained her energy.

In our initial meeting, she assured me that, anger at her father aside, her life was going really well, and there was nothing to complain about. Thirty minutes into the session, she realized that her anger was just a cover for a deep-seated anxiety and sadness. Throughout her childhood she'd felt ignored, hurt, and rejected by her father, which left her with the core belief that she was unlovable and just not good enough.

As a teenager, Judy rebelled. She skipped school and experimented with drugs and sex, which only led to further punishment and neglect by her father. Her first husband, whom she married in her early twenties, was emotionally unavailable, and when he drank, which he often did, he became physically abusive. "It was as if I'd married my father," she told me. The beatings and the marriage ended after five years, when Judy's husband had for the first time turned his violent anger on their children, giving her the strength to finally leave him.

After the divorce, Judy became extremely ambitious, worked very hard, and was soon called Miss Overachiever by her friends and family. At first glance, you could say that she'd turned her life around. Yet her core beliefs of not being good enough still kept weighing her down. Judy admitted that for many years she'd felt stressed and anxious, often unable to fall asleep or turn off her mind. She compensated for her anxiety and insecurity by overextending herself at work, staying in the office longer than anyone else, and refusing to allow herself to relax or have fun—even on the weekends. Although she'd advanced to become a widely respected manager of an advertising company, she didn't dare speak up during group meetings because she feared that nobody would really be interested in what she had to say.

When I asked Judy about her true passions, she broke into tears and sobbed, "I always wanted to be an artist, a painter. I know that I have talent, but I haven't made the time to sit down and paint again. I think I'm worried that people won't like my pictures, and I've never believed that I could do art just for myself, for my own pleasure." This is when she realized that there was a much bigger and deeper issue she needed to deal with than the anger with her father.

Judy's example shows how the experiences and imprints of our early years continue to influence and drive us although we might not be consciously aware of it. Look at the situations that caused you to be anxious and insecure during different stages in your life—from childhood all the way to the present. Do you notice that they have something in common? That they are not separate, unrelated events but share certain themes, patterns, and triggers that you responded to with the same thoughts, feelings, and behaviors?

In Judy's case, one of her major patterns was that she felt unworthy and insignificant when dealing with people who appeared more powerful, more capable, or smarter than she thought she was. Like most people, she merely knew how to ignore or cope with these patterns, rather than address their deeper-seated root causes. She felt safe and in control only when she worked harder than everybody else and denied herself any form of self-expression. Ultimately, these coping mechanisms caused her to feel even less empowered, less worthy, less safe—and more anxious. But rather than acknowledging her own problems, which she was too afraid to do, she focused on her anger toward her father, who admittedly had given her ample reasons to be upset with him.

Judy was able to recognize and break through the root causes of her anxiety and insecurity. Now she acknowledges herself as a very talented artist, paints regularly with a group of friends, and is looking forward to exhibiting her work in an art gallery. By the way, as soon as Judy realized that she needed to find peace and love for herself, her anger toward her father completely disappeared, creating space for her to feel forgiveness and compassion for him.

When a tree continues to produce unripe or flavorless fruit, just polishing the fruit or coating it with sugar won't really solve the tree's problems. As T. Harv Eker, bestselling author of *Secrets of the Millionaire Mind,* likes to say, "The roots create the fruits. Which is why how we do anything is how we do *everything.*" Just like Judy, you've probably found out that working harder, finding a new job or partner, starting an exciting hobby, or getting angry at somebody else didn't provide you with real, permanent solutions for your anxiety patterns. Why? One factor never really changed—you. A wise person once said, "Wherever you go, there you are." So how can you really change and attend to the roots of your anxiety? The answer resides in your subconscious mind.

THE SUBCONSCIOUS MIND: FRIEND OR FOE?

Your subconscious may seem to be an obscure and rather scary part of your mind that is out of your control, causes you a lot of trouble, and therefore isn't trustworthy. You may place your trust in your intellectual and analytical capabilities and be unaware of the enormous potential that resides within this deeper part of your consciousness.

The relationship between the conscious and the subconscious mind has been compared to an iceberg; the tip (the conscious state) is above the surface and the massive bulk (the subconscious) is underneath. The conscious mind is the seat of cognitive learning and is responsible for our awareness in the waking state—thinking analytically, creating logical order, wondering about cause and effect, and asking "why" and "how" to arrive at rational conclusions. The conscious mind makes choices based on facts and directs the body to move.

The subconscious mind usually operates beneath our normal consciousness. One of its major functions is to *filter and interpret* the vast amount of information surrounding us and feed the conscious mind only the tiny fractions that seem relevant for our safety and well-being. It does this for a good reason. Consciously, we can compute only small amounts of information at one time, but subconsciously, we can keep tabs on our surroundings, pick up subtle cues from others, and notice small external and internal changes—all without our conscious awareness. For example, we're able to feel someone staring at us or see a friend and sense right away, without exchanging a word, that something is wrong. Important aspects of our perception, such as first impressions, chemistry, or intuition, are not based on logical considerations but stem from the input of our subconscious.

Another important task of the subconscious mind is *creating emotions,* which it often does without the input of the conscious mind. This explains why emotions can appear so irrational, inappropriate, and out of control. On your way to work on Monday morning, you're sure that you woke up on the wrong side of the bed; everything and everybody irritates you. But by lunchtime, even though nothing external has changed, you're in a splendid mood and whistling your favorite tune. Or, you suddenly feel anxious before a second date—not just a little bit nervous, but heading toward full-scale panic mode. The intensity of the feeling doesn't make sense to you, especially since you had such a blast on your first date with that person.

Another task of the subconscious mind is *filing and storing all our memories.* Just take a moment and think about the bedroom you grew up in. Do you remember the color of the walls or what was on your bed? Since you probably haven't thought about this room in some time, you'll have to access the information from the place it has been stored. To prevent our conscious mind from being overloaded with too much data, our subconscious keeps most memories out of our awareness until we consciously reach for them.

To protect us, the subconscious mind also *suppresses memories* that appear too emotionally overwhelming or damaging. Many people who were abused in their childhood don't remember what happened until, when they are adults, something triggers a specific memory, which brings the abuse to the conscious surface. Amnesia after an accident is another example of the subconscious mind's supportive and kind mechanism.

Emotions and memories are stored not just in our subconscious mind; they're also transferred into our cells. Some clients have told me that they first became aware of their stored emotions during a massage, acupuncture, or chiropractic treatment. Sadness, anger, or fear spontaneously rose to the surface without any conscious thoughts acting as triggers. Other clients shared that while receiving bodywork they suddenly remembered a traumatic memory they'd suppressed since childhood. Once fear and anxiety are stored in our body they can cause serious physical problems such as chronic pain, high blood pressure, heart disease, and autoimmune disorders. These physical challenges can be viewed as a sort of wake-up call—communication from the subconscious mind informing us that it's time to address unresolved emotional issues. For many of the individuals I have worked with, physical complaints have been the starting point of their emotional and mental healing journeys.

The subconscious mind doesn't only use the body as a convenient storage place or communication device. It also masterfully *oversees and coordinates the body's several trillion cells,* so they're working seamlessly together and can continuously adapt to rapidly changing conditions. Just imagine how impossibly tedious it would be to consciously regulate your breathing, heart rate, liver function, or digestion. Even relatively simple tasks like walking or lifting your arm require the precisely coordinated flexing and relaxing of more than a dozen different muscles. While the conscious mind gives the executive order to take a step or raise an arm, it's your subconscious mind that translates these simple commands into their complex details.

This brings me to another function of the subconscious mind. Have you ever noticed that most of the time you don't remember how you drove yourself to work or how you ate that sandwich last night while watching TV? As you were thinking about the daunting to-do list of the day, your hair was somehow washed and your teeth brushed. The subconscious mind *oversees all automatic behavior and patterns* and allows you to occupy your conscious mind with something else. In fact, most daily activities are regulated by the subconscious mind. Consider how much more time you spend thinking about the future or the past without paying attention to the present moment, yet you're still able to avoid accidents, feed yourself, look presentable, and get most things done. Now you can appreciate the amazing, "mind-blowing" abilities of your subconscious.

The many complex tasks and responsibilities of the subconscious mind make its power and enormous potential apparent. The subconscious has really only one flaw, if you will. It needs our *conscious* guidance to fully utilize its potential and operate in a way that is supportive and harmonious with our entire being. Some compare the subconscious mind to a loyal, extremely talented servant who faithfully continues to perform the same tasks repeatedly until told to do something different. When we learn how to consciously work with our subconscious mind, we can change faster and perform better on all levels—mental, emotional, and physical. It's through conscious-subconscious collaboration that we are able to access our true potential and gain a deeper understanding of who we truly are.

HOW OUR SUBCONSCIOUS SCARES US

You're in a hurry, and of course your keys are hiding again. You look for them everywhere, becoming increasingly anxious. Finally you discover them right where you always put them. Hadn't you checked there before at least twice?

Or maybe you're on your way to an interview. You feel good until you notice that mustard stain on your shirt. All your confidence slips away, and you start to panic. You're sure that you will make a terrible impression, because all the interviewer will notice about you is that stain—just as you do.

Why is it that you can't see certain things you want to (your keys), whereas other things you want to ignore (the mustard stain) are all you can focus on?

Every second of our lives, we're surrounded by an incomprehensible amount of information. As I mentioned before, we need to filter out a large portion to make sense of the world and not become completely fried. But how do we distinguish the tiny fraction of information that is relevant from all the remaining input that needs to be ignored? If we tried to make these distinctions consciously, we wouldn't be able to do anything else. Literally all our focus and energy would be devoted to deciphering and sorting every single detail in and around us. This is where our subconscious mind comes in and employs specific filters to separate what it perceives to be as important to us.

In a study conducted at Columbia University in New York, volunteers were shown pictures of random people with neutral expressions. The researchers also displayed random images of people with fearful expressions. The images with the fearful faces appeared and disappeared so quickly that the volunteers weren't consciously aware of them. However, functional magnetic resonance imaging (fMRI) scans—which measure changes in blood flow—clearly demonstrated that the brain had registered the fearful faces, even though the subjects denied seeing them.[1] This study shows that our subconscious filters and processes information, and is also able to perceive external input much more quickly and in more subtle forms than the conscious mind can.

Subconscious filters consist of memories, emotions, inner conflicts, and beliefs. They delete, distort, and generalize information that passes through them and leave us with a condensed and altered version of all that surrounds us—an *internal interpretation* of reality (see figure 2). Since most people are not consciously aware of their subconscious filters, they're also unaware that their view of the world is basically just "made up." Which also means that whatever you think *you are* is just a fraction of the truth.

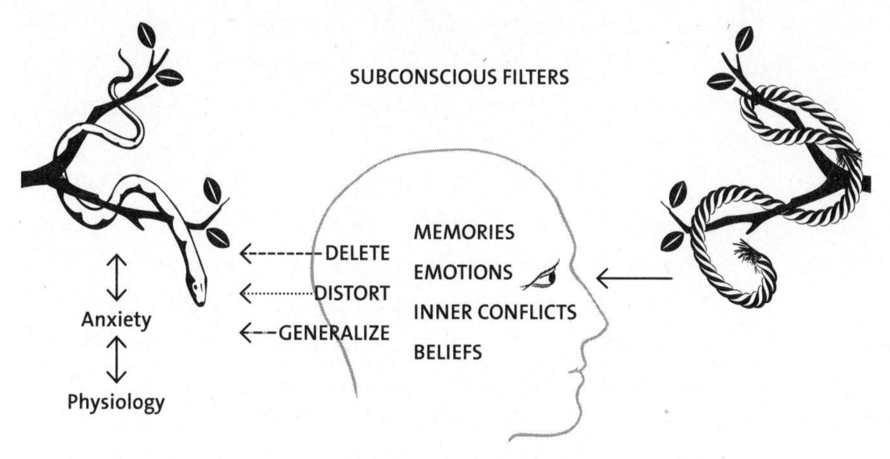

FIGURE 2: How our subconscious creates fear and anxiety

Let's have another look at the snake/rope example. Say you didn't sleep well the night before your walk through the woods because your noisy neighbors kept you awake. You've been on edge all day and already had an argument with your spouse. From the perspective of your subconscious, you're already more vulnerable than usual and, therefore, in need of protection. When you spot that thing hanging from the branch, your subconscious quickly cross-references this image with memories of actual events or scenes from a scary snake-filled movie you once watched. As your subconscious filters and processes the external information, it transforms the visual input into an internal interpretation, transforming the rope into a snake. To protect you, the fight-flight-or-freeze response kicks in, preparing you to defend yourself, run away, or become motionless and invisible to this perceived predator. Finally, after a closer and more conscious inspection, you realize that the snake is a rope. You are safe.

Why does your subconscious make you overlook the keys you are desperately searching for and magnify the mustard stain you don't want to see? Well, in both cases the subconscious mind is on a mission to protect you. By activating the anxiety response, you're being prepared for the negative consequences of being late, which could be embarrassment, criticism, or rejection. As your subconscious shifts your awareness from the present to a possibly unpleasant future, most of the available information of your surroundings (your keys) gets deleted. The same intention, to keep you safe, is also true for the mustard stain on your shirt. Your subconscious distorts and blows up the stain to get you ready for the judgment and rejection that might await you. Logically, you need to concentrate on what is right in front of you—finding the keys or focusing on the agenda of your meeting; however, subconsciously, you're already bracing yourself for the worst.

Your response to situations like these depends on the fabric of your subconscious filters. Your fear and anxiety filters dictate how you interpret the danger or safety of your reality. The more prominent these subconscious anxiety filters are, the faster and stronger you react to potential peril such as misplacing your keys or staining your shirt. Your reaction creates more stress, which in turn increases your chance of overlooking your keys and spilling more food.

Remember the anxiety switch in your brain? On a subconscious level, this switch comprises filters that alter your internal perception of yourself and the world in a way that potentially makes you more susceptible to experiencing fear and anxiety. So it makes sense that to break through these emotions and their ensuing behavioral patterns, you need to consciously remove and replace these subconscious filters.

Removing the filters doesn't mean you will permanently turn off or even dismantle the anxiety switch. As I said before, fear and anxiety are normal and important parts of life. You don't want to abolish your ability to create these feelings, because they provide you with valuable information and are powerful catalysts for continuous growth and self-empowerment. But what if you could convert the anxiety switch into a dimmer switch—one you learn how to operate with increasing proficiency?

THE MAJOR SUBCONSCIOUS ROOT CAUSES OF FEAR AND ANXIETY

Now you're aware that our reality and everything we feel and do is largely determined by our subconscious mind and its filters. Usually, the subconscious mind switches and exchanges filters according to the circumstance. For example, one day you might feel quite optimistic and live in the glass-half-full reality. In this state of mind, you might expect great outcomes and opportunities from every situation. Then there are days when you're far more pessimistic and the glass looks half empty; if your outlook is really bad, the glass is completely empty or nonexistent. On these days, all you notice are obstacles and shortcomings. The easier it is for your subconscious to switch filters, the greater your emotional and mental flexibility. However, you've probably noticed that the longer you've been struggling with fear and anxiety, the less emotionally and mentally flexible you become. This is because these anxiety filters have become more prominent, entangled, and deeply anchored in your subconscious.

Three particular aspects or filters of our subconscious can be regarded as the root causes of fear and anxiety: *inner conflicts, stored emotions,* and *self-limiting beliefs.* To break through fear and anxiety and to shift into an awareness of self-empowerment and emotional freedom, all three root causes need to be addressed.

ROOT CAUSE 1: INNER CONFLICTS

For people dealing with fear and anxiety, it often seems like there's an inner battle being waged between two sides of themselves. Most of the time, they feel as though they're condemned to watching the battle rather than being able to influence it, let alone end it. Have you ever noticed that you are in conflict with yourself? One moment you feel quite confident and optimistic, ready to take on any challenges that may present themselves to you, and then suddenly you find yourself anxious and insecure, seriously doubting that you're capable of doing anything right. What is this conflict about, and who started it?

Over the natural course of our personal evolution, we develop a variety of personas and identities, which are rooted in our subconscious mind as so-called parts. Depending on the situation and the people we're with, we automatically slip in and out of these identities. Our identity as a mother or a father differs from the one we inhabit when we visit our parents and step back into the role of daughter or son. The persona we adopt during our job is different from the one that comes forth when we're with our spouse or friends. Most of these parts or facets of our subconscious coexist and work together without any conflict, thus allowing us to switch hats quickly and easily.

Inner conflicts occur when two parts of our subconscious mind seemingly have opposite agendas and ideas for what is best for us. Let's say a fearful part of you wants to make sure that you're safe and avoid pain while a confident, optimistic part of you has pleasure, success, and rewards in mind for you. While one part of you focuses on survival, the opposite one wants you to excel and thrive. Or have you ever listened to an inner argument between a positive, encouraging voice and a judgmental, very pessimistic one? The inner critic—who may sound like a scolding parent or a teacher who is reprimanding you—forces you to listen to old tapes from your childhood, such as "You're not good enough," "Who do you think you are?" or "You will get in trouble for this for sure!"

A conflict between two subconscious parts often shows up as procrastination and inconsistent, even self-sabotaging behavior. You forge one step forward and retreat two steps back; you come up with promising ideas and impactful commitments, but then find yourself never following through. For some, inner conflicts feel like accelerating a car and putting on the brakes at the same time, which uses a lot of energy to make very little progress. For others, these inner conflicts are that little pebble in the shoe that makes moving forward difficult. In either case, they eventually make you feel incongruent, insecure, and stuck. How can you solve these subconscious conflicts?

In the past, you probably just wanted to get rid of the anxious, insecure, or self-bashing side of you. But by eliminating a part of yourself—even if that part is negative, critical, self-sabotaging, or anxious—you would actually cause a fragmentation of your subconscious mind, which is the opposite of healing and wholeness. You probably noticed that the harder you tried to ignore or eliminate that part, the stronger and more obnoxious it seemed to become, until it was impossible for you to mute its voice and feelings. In chapters 6 and 7, you'll learn how to resolve anxiety- and insecurity-driven inner conflicts by reintegrating the part of you that has been holding onto these emotions, which is one of the most powerful ways to create lasting wholeness and inner peace.

ROOT CAUSE 2: STORED EMOTIONS

Racing for its life, an antelope is being chased by a hungry lion across the savanna. The lion is set for the final attack when the antelope, through a desperate move, manages to escape. Once the immediate danger is over, the antelope starts shaking vigorously, jumping up and down several times before it calmly trots off. You may have seen your dog launching into a full-body shake after a visit to the vet. I watch my cats doing the same every time I abruptly end their hunt for food by taking them off the kitchen counter. Originally I interpreted the cats' shaking as an expression of disgust with me. Then I learned that the reason for this behavior is that animals are literally shaking off the anxiety and emotional charge that the previous, stressful situation created. By immediately getting the unwanted energy out of their system, they find closure and resolution with what happened. Once again, nature proves to be very clever.

Babies or small children still exhibit this healthy instinct. It shows up in their boundless ability to express emotions without restraint the moment they're born. As they grow up, this natural response of freely releasing emotions is no longer appreciated, and it's discouraged by adults. Little boys are told to toughen up and stop crying. As a friend of mine said, "Once they hit kindergarten, they often adopt these blank expressions so as not to betray their emotions. They stand with their hands in their pockets, little tough guys. It's heartbreaking." Little girls also work very hard on not being perceived as oversensitive cry babies to avoid being teased or rejected. In school, children quickly learn that unless they sit still and suppress the sudden impulses to get up or speak up, they will have to face unpleasant consequences. Very early in their lives, they come to understand that it's no longer appropriate to express or even notice emotions. To be accepted and fit in, they must learn how to squelch and suppress their feelings.

Wouldn't you agree that at least some of this pressure to emotionally conform also affected you? And isn't it also true that as an adult you try to hide emotions such as anxiety or worries? Maybe it's because you believe that to express them would be seen as a sign of weakness or that nobody would like to listen to your worries and fears. Maybe you decided to not think about your doubts so that you wouldn't give them more attention. There are countless reasons to avoid feeling and expressing fear and anxiety, but the outcome remains the same: you build up a backlog of unresolved emotional energy.

You're probably asking yourself now, "Why is it so important to attend to and release these old emotions? Shouldn't I focus on the present and the future?" I agree that spending too much time in the past can prevent us from fully experiencing the present. However, think of the energy it takes to suppress those emotions, to shove them down. It's like pushing on a coiled spring—the harder you press, the greater the force of the spring that's trying to bounce back at you. All this unresolved emotional baggage depletes your energy, weighs you down, makes you feel powerless, and can lead to severe physical problems. By releasing this stored anxiety, you're not only freeing yourself from an emotional burden, you're also recalibrating your subconscious mind, which allows you to be more flexible and resourceful in choosing your emotional responses.

How do we get rid of stored fear and anxiety? In the next chapters, you will go through several processes that will allow you to easily and effectively release emotional baggage and create a clean slate on the subconscious and cellular levels.

ROOT CAUSE 3: SELF-LIMITING BELIEFS

Self-limiting, unsupportive core beliefs are possibly the most important and, at the same time, most underrated causes of fear and anxiety. In general, core beliefs act as our personal laws of the universe. They shape how we view and feel about ourselves and the world, and they determine the choices we make and actions we take. The foundation of our core beliefs can be either our most powerful internal resource or our highest obstacle.

Our lives are constantly affected by our core beliefs, even though we don't necessarily know what those beliefs are about. I've heard many clients proclaim that they don't really have a limiting belief; they just *know* that things never work out for them, that nobody can be trusted, or that they always will be alone. Many of our core beliefs were anchored in our subconscious mind before we entered adolescence. During these early years, our subconscious mind is on a mission to figure out who we are and what our world is about. Experiences and imprints are collected by the subconscious, sorted according to their patterns and commonalities, and eventually assembled to form an understanding of the world and how to navigate in it. Just like we assemble the seemingly unrelated pieces of a jigsaw puzzle to reveal the whole picture, our subconscious takes the pieces of information it has available to form a picture of our reality that explains the past, helps us function in the present, and predicts the future. As these pieces are put together, core beliefs are formed.

In accordance with the prime directives of the subconscious, our set of core beliefs is designed to keep us safe and to help us experience pleasure. Depending on our early imprints, these beliefs may place a stronger emphasis on either safety or enjoyment.

Usually, we don't consciously choose our core beliefs. Instead, they are largely based on other peoples' beliefs or how we interpreted their actions. Here's an example. When I was eleven years old, right before I was about to enter the *gymnasium,* the German equivalent of high school, my family went on vacation to southern France. I was cheerfully playing on a sandy beach when my parents solemnly approached me to let me know that my former teacher considered me "a late bloomer." At first the news didn't bother me because I was having so much fun and didn't know what a late bloomer was (which in itself probably was a sign that I was one). But later, when my parents and I talked about it more, I understood that my teacher had expressed serious doubts about whether I was even smart enough to succeed in the *gymnasium.* I'm still grateful that my parents didn't fully buy into this teacher's limiting beliefs of my intelligence and sent me to high school anyway. However, I also felt their worries—and their pressure when I actually came home with my first D in math.

For what seemed an eternity, their scolding, threats, and lectures told me that I was doomed for the rest of my life if I didn't get better grades. It was pretty painful and scary. Looking back now, I realize that before that time, I used to be a happy-go-lucky, daydreaming, savor-the-moment kid. Nothing seemed too dangerous or serious to me (especially not school), and the world was full of adventures and possibilities for fun. This set of core beliefs was quickly replaced by "You need to work harder than others, because you're not smart enough." My parents had only good intentions and wanted to make sure that I didn't fail in life. However, as I picked up their worries and doubts about me, I became very stressed and anxious. I couldn't sleep before exams, and despite excellent grades I continued to question my intelligence.

Two doctor titles and many other plaques on my wall later, I finally realized that I couldn't outrun or outsmart this limiting belief. This is when I learned how to communicate with my subconscious mind to deprogram a belief that no longer had any validation or truth for me.

"I am an anxious person" and "I am not good enough" are two of the most common fear- and anxiety-driven limiting beliefs. Like other limiting beliefs, they lead to a tunnel-vision perspective of yourself and the world. Anxiety and insecurity become the basis for your identity and the way you perceive reality. To let go of any limiting belief, you need to release your attachments to your old identity. It may seem safe, or at least familiar, to believe that you're not good enough or that you're unable to change. But the truth is, as long as you're invested in the idea that these beliefs determine who you are, your inner foundation remains very fragile and the size of your world confined and limited.

• • •

Bhagwan Shree Rajneesh, the great mystic and spiritual teacher, wrote, "When fear comes, just sit by the side and look at it and say, 'I am not fear' and see the difference. Immediately you've caught the very root of fear. It is no more nourished. You feed these emotions by being identified with them." The processes described in this book provide you with the opportunity to peel off the layers of inner conflicts, stored fear and anxiety, and limiting beliefs that have kept you identified with these emotions and prevented you from realizing your true nature and accessing your untapped power.

Just the thought of letting go of old, familiar ways can bring up strong resistance. The path into unknown territory can appear more frightening than staying stuck. "Who will I be if I'm no longer afraid? What if nobody likes the person I become?" Don't worry. I have never encountered anyone who, after breaking through fear and anxiety, was eager to go back. Changing is much the same as blowing up a balloon—the resistance is the greatest right at the beginning, when you have to blow hardest to get the balloon out of its deflated state. When its shape is more rounded, it's much easier to fill with some additional air. As with filling the balloon, the first move from the anxious and insecure state of mind requires the most energy and commitment. This is why it's so important to have strong reasons to want to change and to have goals that lead your focus beyond the problem; the next chapter will help you determine your reasons for change and set your goals.

PART III

Choice

CHAPTER 5

How to Find Out What You Want and How to Get It

AS I HELPED countless people break through their external and internal obstacles, I found that success directly correlates to a person's determination, commitment, and ability to stay focused on what lies beyond the obstacle. Architect Frank Lloyd Wright once said, "I know the price of success: dedication, hard work, and an unremitting devotion to the things you want to see happen." This quote can be summarized in one word: motivation, the necessary driving force for any change. Only when you're sufficiently motivated will you find the strength, flexibility, and endurance to truly overcome the barriers that block you from your goals. But how do you get motivated, and how do you stay that way? It all starts with making a clear choice about what you want and what you are no longer willing to accept.

MOTIVATION: THE POWER OF PUSH AND PULL TO CHANGE

Motivation is fueled by the reasons why it's good for you to change. The better those reasons are, the more motivation you'll have at your disposal. Because motivation is an emotional force and, therefore, largely generated by the subconscious, these reasons don't need to make sense intellectually. They don't even have to be reasonable.

There are two kinds of motivation: *away from (push)* and *toward (pull)*. When you're motivated to move toward a goal, you're motivated by the positive aspects of reaching it. Why do you *want* to change? What makes you excited about this desired outcome?

Toward motivation keeps your intention *in tension.* Imagine a rubber band that you've attached to your future. The toward motivation pulls you forward and keeps you on track. The one downside or limitation of toward motivation is that, for some people, it does not seem to be sufficient to get them out of their stagnation. Either they can't fully imagine what a positive and exciting change of themselves and their future could look like, or they believe that the gap between where they are now and where they want to be is too wide to bridge.

This is where the other force, the away-from motivation, comes in handy. The away-from motivation focuses on why you *need* to change. This inner force pushes you, rather than pulls you, toward your goal and is generated by your desire to avoid any kind of pain, physical or emotional. Anxiety in itself can function as an away-from motivation. You may have found that a certain amount of stress and anxiety is the reason you've been able to succeed, or to at least keep your head above water. A looming deadline, peer pressure, a demanding boss, an unhappy spouse, or financial challenges can all be strong forces motivating us to take action.

However, being motivated by what you want to avoid also has its severe shortcomings. I'm sure you've noticed that this away-from energy can be quickly draining and rather short-lived, resembling more the efforts needed for a sprint than a long-distance run. After you've successfully dodged the bullet and circumvented disaster, you may find yourself without the energy and real inclination to continue to move forward.

Procrastination is a classic example of this self-defeating pattern. You postpone and ignore the tasks at hand until the anxiety and pressure become unbearable, and then you explode into frantic action. As soon as that battle is over and your positive intentions to stay on top of things are smothered by exhaustion, you're back to immersing yourself in the comfort of avoidance and denial—until the next explosion. As a physician working in a cardiology department, I noticed a similar phenomenon. After the shock of a first heart attack dissipated, many patients went back to a life of stress, fast food, and even cigarettes until acute chest pain forced them to pay us another visit. As a colleague of mine said, "Denial is the greatest risk factor for a second heart attack."

None of us is exempt from this type of behavior. To some degree, we all have a tendency to stop taking care of ourselves, returning to old grooves as soon as the agony and discomfort that propelled us in the first place are gone and we feel better. Although it really doesn't make sense to stop moving forward and drop all the positive resolutions, efforts, and habits that got us to where we want to be, this form of self-induced regression is much more likely to happen if the progress and change were only motivated by the avoidance of pain and suffering.

To move out of the inertia of being stuck and consistently forge on toward your goals and the fulfillment of your dreams, you're best served by employing a combination of toward and away-from motivations. If one force pushes you away from the pain and suffering of your starting point and one pulls you toward your destination with excitement and desire, you will be able to reach your goals more quickly and easily.

THE ESSENTIAL GOAL-DEFINING QUESTIONS

The following exercise will help you to consciously build, direct, and apply away-from motivation and toward motivation to generate the energy you need to break through fear and anxiety and expand into your empowered self. By answering the questions below, you'll define a goal with inherent momentum, which means that it's equally motivating and exciting for your conscious and subconscious mind and will inevitably lead you to success.

The goal-defining questions are:

1. Where are you now?
2. What do you want?
3. How will you know that you've reached your goals?
4. Why do you want to reach your goals?
5. Who is this change for?
6. What will you lose if you get your desired outcome? What will you gain?
7. Which of your qualities and strengths will help you reach your goals?

Let's look at these questions and how to address them in more detail. Take a deep breath, open your mind and heart, and begin.

QUESTION 1: WHERE ARE YOU NOW?

This question is all about building a strong away-from motivation, but it is not meant to focus your attention only on the external circumstances you're unhappy with. As you've probably noticed, anxiety tends to direct your attention toward potential dangers and problems outside of you and beyond your immediate control. And because you can't change what's beyond your control, you feel a greater sense of powerlessness. You might even feel victimized.

However, if you want to harness the power of the away-from motivation to break through fear and anxiety, you need to shift your focus away from dwelling on the failures of the past or worrying about the other shoe dropping in the future, and toward the negative impact these emotions have had on you and your life. So let's take an inventory and define the starting point of your journey of change and self-empowerment.

Create a Powerful Away-from-Anxiety Motivation

List all the things that no longer work for you in your struggles with fear and anxiety. Focus mainly on how you feel inside and not so much on what is going on outside of you. For example, "I feel drained, empty, anxious. I have no self-esteem left . . . ," rather than, "My life sucks. My boss is horrible. I'll lose my job, and I won't have enough money."

Answer the following questions. Don't contemplate or analyze; just write the first answers that come to your mind. Again, you want to gain momentum and build away-from motivation and not feel discouraged or even paralyzed by the blocks and burdens of the past.

- **What emotional and behavioral responses to certain people or situations pose a problem for you?** Examples: I worry when my kids are out with their friends. My mind is racing with self-doubt and judgment. My entire body aches with tension before I enter a board meeting.
- **What did or do you not allow yourself to do because of anxiety?** Examples: I didn't speak up when I was treated unfairly by my colleague. I don't tell my spouse how I really feel because I am afraid he (or she) would criticize me. I stopped calling my friends because I believe they think I'm no fun to spend time with.
- **How much have fear and anxiety cost you (not necessarily monetarily)?** Examples: My life has shrunk to the size of my office and my bedroom, and I feel really limited by my shriveling world. I've stopped trying to advance at work, which makes me feel like a loser in the eyes of my family. I've gained weight because I eat comfort food to make myself feel better.
- **Which aspects of your life have been negatively affected by your fear and anxiety? What will your life look like in five years if you don't change now?**

Examples: I'll have lost my job, my marriage, and most of the things that are important to me. My health will be even more affected by the stress and worries. I'll have no hope that I can ever have a different life.

How do you feel after answering these questions? Do you notice an internal push building, telling you that the time is now to start moving away from the fear and anxiety that have kept you stuck?

Know How Far You've Come

In addition to creating breakthrough momentum by using the away-from motivation, there's another reason why this first question—"Where are you now?"—is so important: keeping track of where you started will become even more significant to you as you make progress toward your goals and after you've reached them. In the process of making progress, we often forget where we actually came from and how far we've come. The human mind is conditioned to always want more, which, in itself, is a very good trait. On the downside, it can also lead to ongoing discontent and impatience. It often astounds me that as soon as people feel better, a kind of amnesia eclipses the memories of how miserable they were a mere few months prior, and they stop appreciating the amazing changes they have been able to achieve.

Cathy, one of my clients, called me one day because she felt that she really hadn't progressed, that she was still in the same place she'd been when she started working with me. During our first session, a few months before that call, she wasn't even able to go on walks because of pain and an overwhelming sense of exhaustion. She felt paralyzed by anxiety and low self-esteem, and she was isolating herself more and more from her friends and family.

In that first session, Cathy told me that she'd pretty much given up hope of ever spending quality time outdoors again. When she recently called me to complain that nothing had changed for her, she'd just returned from a fabulous weekend of kayaking and camping with friends in the San Juan Islands. After the kayaking trip, the discontent that prompted her call came from not yet having found a romantic relationship. All Cathy was focusing on was what was not yet working in her life, making this lack her reality, rather than appreciating how far she actually had come. When I read to her how she'd replied in our first session to the question "Where am I now?" she became very quiet and finally said, "Thank you. This really helps. Now I realize how much I've actually healed and what amazing potential I must have inside. If I was able to overcome these physical and anxiety problems, I can solve any other problem, as well."

After you've worked with and broken through fear and anxiety, look back on your journey and appreciate the progress and the achievements you've made. This increases your sense of confidence and self-appreciation, and it will also motivate and encourage you to continue to grow and expand your life.

QUESTION 2: WHAT DO YOU WANT?

This is probably the single most important question when it comes to any form of change, and for many, it's also the hardest one to answer. As I've already described, our subconscious has two main areas of focus and motivation: (1) to watch out for potential danger and avoid pain and (2) to look for opportunities to experience joy and pleasure.

The Space Beyond the Board

Have you ever tried to break through a one-inch wooden board with your bare hands? Even if you haven't, you can probably imagine how your first instinct is to focus on the hard obstacle. The problem is that if your focus stays on the board, you can't break through it, because right before your hand reaches the wooden surface, something inside of you yanks back, just for a few milliseconds, as if to say, "Are you sure that you can or want to do that? Are you sure that this won't hurt?" As your hand slams painfully against the hard surface without affecting the board at all, these fears seem to be confirmed. Then the next time you try to break through the same board, it appears even thicker, and this doubtful voice is probably even louder and more assertive. While your resolve and your strength weaken, the only thing that seems to break is your belief that you can actually smash this board into pieces.

To succeed with any breakthrough, you need to focus on the space beyond the board and imagine that your hand can cut through the wood as if it were butter. What matters is the destination that is five inches beyond the obstacle.

What You Focus on Increases

In a fairly recent study, participants were tested for the level of pain stimulated by a computer-controlled heat pump.[1] Researchers told the subjects to expect different levels of painful heat at specifically timed intervals. The shortest interval (seven seconds) signaled the least pain stimuli (and therefore the least discomfort); the longest interval (thirty seconds) signaled the most severe heat-induced pain stimuli. The researchers used fMRI to measure the changes in subjects' brain activity.

After one or two days of training, the researchers began to mix up the signals without informing the participants. Based on what they'd been told and had experienced, the subjects expected a certain temperature, but they actually received a higher or lower temperature stimuli. The fMRI results showed that when people expected to endure severe heat, they sensed a significantly higher level of pain than when they anticipated only mild discomfort. You've probably experienced this phenomenon yourself. When you're told—for example, by your dentist—that something will hurt, you focus on the pain you'll feel, and you'll wait for it to show up.

In the same way, the more we expect to feel anxiety, the sooner we'll feel it. What we focus on magnifies. When we believe that we're incapable and insecure or that the world is a scary and unfriendly place, we subconsciously look for evidence that can corroborate these limiting ideas. Most of us spend more time and energy focusing on our problems than asking ourselves what we would like to have instead and how we could achieve it. This way, we don't provide our mind with a new goal, and we don't mobilize and utilize the pulling force of the toward motivation.

Think about a time in your life when you *really* wanted something, whether it was a new car, a house, or that amazing person you were attracted to. When you made up your mind about what you wanted, you probably saw the exact car everywhere, noticed "for sale" signs on numerous homes, or felt your heart skip a beat when you spotted in the crowd someone who looked similar to that special person. This is one of the great benefits of consciously defining your goals: when you know what you're looking for, your subconscious mind searches tirelessly for opportunities for you to get it.

"What do I want?" I know that for many, this question appears almost too large to contemplate, especially if you had been fixated on what you don't want. I can hear you asking, "What if I don't know, or what if I want the wrong thing?" There is no such thing as a wrong answer; however, some answers may be more in alignment with your conscious and subconscious mind than others. So let's address this question in steps to fully engage and excite your head and your heart.

Four Steps for Creating a Powerful Toward Motivation

1. **Choose the opposite.** Go back to the inventory you just compiled, the list of all the feelings and aspects of fear and anxiety that you're eager to change. On a separate paper, write the exact opposite to each item you've already listed. State the desired outcome in positive terms. If you define your outcome as, "I don't want to feel afraid anymore," or "I want to be free of anxiety and doubt," a large portion of your energy and focus will still go toward fear and anxiety. So phrase your intention in a positive way, such as, "I want to be at peace" or "I choose to feel calm, centered, and confident."

2. **Imagine your future. What will it be like? What will you allow yourself to do?** Now go beyond the lists from question 1 and focus on other ways you want to feel about yourself and your life. Choose words that aren't too abstract. "I want to be happy" seems to be a desirable goal, but from the subconscious point of view, it may be too vague or too generic and, therefore, not as strong a motivation as it could be. The goal is to be as elaborate and specific as possible about what breaking through fear and anxiety will mean to you. Go through your daily life and create a new future vision of yourself. For example, "I wake up in the morning rested and rejuvenated. I feel positive and energized and look forward to what the day will bring to me. I experience myself as a person who is full of potential and able to meet any challenges with ease and competence. People enjoy my company, and I am fully present in the now, enjoying every moment . . ."

3. **Describe what you will feel about yourself and your life when you've moved beyond fear and anxiety into self-empowerment.** Will you be calm and relaxed? Optimistic and hopeful? Confident and self-accepting? Will you be excited about the great opportunities life brings? Appreciative for the blessings you already have? At peace with the past?

4. **Engage your senses.** What will you see, hear, smell, and taste when you've reached self-empowerment? By imagining these things, you're adding sensory substance to your goals, which makes them even more desirable and "real" for your subconscious mind. For example, you aim to approach your life with more confidence and ease. Imagine your body feeling relaxed and comfortable while you get dressed, the smell of freshly brewed coffee or tea greeting you when you enter the kitchen, the self-assured sound of your voice as you talk to your boss, or the warm sensation in your heart when you look into the smiling eyes of your loved one. The more vividly you can imagine being your new, empowered

self and the more excited you become about this vision, the more your subconscious will support you becoming it.

Uncover Your Inner Resources

You may be thinking, "What if I don't know how what I want feels or looks like? And how can I correctly do these steps to clearly define what I want if I have never had any of these positive feelings?" Don't worry. There's more you can do to become clear and motivated.

Let's say your goal is to be peaceful, confident, or optimistic; however, you find that you have a hard time imagining these wonderful feelings because you're convinced that you've experienced only the lack of them, in the forms of anxiety, insecurity, and uneasiness. Now is that really true? Haven't there been moments in your life when you basked in these positive feelings, even if those times were brief?

We all have an enormous reservoir of past experiences stored in our subconscious. What we need to do is to bring the positive memories to light. You might recall the calmness that overcame you when you were somewhere in nature, in a church, or in a temple. You might remember the delicious peace you felt on a quiet Sunday morning while you were gently drifting back and forth between being asleep and awake. You might bring to mind the moment of pride you felt on your graduation day, the confidence you felt after your first promotion, or the overwhelming joy you felt when you first glimpsed at your newborn child. And you may recover the memory of your favorite pet, who used to look at you with unconditional love and adoration. For the subconscious mind, the circumstances aren't as important as the energy and quality of the emotion they evoked. Remembering, reliving, and embracing even the briefest instances of positive feelings are sufficient for your subconscious to comprehend what you would like to experience more of in the future.

As you consult your memory to tap into positive, enticing emotions, intentionally immerse yourself in the past. Allow your mind and your body to fully reexperience the events and their circumstances using the following steps:

1. **Take a stroll down memory lane** and revisit empowering, uplifting, or calming episodes in your life. Make a list of those special moments and focus on how you felt during those times.
2. **Try to describe those feelings** and then notice where you can still sense them in your body. As soon as you register such a positive sensation in

your physical body, your subconscious mind designates this emotion as a resource that is instantly available to you from now on.

3. **Repeat this process with several different memories,** so you can stock up on these resources until it's fairly easy for you to access the desired emotion.

By the way, to reassure your skeptical side, let me tell you that recalling positive situations and the emotions connected with them has nothing to do with living in the past or pretending. All you're doing is instructing your subconscious about what you want, so that you can steer it more precisely toward your goals and preferences. As I've said before, I believe that our subconscious is in many ways superior to our conscious mind, but it still requires our conscious input to operate and support us in the most beneficial way.

Closing the Gap

Despite all your efforts, if you have felt anxious and insecure for a long time, you may not be able to imagine how it will feel to be confident and joyful again. The gap may seem so wide that you can't envision leaping across it, let alone believe you'll ever be on the other side. If this is the case for you, it can be very useful to define the substages that will bridge the gap between where you are now and where you want to end up.

For example, focus on feeling a bit of hope or being a little calmer or more relaxed for at least part of the day. Then focus on being willing to give your inner-change work a good effort. Once you have been able to climb to higher emotional levels, you can then concentrate on appreciating some of the success you've had so far, which will get you closer to confidence and self-empowerment.

Don't rush or push yourself. Take your time and make sure that each of the emotional stepping stones you're advancing to feels solid and stable. Patience is a powerful ally on your path to change. As you contemplate your goals, keep in mind that at any time you can go back and adjust them. With a greater understanding of yourself, you will gain greater clarity of your ambitions and desires.

QUESTION 3: HOW WILL YOU KNOW THAT YOU'VE REACHED YOUR GOALS?

Although it may appear redundant at first glance, this question is different from the previous one, "What do you want?" The former provides the general direction. If you don't know where you want to go, it's difficult to know if you've arrived. The question "How will you know that you've reached your goals?" asks you to focus on specific convincers, the evidence that clearly indicates to you that you've reached your destination and accomplished your intentions.

How You Know You Are in Paris

As an analogy, let's say you want to travel to Paris. As soon as you spot the Eiffel Tower, you know that you've arrived in the City of Lights. This landmark is what convinces you that you're in Paris. But would just knowing you're in Paris fulfill your dreams of traveling there? Would you then turn back toward the airport, telling yourself, "Been there, done that"? Probably not, because arriving in Paris isn't enough for you. There's so much more you want to explore and experience: the Louvre, Notre Dame, Sacré-Coeur Basilica, and all that delicious food.

Convincers are the landmarks, the specific ingredients that make the difference between where you are now and where you want to be. They need to be specific, enticing, and, ideally, measurable. Convincers give your motivation toward your destination an additional boost.

Your "what do you want?" goals could be to feel confident and relaxed and to go about life in self-empowered ways. What would demonstrate to you that you've achieved these goals? Maybe you are able to stay calm and secure during a performance review with your boss. Maybe you can talk comfortably with complete strangers during a party. If procrastination is a part of your anxiety challenge, perhaps you've paid your bills on time and followed through with all your commitments for at least three months in a row.

Convincers define in more detail the parameters for success. We all thrive on success, on achieving what we've set out to do. Success reassures us that we have potential and capabilities. It provides us with the motivation to keep going or aim for even higher goals. But what or who usually defines success for you? Are you truly self-reliant and do you decide for yourself whether you've succeeded or failed? Or do you tend to let others make that call because you don't have enough trust in your own judgment? There is hardly anything more personal than the journey of growth and self-empowerment on which you've embarked, so it makes sense that only you can define what success means to you.

As you go through this very personal process, you may have moments of doubt and discouragement, wondering whether you're on the right track and whether you've made any progress at all, despite your efforts. Some people in your life won't appreciate and approve of your changes, your newfound confidence and inner peace, as much as you would hope for, which may further add to your uncertainty. Others may passionately tell you what they *know* is best for you, expecting you to accept and comply with their "brilliant" ideas. Having a clear concept about some important end points of your inner journey will help you stay focused, unwavering, and motivated on *your* goals until you reach your destination.

Three Steps for Defining Your Convincers

1. **Imagine how you will interact differently with the world around you when you've reached your goals but nothing outside of you has significantly changed.** The people in your life, job, and the place you live are all still the same. How would you act differently around these people and in your normal environment once you've reached your goals? For example, you might say, "I would speak more openly and directly with my spouse," "I would no longer take the grumpiness of my coworker personally," or "I would be able to go to sleep in a clutter-free bedroom."

2. **Pick a few challenging situations that have often triggered fear and anxiety for you. Imagine how you might feel about and deal with these challenges in a different, more resourceful way.** What responses to these challenges would convince you that you've changed and reached your goals? And how many times would you have to experience these positive changes to trust that they are permanent? Find the balance between realistic and fantastic. In other words, create a vision that is believable and exciting at the same time. For example, "I could say no and create healthy boundaries when my boss asks me to work overtime on the weekends," "I would tell my neighbors to turn their music way down if they were blasting it again at 2:00 a.m.," "I would calmly watch my kids leaving for their overnight camp, knowing that they will be alright, and would enjoy a nice evening with my spouse."

3. **Set up motivational intermediate convincers.** There's always a way to get to where you want to go. Maybe you're more comfortable with defining intermediate goals that keep you focused and on track or taking smaller steps at first and moving through a series of solidifying resting places between where you are now and where you want to be. What smaller goals would you like to

reach in order to prove to yourself that you've gained ground and made some progress? For example, "I would go to the grocery store in sweatpants and still feel good about myself," "I would openly share with my friends that I am working on breaking through my fears and insecurities," or "I would admit to others when I have made a mistake or was wrong."

Whether you like to focus on one intermediary stepping stone at a time or feel ready to take greater leaps, the pace of this journey is totally up to you. Convincers help you along the way by making your successes more real and believable, thus reenergizing your motivation to go even further than you thought possible for you.

QUESTION 4: WHY DO YOU WANT TO REACH YOUR GOALS?

To paraphrase Anthony Robbins, a well-known life strategist, writer, and inspirational speaker, "The more powerful the *why* you decide to do anything, the greater the likelihood for you to succeed." Any change and growth usually stirs up some inner resistance. Maybe you're concerned that people will no longer like you after you've changed, or you doubt that you really deserve a better life. Or maybe you're tempted to slip into the familiar grooves of old habits because it feels more comfortable there than it does to change. Maybe you're telling yourself impatiently, "This is too hard" and let the momentary lack of trust and drive break your momentum. These are just some of the usual suspects, which, if you don't have strong enough reasons to maintain your goals, might tempt you to give up and retreat to the old comfort zone. The *why* question is your litmus test for finding out whether or not you're ready to jump off the fence and truly go ahead and change. Is there enough energy behind your decision to move forward?

Behind most of our activities is the driving force of a powerful *why,* which keeps us going even during times when we would rather stay in bed or take a vacation. The *whys* are closely connected to our core values and function as a stable, foundational current, although they are not always in the forefront of our minds.

How many mothers or fathers do you know who've forgotten what it means to relax and let themselves be taken care of because during the few moments they're not changing diapers, cooking, cleaning, driving to soccer practice, and maybe working at another job, they're thinking about what else needs to be done? How many small business owners do you know who sacrifice all their time and energy to keep their enterprise going? What about diehard marathon runners who repeatedly endure the pain and agony of grueling, long-distance races? How many of those people actually gave up their kids, their businesses, or their runs?

None of them, right? Or at least they didn't without extenuating circumstances. But while they pursued their missions and objectives, there were also those moments when they had to dig inside and somehow find additional energy and resources to get over obstacles and keep themselves forging forward. And when the greatest push and effort were required—just when they were digging the deepest—a little voice inside asked, "Why am I doing this?" Their answers could be, "Because I want my kids to be happy and healthy," "Because I want my business to succeed," or "Because I love to run, love to finish." I'm sure you had similar experiences yourself. The strength and resilience of the human spirit is astonishing. And it's the *whys* behind what we do that allow us to tap into that strength.

Twelve years ago, realizing *why* helped me go beyond my perceived limitations and ultimately change my life. I was in the high desert of New Mexico at a kundalini yoga retreat. It was my birthday, and I was bracing myself for a long day of meditation and exercise with 1,600 other yogis and yoginis. Soon it became clear that, unlike us, the air wouldn't move all day. By 9:30 a.m., the temperature had climbed to 100 degrees.

Still, I felt ready for the first of many challenging and invigorating meditations. Keep in mind this was not the sitting-on-a-pillow-and-letting-your-thoughts-float-away kind of meditation. Part of the philosophy of this retreat was that by going through physically demanding exercises, we could overcome mental blocks and clear our psyches of emotional baggage. I admit this was a rather heroic approach, given the heat and the fact that each posture is supposed to be held for either thirty-one or sixty-two minutes straight. But it worked for me. As soon as the amnesia kicked in, letting me forget the pain, I decided to return each year.

The facilitator didn't know it was my birthday, so he didn't cut me any slack—and I am certain he wouldn't even if he knew. The first meditation he introduced involved holding up our arms at a sixty-degree angle while chanting a specific mantra and locking eyes with the person sitting opposite us for *only* sixty-two minutes. Murmurs of disbelief and nervous laughter went through the room. Everybody held onto the slim hope that the facilitator was joking.

But since he never joked and offered not even the faintest smile, all we could do was to surrender to our inevitable fate.

During the first ten minutes, I remained optimistic. Maybe it wouldn't be that hard after all. But the struggle soon began. My arms started to feel really heavy, and my neck and shoulders tightened into knots. Waves of shooting pain pulsated from my hips and lower back, while my calves and feet started to numb.

A familiar, seductive voice first whispered, then pleaded, "This is too hard. Why don't you just sit this one out? You can end this agony right now. Just go to the bathroom. Don't you have to go anyhow? It's your birthday. You shouldn't suffer like this." This coercion didn't make it any easier to remain steadfast. All too quickly, I had to find very powerful *whys* to be able to maintain this meditation for fifty more minutes. First, I reminded myself that getting up now would be giving up in front of 1,599 people, which would be quite embarrassing. I also didn't want to honor my birthday by being defeated by a yoga meditation (albeit a grueling one). My goal was to strengthen my inner focus and my ability to overcome discomfort through commitment. I tried to recall how amazingly cleansing, empowering, and uplifting it had felt every time I'd been able to master such a meditation.

But then I recognized the biggest *why*. It was sitting right in front of me in the form of an amazingly beautiful woman who had offered to be my yoga partner on this special day. As far as I could tell, she hadn't moved at all but remained completely still—like a rock. She was looking at me with honey-brown eyes and even wore a little smile on her angelic face. Could she tell that I was struggling? Was she amused by me, or was she trying to beam me support through that smile? All of a sudden, I felt a surge of renewed energy and determination rising up from somewhere deep inside of me. Part of it came from the thought "If she can do it, I can do it."

Beyond that, I knew I wanted to hold the pose for *myself*, but I also didn't want to disrupt the woman's concentration and resolve. It was no longer only about choosing the goal of enlightenment over comfort; now the stakes were higher and the *whys* more potent. I was determined to give my best to support—and hopefully also impress—my partner, at least a little bit.

It worked. I was able to move through that meditation and seven similar ones with surprising ease. Four years later, I also convinced my beautiful partner to marry me.

What Are the "Whys" for Your Breakthrough?

Although it may appear perfectly obvious to you why you want to change and overcome fear and anxiety, take this opportunity to further amplify this powerful resource, which can lift you beyond the perceived obstacles you may encounter along the way.

1. **List all the reasons for you to break through fear and anxiety and empower yourself now.** Think about the positive effects this outcome will have on your life and how the changes you're making can also benefit the people you care about. Spend some time considering how remaining where you are right now would negatively impact your life. It's perfectly fine to repeat answers from the previous questions and to notice whether you can generate an even stronger sense of motivation and determination in this process.

2. **Think ahead to possible future points of resistance.** Determine the whys you'll need as leverage to overcome these obstacles. What are the most convincing reasons for continuing to make every effort to reach your goals? For example, you may already foresee that one day you'll tell yourself that it's selfish to focus so much on yourself: "I shouldn't be that selfish. What about putting my job, my family, my friends first?" Your *why* response could be that by taking care of yourself and by being well and at your best, you're also getting ready to be of better service and support to others.

Or you may predict sabotaging self-talk, such as, "This is all too ingrained and too difficult to overcome." Think how you'd like to counterbalance this doubt, and formulate a strong statement that keeps you committed to your growth, such as, "I've created these patterns, and therefore I can uncreate them. By continuously working on myself I can establish new, empowering patterns and soon be in charge of my thoughts, my feelings, and my actions, which puts me in charge of my life."

I know I've said it before, but it's so important that it bears repeating: to get the subconscious mind involved, make sure that the *whys* are not only logical and reasonable by nature, but that they also elicit a strong emotional response for you. The best arguments matter only if they matter to us.

QUESTION 5: WHO IS THIS CHANGE FOR?

Are you mainly thinking about yourself when it comes to reaching your goals, or are you equally, or even more, motivated to make someone else happy? You may believe that it's much more honorable and evolved to think first and foremost about others, even when it concerns your personal goals. You want to make sure that the important people in your life benefit from your changes, not only because you care about them, but also because you want them to approve of you.

However, having other people in mind during your own breakthrough process can prove distracting. It may even lead to confusion and inner conflicts about what you'd like to accomplish versus what others want you to do. Let's face it—creating a goal that is mainly designed to please others doesn't really get you any closer to feeling confident and positive about yourself.

The man who decides to stop smoking because he wants to get his nagging wife off his back eventually begins to resent his spouse every time he longs for a cigarette, and sooner rather than later, he starts smoking again. If your main reason for letting go of fear and anxiety and becoming more empowered is to make your family happy, to impress your boss, or to have more friends, you're making your outcome dependent on other people's approval.

This is not to say that you shouldn't consider how your relationships might be affected by your personal growth. As I mentioned before, you wouldn't feel as motivated to change if you were worried that these changes might jeopardize your marriage, your job, or other parts of your life that are important to you. In my experience, profound change and self-empowerment are not always immediately appreciated by those around us. You may initially feel encouraged and supported in your efforts to find your true, confident self. But at some point, the people who were used to dealing with that smaller, more insecure person may turn out to be a little disgruntled as you're speaking and standing up for yourself in a more self-empowered way. If others' approval is a large part of your motivation and you're not receiving the positive feedback you were hoping for, you could potentially judge your growth as a mistake or a failure and, at the same time, start to resent those who aren't applauding your changes.

Determining whether you're mainly self-motivated or whether you're making improvements for others' sake is crucial. You're much more likely to stay focused and overcome any resistance that presents itself along the way if the driving force of the journey to change comes from within you. This doesn't mean that you shouldn't ask for and receive encouragement and support while you're working on yourself. The people who care about you can serve as catalysts, now and then providing that extra boost of energy to keep you going. Yet the primary energy and motivation needs to come from within you and be for you.

QUESTION 6: WHAT WILL YOU LOSE IF YOU GET YOUR DESIRED OUTCOME? WHAT WILL YOU GAIN?

There are two aspects of asking yourself what you will lose when you reach your goals. The first one can further boost your away-from energy by renewing your awareness of the things you no longer desire and accept, such as anxiety, insecurity, or indecisiveness. It can help you move beyond your previous answers and access an even deeper level of realization of what you want to change and let go of. The second aspect addresses one of the major blocks to change, which is the fear of doing so. It is a law of nature: change is inevitable. However, when and how it occurs is largely dependent on the degree to which you allow fear of change to hold you back.

Robert, a highly intelligent young man, breezed through high school with straight A's and great ease. However, when he started college, something inside him changed, and within a few months, the optimistic and interested student became increasingly anxious, insecure, and indecisive. He became so overwhelmed with anxiety and obsessive thinking that he needed to take a leave of absence from school. He could no longer manage the daily stresses of being a student. Moving back with his parents combined with the inertia that came with taking the leave only aggravated Robert's anxiety and sense of powerlessness. Yet, surprisingly, a part of him accepted this situation as more bearable than going back to college and facing the challenges of interacting with fellow students, trying to grasp new subjects, or taking a test and possibly failing.

His mother was very distraught about her son's sudden deterioration and tried to help him by dragging him from one psychiatrist or counselor to the next. Robert didn't really participate in the sessions and insisted that his issues were so complex that nobody would be able to understand or help him. His resistance to change was greater than his desire to feel better. The driving force to even consider any form of therapy was his mother's persistence. As soon as the therapists touched on a subject Robert wasn't comfortable addressing, or if they asked him to do some self-improvement homework, he decided to discontinue the sessions.

Robert's example shows how powerful the fear and resistance to change can be. Despite all the pain of being locked into fear and anxiety, the fear of having to suffer the even greater discomfort of actual change squashed any motivation to move forward.

Fear is usually the fear of losing something of value. So what are you afraid of losing when you reach your goals? This question is extremely important because it will help you to identify possible secondary benefits for staying stuck in fear and anxiety, which could end up leading you to self-sabotage your efforts to change and grow. Robert was facing three major aspects of the fear of change: the fear of losing face through potential failure, the fear of losing safety, and the fear of losing love and attention, which he received in ample ways from his mother and anybody who was trying to help him.

Take some time, be completely honest with yourself, and contemplate the possibility that a part of you prefers the uncomfortable place you're in because it's a comfort zone. Consider the following:

- Does the possibility of failure appear more threatening and unpleasant than staying stuck in the place you're in right now?
- Do you believe that anxiety actually gives you a certain edge that makes you perform better and helps you succeed, or provides for your own safety and that of others?
- Do fear and insecurity give you a conscious or subconscious excuse to not fully show up in life and to turn your back on your dreams, which may appear to be safer than changing because you won't be judged, criticized, or disappointed?
- Do you get more attention and support from others by staying where you are?
- Are you afraid that there will be nothing left of you if you let go of the anxiety?

Notice any potentially hidden agendas that may run like an undercurrent in your subconscious. Once you've detected secondary benefits for not changing, consider whether they truly *benefit* you more than reaching your goals. For example, is it really true that it's safer to stay stuck than to pursue your goals and dreams? Is living your life from a place of fear and doubt—and believing that you're not good enough or that you're powerless—the best way to stay out of harm's way, let alone enjoy your life? And is there really such a thing as failure, or are there simply opportunities for you to learn and grow?

Aren't there better ways for you to get attention, love, and support? Wouldn't you prefer to be recognized, respected, and appreciated for your true empowered self instead of for your limitations? And even beyond that, wouldn't you rather give yourself the attention you're craving instead of needing to get it from somebody else? Noticing and addressing these deeper concerns right at the beginning of your breakthrough work, lifting them from the subconscious to your conscious awareness, will make the entire process go much more smoothly.

The question about the gains of change is more straightforward. Except when applied to body weight, the word *gain* has a positive connotation for most people. It's a natural desire to acquire more and to keep it. Thinking about the benefits you will gain by reaching your goals increases your level of toward motivation. It may be tempting to go easy on yourself and recycle answers from previous questions about how reaching these goals will positively affect your life. Instead, dig deeper to see whether you can find even more enticing reasons and greater benefits for breaking through fear and anxiety, benefits that could also counterbalance your concerns about change. Imagine what it would mean for you to gain inner peace, the courage to start something new, the strength and clarity to fulfill your dreams, and the freedom to be yourself.

Eventually Robert felt that the pain of being stuck was greater than the imagined pain of changing—a shift that coincided with his mother losing some of her patience with him. He decided that he was too young and too talented to give up on himself, and he started to focus more on what he could gain from working on himself. This decision made Robert stay in therapy and return to college.

QUESTION 7: WHICH OF YOUR QUALITIES AND STRENGTHS WILL HELP YOU REACH YOUR GOALS?

A goal that can't be reached is nothing but a pleasant dream that eventually will turn into the nightmare of failure and defeat. This is why, no matter how exciting and motivating the goals you've created seem, you need to ask yourself, "Do I have what it takes to reach them?" I know that if you've been feeling trapped in anxiety and insecurity, you may have had your serious doubts about that, but only if you address these doubts now will you avoid getting stuck in them later. That's what makes this question pivotal.

We all have an enormous potential inside us that has helped us reach two of the most challenging milestones in life: learning how to walk and to talk. Can you imagine how difficult it was to move your whole reality from the horizontal to the vertical? And what effort it must have taken to form words with your mouth and vocal cords? At that time, you didn't have a mind-set of doubt and limitation. Otherwise a few painful falls on your face and unsuccessful attempts to communicate would have been enough for you to decide that it was all too difficult and that you simply didn't have what it takes to grow up. When you were a baby or toddler, succeeding was the only option, and you pursued your goals with a relentless tenacity and a steadfast belief in yourself. Nothing could stop you. Sure, there was frustration, but there was also the enormous joy of discovery, learning, and mastering each phase of these challenges. So you already know that you were born with enormous potential.

I'm certain that walking and talking haven't been your only successes in life. You've probably just failed to acknowledge your wins. Unfortunately, this is a very common oversight, which has been often disguised as modesty and humility. Don't get me wrong—being modest and humble can be virtues and signs of character. However, many people believe that they can't appreciate their successes unless they make the news or do something massively beneficial to humankind, such as finding the cure for cancer or solving the world energy crisis. Anything less than that is just "normal." How uplifting and encouraging is that? If you want to get ready to break through fear and anxiety, now is not the time for making yourself smaller. Now is the time to examine your past successes and identify the strengths, knowledge, qualities, and tools that enabled you to achieve them.

If you've ever explained to someone how to tie shoelaces, swim, or ride a bike, you know how challenging it is to teach these "ordinary" skills. You may even recall how challenging it was for you to learn them yourself. When all the frustrating trials and tribulations were finally over and you had reached that sweet moment of success, weren't you overcome by an almost intoxicating mixture of excitement, joy, and pride? Well, if you don't remember that, you may at least have witnessed with great elation your own children passing through these milestones. You've had countless successes and achievements in your life—the first time you were able to write your name, the first time you went to school by yourself, the first time you drove a car—most of which you ignore or belittle. All of them have one thing in common: you made them happen by applying your personal success strategy.

Your strategy for success is the combination of the specific qualities that have helped you move from the questions to the answers, from problems to solutions, from challenges to achievements. In fact, you've developed a strategy for pretty much everything: how to brush your teeth, how to show your spouse your affection, how to barbecue a hamburger. Over time, you've probably improved and perfected your approaches to achieve better and more satisfying results. So when it comes to learning more about your success strategy and how to reach your goals, you can refer to a large number of past experiences. All you need to do is to ask yourself the right questions.

What are your successes? What goals have you already been able to reach? Again, don't think in terms that are too grandiose. Every test you passed, every obstacle you overcame, every new skill you learned can be included in your list.

Which of your personal qualities ensured your success? For example, do you like to analyze and evaluate your options thoroughly to avoid running into obstacles? Are you at your best when you begin right away and figure things out as you go along? Are you quick on the uptake and able to learn from others' success strategies? Was it your tenacity or your creativity that made you achieve your desired outcomes? Were curiosity and your talent for thinking outside the box part of your success strategy? Were you relying on your ability to stay up all night and mobilize the necessary energies when it mattered the most? Do you know how to ask for help, or are you proficient at delegating?

It's a very good idea to also ask the people who know you well for their opinion about your success strategies. You may be surprised what your parents or siblings can tell you about resources you already had as a child but may have forgotten about.

How can you now benefit from these qualities? Which of your strengths and strategies can support you during your breakthrough? And how specifically can you utilize them as you're moving forward on this journey of self-empowerment? For example, your analytical capabilities allow you to thoroughly examine how to apply the insights and tools of this book to your life in the most effective way. Curiosity and tenacity can keep you motivated, focused, and help you to make your healing and growth a priority. With your ability to ask for help, you can engage a friend to become your accountability partner and help you to stay on track.

As you answer the preceding questions, treat yourself with generosity, encouragement, and open-mindedness. This way you will gain the awareness and confidence that you have what it takes to make your goals your reality.

Rest assured that, at this point, it's perfectly OK for you to still have thoughts such as "I'd better not get my hopes up. I'll just get disappointed again" or "Others may be able to succeed, but not me" or "My problems are way too big to ever get resolved." As you know, a part of you has been struggling with doubts, insecurities, and the fear of failure. Let's start talking to this part.

CHAPTER 6

Look Who's Talking!

ADDRESSING NEGATIVE SELF-TALK AND MIND-RACING

WE'RE CONSTANTLY TALKING to ourselves, but it might not be out loud. Some inner self-talk can be a way to consciously work through a problem, analyze what just happened, evaluate the pros and cons before we make a decision, or rehearse how we'll act or respond in an upcoming situation. Conscious self-talk allows us to cheer ourselves on, listen to an internal mentor's voice of reason, or review the kind words of a supportive friend. However, a large portion of our self-talk bubbles up from our subconscious mind without us being fully and consciously aware of its details. It appears more as background noise or mind chatter—like the humming of the refrigerator, which we try to tune out and ignore because we find it annoying.

And then there is negative self-talk, which plays a major role in how we create fear and anxiety. You're probably familiar with that voice that rises from somewhere deep inside your subconscious. For some, it sounds worried and insecure; for others, it sounds nagging or whiny, critical or angry. At times it doesn't even sound like your own voice at all; it may remind you of a scared child, a parent, or a teacher. You don't seem to choose the limiting, anxiety-triggering, or self-sabotaging thoughts, nor do you seem to be in control of them.

Negative self-talk can also be more obscure than the previous examples. You know how every now and then out of the blue you can feel completely overcome by anxiety? You start frantically searching for obvious reasons for your worries, but nothing around you has changed enough to warrant this emotional tailspin. So how and why did you end up in it? You may be surprised to discover that, most of the time, a series of anxious, negative thoughts that were subtle enough to fly under the radar of your conscious mind preceded the feelings. In other words, you freaked yourself out without even noticing it.

THE THREE TYPES OF ANXIETY-TRIGGERING SELF-TALK

I distinguish between three different types of negative self-talk—three different subconscious voices—that trigger fear and anxiety:

1. "What if" and "what was" talk
2. Self-bashing talk
3. Bashing-others talk

"WHAT IF" AND "WHAT WAS" TALK

This inner voice says history was a disaster that will only repeat itself. Or it tells you that, this time, whatever it is you're doing or about to do will definitely go wrong. It lays out in painful detail why you or those you care about are destined to failure, pain, and suffering—and why it's probably your fault. Sometimes anxiety-triggering thoughts can flash through your mind in terrifying images that are too incoherent to comprehend, too rapid to distinguish one from the other, and too many to escape from.

A client once told me that she often feels as though her mind is like a runaway merry-go-round, spinning faster and faster as if trying to outrun itself. As it spins, she becomes increasingly anxious and confused. Her mind stops racing only when she finally falls asleep after an exhausting day of circular and often catastrophic thinking. As soon as she wakes up the following morning, the ride begins again. Sound familiar?

Regardless of whether the negative self-talk races so quickly that we can't catch the words or follow the train of thought, or whether it moves more slowly, its concerns, doubts, and fears usually circle and cause us to obsess about a fairly small number of topics. The chain of negative thoughts can start with a mere reflection on an event in the past, present, or future. This can be followed by a self-doubting "I should have" or "I can't," which creates a sense of unease. Further accelerating the downward momentum are deep regrets about things that already occurred and worried, what-if assumptions about the possible disasters and failures that haven't yet happened.

The arguments feed off each other, confirming and expanding on the negativity of the previous ones. And all the while, you're losing touch with *what is* and getting lost in the "reality" of *what if* or *what was.* With every thought, the emotional charge increases, taking you on a slippery downward spiral of potential problems and limitations that ends in a dark pit of gloom and doom. By the time you hit bottom, you feel utterly inundated and deflated by anxiety about the fictitious facts that a part of your subconscious mind has just created.

SELF-BASHING TALK

As you probably know too well, self-talk, by nature, can be very judgmental. You doubt and criticize yourself, constantly wondering what faults and flaws other people may discover about you. Let's be honest: how often have you been rude to yourself, calling yourself stupid, fat, ugly, a loser, not good enough? How often have you blasted yourself with derogatory insults that you'd never dare fling at anyone else because your words would hurt them or because they'd cut you out of their lives or would punch you? How often have you shown respect and consideration to others and treated yourself with contempt and disregard?

I routinely ask my clients to carefully listen to and actually write down their negative thoughts. Most of them are surprised to realize how frequently unfriendly thoughts about themselves flash through their mind. But what really shocks them is what they hear themselves saying about themselves. "How can I be so mean and cruel to myself?" is a very common reaction.

BASHING-OTHERS TALK

Another form of negative self-talk is judging and bashing others, which at first may appear less self-destructive than judging and bashing yourself. What most people don't realize is that the subconscious mind takes *everything* personally. So when you're on the road yelling at an obviously clueless driver or you're at work contemplating the utter incompetence of your new coworker, your subconscious registers only feelings of anger and disdain. It is unable to determine whether you're upset with somebody else or yourself. This explains the old saying, "Resentment is like taking poison and waiting for the other person to die."

Judging others doesn't have to lead to anger to count as negative self-talk. Whether you're judging others through comparison, gossip, envy, or *Schadenfreude*—a German expression describing glee in response to another's misfortune (we Germans must be good at it to have invented a word for it)—from the perspective of the subconscious, you're just bashing yourself. And when you consider that, in most cases, being judgmental of others actually stems from a deep insecurity within yourself, you can imagine the detrimental impact such a mental diet can have.

• • •

You might say, "Well, I just can't help it. My self-talk is automatic, from some place in my subconscious and, therefore, out of my control." But is that really true?

WHERE DO NEGATIVE THOUGHTS COME FROM?

Some schools of thought suggest that negative self-talk stems from our ego, or the "monkey mind," which is best ignored or fought by saying to ourselves, "Delete, delete, delete," or "Stop! I don't want to listen to you," or simply, "Shut up." Ignoring or fighting negative self-talk may work sometimes for some people. However, rejecting a part of ourselves doesn't really lead to a greater sense of wholeness and self-acceptance. Instead, wouldn't it be better if you understood where these insecure, doubtful, critical, and anxious thoughts really come from and what they are trying to achieve? Once you do, you'll probably realize why ignoring or scolding this part of you doesn't work in the long run.

Ryan is a good example of someone who felt trapped in negative self-talk and the feelings that came with it. He was a young salesman who had everything going for him: a promising career; a loving wife; two healthy, beautiful children; a life that seemed filled with exciting new possibilities. However, Ryan's internal world didn't reflect that life at all. Since he'd started his own family, he'd struggled with negative, self-defeating thoughts: "Life is hard. I don't think I can ever have what I want. What if I don't meet the next quota and get fired? How will I take care of my family? Maybe they don't care about me anyhow. Maybe they will leave me when I can't provide for them—just like all those 'friends' who don't call me back."

These negative self-talk loops seemed ever-present, regardless of whether Ryan was working, playing with his kids, or trying to enjoy a game of tennis. This constant negativity and shifting between anxiety, insecurity, and depression consumed his energy so that on weekends often all he could do was stay in bed. He saw therapists and had tried antidepressants, but nothing seemed to make a difference. Eventually he started to get frustrated with himself for not being able to make himself feel better, for turning into what he saw as a useless member of society who was just taking up space.

At the time Ryan started working with me, he'd been stuck in that state for several years. When we talked about his childhood, he shared with me that although externally everything appeared quite normal, he'd never felt that anyone really cared about him. He was the youngest of five brothers and had a hard time relating to any of them. His father was mostly absent because of work, and his mother was busy taking care of a big household. Neither parent had the patience or awareness to notice that Ryan was a rather sensitive boy and needed more attention and support than they were giving him. All his basic needs were met; however, there was no warmth, love, or comfort in his home. His parents' behavior was mostly indifferent, neither praising nor punishing, leaving their kids without guidance or reassurance.

The lack of support and attention from his parents had greatly affected Ryan. Since early childhood, he'd felt sad, anxious, and lonely. What made it worse was that he couldn't figure out whether they were incapable of giving more or whether there was something wrong with him for wanting more. At some point, he decided to escape this rather cold family mold. With his eyes set firmly on very specific goals, he forged through high school and college with great discipline and ambition.

In his thirties, Ryan became by far the most successful member of his family and could have enjoyed all his achievements, but the anxiety, sadness, and negative self-talk of the past caught up with him. His growing negativity seeped into his work performance and into his relationship with his wife and kids, often leaving him feeling isolated and rejected just as he had growing up. Why did all these old feelings and patterns resurface at the best time of his life? How could he still feel so bad about his life and himself after all he'd accomplished? Intellectually it didn't make sense. From the perspective of the subconscious mind, however, it does.

Here is why young minds matter. Before the age of ten, your mind is like a dry sponge, soaking up any information from the outside that appears relevant to answering the three basic questions for your survival: "Where do I belong?" "What am I about?" and "What's for dinner?" At that age you're rather powerless when it comes to feeding yourself, paying a mortgage, or dealing with perceived outside danger. You're highly dependent on the acceptance and support of your providers and protectors—mainly your family. A series of scary or confusing experiences during these early years can shake up your trust and confidence. Maybe you were reprimanded or criticized and didn't understand what you had done wrong. You may have been told that you would never amount to anything or just felt that whatever you did, it was never good enough. Maybe you were made fun of, didn't get enough attention, or were left crying alone for what seemed like an eternity, though in reality it may have been for only a few minutes. Or you may have felt like Ryan—unloved, unwanted, and not belonging.

When you were that small and vulnerable, negative messages and sentiments were entering your subconscious mind in osmosis-like fashion. It doesn't take major trauma for you to doubt and wonder whether you're really safe or whether you're good enough, loveable, able to fit in, and can really count on a daily dinner. Many of my clients grew up under completely "normal" and rather uneventful circumstances. But unlike their siblings or friends, their parents' expectations or judgments, their teachers' disapproving remarks, or the pressure of having to fit in with their peers left them with deep imprints of worry, pain, and insecurity. I often reassure my clients that there is nothing wrong with them and that they are not too sensitive. Rather than seeing themselves as flawed or weak, I ask them to feel good about their astute awareness and their courage to recognize and admit to themselves that there are wounds of the past that need to heal.

Like Ryan, you may have a part of your subconscious mind that still holds onto anxiety and limiting beliefs that stem from your childhood. Have you ever wondered why certain situations or people can make you feel small, vulnerable, and helpless? Why do certain triggers bring up the same negative thoughts and deflated feelings that you frequently felt when you were much younger? You want to disappear when you're about to give a presentation, convinced that everyone will notice that you're an inadequate fraud. When your spouse is busy and preoccupied, you feel rejected, unloved, and afraid of being abandoned. You revert to the pouty, defensive attitude of a teenager when you get that reproachful look from your parents for arriving late to Sunday family dinner. Or you blurt out a self-derogatory comment when somebody gives you a compliment, because you were told that feeling good about yourself is arrogant and off-putting. Doesn't all such behavior appear immature and inappropriate, making you sometimes shake your head in disbelief?

These childlike reactions make sense only when you realize that they're driven by a part of your subconscious that is stuck in the past. This part may still perceive you as a young, small, and rather powerless kid. It doesn't recognize that you've become a self-reliant adult and that your life is safe and enjoyable. Until now, you probably haven't consciously realized that this younger self exists. But listening to your negative self-talk or recalling those moments of involuntary immaturity probably makes you understand that a part of you still hasn't fully grown up.

Why does this childlike subconscious part continue to create negative self-talk and old self-defeating patterns—even though this behavior just reinforces pain and anxiety and doesn't allow you to be happy, confident, and able to enjoy your life? The answer is simple: it doesn't know any better because it has never been properly guided, encouraged, and reassured. This younger self believes that the same reasons that warranted anxiety and insecurity when you were a child are still valid today—and that you're still lacking the strength, skills, and knowledge to deal with them any differently. The anxieties and limiting beliefs that are fueling negative self-talk can be deeply ingrained imprints that a part of your subconscious holds onto until it's convinced that you're no longer unsafe—or, as Carl Jung said, "until you've outgrown the problem." The following processes will help you do both.

HOW TO RESPOND TO NEGATIVE SELF-TALK

Let's imagine that you're with a child who is scared. He or she may say, "I'm afraid that I'll fail" or "I'm afraid that I'll get hurt" or "I'm afraid that nobody loves me." How would you respond? Would you shout out, "Delete, delete, delete"? Or "Shut up"? Would you tell the child, "Yes, you're right, you suck and the world is an unfriendly and dangerous place"? Or would you just ignore his or her concerns?

None of those options would be appropriate or helpful. Most likely, the child would feel even more frightened. What you *would* do is comfort and reassure, not merely with intellectual reasoning but with gentle, compassionate kindness from your heart. As a result, the child would feel heard, understood, and, most likely, safe and at ease again.

The part of your subconscious that creates negative self-talk and mind-racing responds in a very similar way because its roots are in your childhood. If you ignore the messages of this subconscious part or try to suppress them with frustration and disgust, it will continue to feel unsafe or even threatened by your efforts to stifle it. To grab your attention, this inner child will intensify the decibels and frequency of its internal cries until you finally get its warnings and take the measures necessary to avoid pain and peril and to stay safe. Remember, this subconscious part is stuck in the past and does not realize yet that you're no longer living in the same circumstances, that you're no longer confronted with the same dangers, and that you're no longer a small child with limited possibilities.

On the other hand, if you pay too much attention to this part of your subconscious and buy into its fears and insecurities, its anxious voice will still become louder, because now you validate its concerns.

So whether you're ignoring, stifling, or buying into the fearful self-talk of the younger self, it will feel confirmed in its beliefs that it is indeed pretty much on its own and that you're not to be relied on or trusted. But don't think this is a no-win situation. There is a better way to deal with this inner, younger part of you, and that is to directly address, reassure, and appease this inner voice.

The following method is a major key to breaking through fear and anxiety and unlocking your untapped potential. It is so effective that, with it, most people can significantly reduce their negative self-talk within a few days. Keep this proven success rate in mind as you delve into this powerful exercise.

STEP 1: TAKE NOTES

Buy a small notebook that you can carry with you at all times, and write down negative self-talk the moment you notice it coming up. This step helps you gain greater awareness of the frequency and the themes of your negative self-talk. Most likely you'll realize that you're simply rehashing the same thoughts with minor variations, depending on the specific situations or issues they spin around. These recurring themes and thought patterns are often reflections of deep-seated emotions, memories, and limiting beliefs. By finding the patterns, you will also shed more light on the root causes of the fear and anxiety you've been dealing with.

Negative self-talk can be disguised as a question, such as, "What if I lose my job?" or "Did I make the right choice?" or "Are my parents disappointed with me?" The negative thoughts behind these questions can be easily unmasked by changing the questions into statements: "I will lose my job." "I didn't make the right choice." "I'm a disappointment to my parents." Turning a worried or insecure question into a negative statement will reveal what you're really afraid of and give you more direct leverage to counterbalance it.

STEP 2: TAKE A REALITY CHECK

After you've jotted down each negative thought, ask yourself:

- Is this thought true?
- Does this thought make me feel good?
- Does this thought help me reach my goals?

Each question acts as a reality check and will help you appreciate that entertaining the thought is hurtful and gets you nowhere.

Let's say you hear yourself thinking, "I look fat," or "I'm not good enough." You may feel that the honest answer to the first question, "Is this true?" would be "yes" or "maybe." But you would probably answer the second two with a resounding "No! The thought makes me feel lousy, and it certainly does not help me reach my goals."

Noticing and immediately questioning the legitimacy and usefulness of the self-talk has two major effects. First, you're mentally taking a step back and no longer identifying yourself with the negative thoughts. You are switching the roles, from being the source of the negativity to being the more objective observer of it. Second, asking these questions interrupts the spiral of negative thinking before it gets out of control and you find yourself in a debilitating state of anxiety. Interrupting a pattern that used to run its course somewhat undisturbed is one of the most powerful methods of change. The moment of interruption is like a healing shock to your subconscious mind, a wake-up call that it can't ignore.

A dog trainer once explained to me that to change a dog's unwanted behavior, such as tugging on its leash in an effort to chase a squirrel, you need to catch the dog at the instant the pattern starts—in this case, the second the dog sights the squirrel and makes the first frantic pull on the leash. At this moment, the trainer first establishes a boundary by telling the dog "no" or "stop." Then he quickly takes out a ball, throws it up into the air, and catches it, immediately diverting the dog's attention. All the animal desires now is that ball, which is in the hands of the trainer—as is the dog. To further solidify who's in charge, the trainer orders the dog to sit down and promptly gives it a treat or verbal praise as positive reinforcement. The trainer assured me that any unwanted pattern can be erased after only a few of these interruptions.

Assuming that our subconscious operates, in many ways, like the mind of a dog would be absolutely accurate and not at all degrading. Any species will respond to boundaries, guidance, and rewards as a motivation to change a pattern. By asking the three simple reality-check questions, you signal to your subconscious that you're taking back the reins and steering your mind into a new, more appropriate, and supportive direction.

In the same way a baby wants to be held in a firm swaddle or children need clear rules from their parents, this younger part of your subconscious desires and requires firm boundaries that will ultimately provide it with a greater sense of safety. However, as with children, establishing boundaries is in itself not enough, because boundaries can be easily misinterpreted by this part of your subconscious mind as a form of dismissal, punishment, or rejection, which might only increase the anxiety. This is why Steps 3, 4, and 5, which follow, are so important.

STEP 3: LOOK AT THE BRIGHT SIDE

A friend, who is an excellent mother, once told me, "After I set a boundary [for my children], I bring my body position to their height, look them in the eyes, and help them focus on the positive aspects of the situation. At the end I always tell them that they're OK and how much I love them." Enforcing boundaries with a child doesn't require withholding guidance, kindness, and love, and neither does enforcing boundaries with your subconscious. You need to treat your subconscious child with the same mindfulness and care that you would an actual child.

The minute you write down the negative thought, also write down convincing arguments that shed light on the opposite, positive points of view. Write down at least three positive thoughts to counterbalance each negative one. If your negative thought was "I'm not smart enough to perform this job," don't just counter with the exact opposite: "I *am* smart enough." Instead, get creative. Talk about all the evidence that proves that you're smart and intelligent. For example, "I have a high-school (or college) degree," "I've been able to solve specific problems," "I've had the following successes . . ." (list examples of successes you've had and problems you've solved).

Here are a few more examples of common negative thoughts and ideas for counterbalancing them:

- **Something bad will happen.** Counterbalances: Right now I'm OK. There've been many times before when I was worried, and everything turned out well. I have the strength and abilities to handle anything that comes my way.

- **My boss doesn't like me.** Counterbalances: I don't really know what my boss is feeling. I'm doing a great job. If I were my boss, I would be happy to have me as an employee.
- **I will never get better.** Counterbalances: I've changed/healed/improved many times before. I'm using this time now to learn about myself and life. My mind is strong, and I'm determined to reach my goals.
- **I will always be alone.** Counterbalances: I'm a good person with many wonderful qualities. Whomever I choose to be with is very lucky. I'm using this time now to become independent, empowered, and my own best friend.
- **My life is so difficult.** Counterbalances: Many good things have happened in my life. I'm growing and improving with every challenge and difficulty. I'm learning to take my life in my own hands and make it easier for myself.
- **This job is killing me.** Counterbalances: I'm taking good care of myself by noticing what is not working for me. I'm a capable person and a great asset for any employer. I know that there are many better opportunities available to me.
- **It's too hard.** Counterbalances: I have the motivation and the strength to reach this goal. Just by staying focused on what I want every day, I'm moving closer to reaching my goal. I value myself too much to give up on my goals.
- **I don't have enough.** Counterbalances: The most important gift I have is myself. I deserve to have more than enough. The world is an abundant place, and I can bring this abundance into my life.

Note that the positive, counterbalancing impact of most answers can be further enhanced by listing specific examples that back up the statement, such as, "I'm doing a great job because I am very reliable, have successfully completed project XYZ, and always seek ways to improve."

Fear and anxiety often come with a very narrow tunnel vision of yourself and the world around you. Yet we all know there is always more than one side to every story. Positive counterbalancing is training your mind to search for and find uplifting and empowering perspectives for any given situation. By doing so, you're consciously guiding the younger part of your subconscious to consider a positive angle on a subject that it previously perceived in only one limiting way.

Soon you're gaining greater openness and flexibility in your perception, so you can move more easily from seeing limitations to seeing possibilities. With every positive thought, you're planting a seed in your mind that supports the growth of your confidence and self-esteem—and the growth of that younger self.

STEP 4: ADD POSITIVE EMOTIONS

In the past, you may have tried to manage negative thinking through positive counterbalancing without great success. Like many other people, you may have given up, frustrated and convinced that the only thing left to do is ignore your thoughts. However, there may be a reason counterbalancing hasn't worked for you yet: you might not have added positive emotions to your positive statements. For the subconscious mind, words have meaning only if they're associated with an image, a sensation, or a feeling. The stronger the emotion, the more profound the meaning. So rather than staying in your head and using this exercise as mental gymnastics or an internal debating club, make sure that you can actually feel and stand behind the positive counterbalancing statements. Make them come from your heart.

I know that feeling positive, kind, and compassionate toward yourself can be a huge challenge, especially when you're struggling with anxiety, low self-esteem, and self-directed anger. It may feel as if you're trying to put out a wildfire with thimblefuls of water or to stir cement with an eyelash. No matter how much effort you put into it, the negative self-talk just keeps on pounding relentlessly inside your head. This is why it's so helpful to remember that the main source of your repetitive negative thoughts is a younger part of your subconscious mind, which is just playing old "tapes" and repeating limiting programs.

Isn't it easier to talk in a calm, reassuring, and comforting way when you visualize addressing a child? By adding kindness and compassion to your counterbalancing positive thoughts, you take on the proactive role of the one who addresses and reassures this inner child. Assuming this role automatically shifts your consciousness and attitude from "I'm powerless" to "I'm taking charge." You're no longer just the victim of your own thoughts; now you can choose what you want to steer your mind toward.

Sometimes I hear my clients complain that they don't really believe in their positive counterbalancing arguments, and that's why this tool doesn't work well for them. It is true that basically lying to yourself (and to your younger self) doesn't get you any closer to yourself or make you feel better. But you don't have to believe 100 percent in all the encouraging things you're finding to say about yourself. Especially at the beginning, it's OK to feel a bit timid or unsure of all the wonderful qualities that make you the amazing person you truly are. What *is* crucial, though, is establishing a connection with that more sensitive and vulnerable younger self and going forward with the intention to deepen that relationship with patience and understanding. Children don't need to know specifically *why* they're loved and safe, but they do need to know that they are. In other words, the intention and energy behind your positive thoughts can carry greater impact than their content.

STEP 5: COMMIT WITH COMPASSION

Your commitment to this five-step exercise is crucial because you don't want to start an inner communication with a subconscious, younger part of you, and then ignore it again. Can you imagine how this would feel to a child? Talk about abandonment!

Yet trying to catch all negative messages, especially if they appear to compete with each other for your attention, can be overwhelming. Instead, commit to counterbalancing seven to eleven negative thoughts per day. By using this method just seven to eleven times per day, most people can significantly reduce negative self-talk within a few days. And the positive results begin immediately. While you're developing a new habit of thinking and feeling positive and optimistic, the younger part of the subconscious mind will feel increasingly calm and secure.

If you're someplace where you can't write down your thoughts, such as during a business meeting or while driving, just walk yourself through the steps in your head. Because it's more effective to spend the time and energy writing and reading your thoughts, you'll benefit from recapitulating a few of them during some quiet time in the evening.

Sometimes you may feel frustrated and upset with this negative and possibly critical voice inside, which is understandable. But rather than pushing this part of you "back into the closet" and out of your awareness, use this frustration to create a clear boundary that lets your inner child know that these thoughts are no longer desirable or helpful. Give yourself and this younger self a timeout by, for example, taking two minutes to simply breathe slowly in and out. Then shift your energy to gentle kindness and compassion while counterbalancing the limiting thoughts. As I said before, like children in general, your younger subconscious self needs to be raised with that special combination of clear boundaries, guidelines, reassurance, and love. Go through this process with patience, mindfulness, and compassion. Don't use it as another opportunity to demonstrate to yourself how hopelessly screwed up you are (or at least a part of you is). Instead, approach this and all the other exercises in this book as demonstrations of how much you care about yourself and how much you're determined to feel better and rise to that next level of your personal evolution.

Ryan told me that by using this exercise and talking to himself just as he would comfort his own children, his negative thought patterns almost completely disappeared within a very short amount of time. What was so eye opening for him was that while he'd been a very kind and loving father, providing his own children with all the support and love he'd missed in his own upbringing, he'd continued to treat himself in the same way his parents had treated him during his own childhood—without encouragement, warmth, and empathy.

"It was amazing to watch how my child self became more and more comfortable and calm," Ryan told me. "The more this part of me trusts in the love of the adult self, the more I trust and love myself."

HOW CAN YOU COUNTERBALANCE FREE-FLOATING ANXIETY?

At this point, you might be thinking, "But I don't hear any negative self-talk. The anxiety is just there, without any thoughts or inner dialogue." You may wake up with tightness in your chest or suddenly feel a sense of uneasiness welling up. In my experience, even in these situations, anxiety is triggered by a series of thoughts in response to an external or internal stimulus (for example, a memory or an anticipation of the future). These thoughts may just pass through your mind so rapidly that you can't compute them consciously. And once the emotion takes over, your outlook on the world and yourself becomes limited and distorted by the anxiety filters. Reality appears frightening although you still don't know why. So your mind ventures off to a fervent search for valid reasons you're in danger. Often, all you can come up with is a *what if* thought, which only confirms that you're probably doomed. So what can you do to prevent the anxiety from taking you hostage?

First of all, a feeling can't take you hostage. It just feels like it can, especially if your conscious mind can't understand its meaning. Let's start with giving the emotion a name. By naming what you feel, you begin to take hold of it. So if you feel anxious but aren't exactly sure what the underlying reason or triggering thought might be, you could begin by saying, "I feel anxious." That's a good start. *Anxious* is a word that can encompass many feelings, most of them negative. So to better manage the free-floating anxiety, you can get more specific: "I feel restless, worried, small, doubtful, overwhelmed, stressed . . ." Finding the specific words that match your feeling will give you valuable information about the triggers and the roots of the anxiety.

By the way, many people confuse excitement with anxiety, because both emotions prompt very similar physiological responses, such as a racing heart, shallow breathing, muscle tension, and so on. However, whether you call yourself anxious or excited makes all the difference in how you evaluate and approach upcoming events, such as a first date, a big presentation, or a move to a new city.

At this point, you've zeroed in on a negative and limiting thought—for example, "I feel worried and restless." This thought might be true, but staying this way doesn't help you reach your goals. So now you can work with the counterbalancing exercise and address that smaller part of you that's the source of these feelings. Think about it: to arrive at this juncture, all you did was put a vague feeling into words.

If you are more inquisitive, you can also be more specific by asking yourself questions such as, "What am I feeling worried and restless about?" "Compared to whom do I feel small?" "What am I doubtful about?" "What appears scary or overwhelming to me?" Sometimes it's quite illuminating to notice what comes up when you say to yourself, "I feel XYZ because . . ." and then just wait for the answer. The more details you capture, the easier it will be for you to counterbalance the thought that describes the anxiety and thus shift the feeling.

By consciously addressing the subconscious source of your negative self-talk, you have started to reconnect and heal that part of you whose reality was defined by fear and anxiety. In this next chapter, you will be able to go even farther and deeper—from reconnection to *reintegration.*

CHAPTER 7

To Wholeness and Beyond

RESOLVING INNER CONFLICTS

HERE IS ONE of the most common challenges people who are dealing with fear and anxiety report: "I'm constantly struggling with myself. Every time I want to change or take a step forward, I hear one voice in my head encouraging me, 'Go for it. You can do it.' But another scared voice says, 'Don't do it. It won't work. You'll just fail and be made fun of.' This argument goes on and on. Usually I end up doing nothing, which makes me increasingly depressed and angry with myself."

Does this challenge sound familiar to you? Are you also finding yourself in the midst of an inner battle? The back-and-forth between anxious, limiting self-talk and confident, encouraging thoughts is just one of the hallmarks of an inner conflict. There are also other signs, which I've listed here, in order of severity.

Self-doubt, indecisiveness, and second-guessing. Isn't it annoying when after you've made a decision you wonder whether you really made the best choice? Even if it's as minor as buying a pair of shoes or ordering lunch at a restaurant, a simple this-or-that decision feels almost like a matter of life and death. Likewise, isn't it frustrating when you come home from work and start analyzing your performance and then beat yourself up for a potential mistake or for making a fool of yourself? Eventually, the fear of failure and rejection becomes stronger than the desire to succeed and enjoy yourself.

Inconsistent, self-sabotaging thoughts, emotions, and behavior. Nobody thinks, feels, or acts the same way all the time; we're always changing our minds. However, if you're struggling with an inner conflict, these mental/emotional flip-flops may appear more pronounced and have a greater impact. One day you might be optimistic and motivated; you start to put yourself in gear to strive toward your goals, drop a habit, or make another significant change in your life. The next day you're thinking that nothing will ever change, that once again you won't succeed, and that you shouldn't even start trying.

Or you hear a tempting voice inside whispering, "Don't push yourself so much. You deserve to give yourself a break. Life is too short." So you procrastinate, or you give up applying yourself to improve.

Or you vacillate between being calm and compassionate when taking care of your kids or your friends and becoming irritated and impatient when it's time to look after yourself. You may watch yourself alternate between feeling like an empowered, self-reliant adult and feeling like an insecure child or teenager. Eventually you become stuck.

Feeling stuck, exhausted, and powerless. If your car has ever been stuck in the mud, you know how an inner conflict can affect you. You're spinning the wheels, trying to somehow gain the traction and momentum to get yourself out, but the harder you try, the deeper you dig yourself in. You may feel stuck only in specific areas of your life, such as your career or your primary relationship—or you may see yourself constantly trapped between two opposing internal forces, destined to slog through the mud for your entire existence.

As I mentioned before, an inner conflict is one of the three root causes of fear and anxiety (the others being stored emotions and self-limiting beliefs). So who is in conflict with whom? Most often, it appears that the battle is fought between a "negative" part in our subconscious that brings up anxiety, worry, insecurity, and shame, and an opposing "positive" side that makes us feel more confident, motivated, and optimistic. While the agenda of the positive subconscious part seems to be about promoting growth, success, and happiness, the negative is usually perceived as the inner obstacle, the weakling, the critic, or saboteur—that which holds us back from living up to our potential. However, viewing an aspect of ourselves as negative and limiting only makes us distrust and resent our subconscious mind even more. And as you've probably realized by now, blaming the subconscious isn't helpful or empowering—and it's not really fair.

To truly resolve your inner conflict, it's important to deepen your understanding and appreciation of subconscious parts in general: how they came to exist, their "job descriptions," and what they're fighting about. Some of this information I've already shared in the previous chapters, but it bears repeating here, in this new context.

THE RISE OF THE PROTECTOR

Imagine our subconscious as a diamond with many beautifully cut facets, each representing a part of our mind that provides us with specific information and resources. As a result of these many different parts, we can comfortably fulfill a multitude of roles at different stages in our lives. We can be a son or daughter, a student, a friend, a parent, an employee, an entrepreneur, and so on. The parts of our subconscious also contain the basis of our personality traits, such as discipline, consideration, sociability, or sensitivity.

These facets of ourselves develop in response to external and internal changes and the emotions these changes elicit within us. As I described in chapter 6, at birth our subconscious was rather simple and unrefined—yet complete. Spongelike, it soaked up any information that seemed relevant to our survival, growth, and understanding of the world. Over time, life happened, and our subconscious may have registered certain events as confusing, scary, or even traumatic. Depending on the frequency and intensity of those significant emotional events, the subconscious added a new facet that looks upon life and the future with caution and concern. Eventually, this part of our subconscious mind can take on the role of the *inner protector*, dedicated to dealing with the dangerous and uncertain circumstances of life.

As you may recall from the previous chapter, the source of fearful, insecure, or critical self-talk is often a younger part of your subconscious that still holds on to the anxiety-inducing experiences of the past. Remember that one of the reasons it has been unable to let go of the past is that this younger self hasn't been properly reassured and told how to view you as anything but small, powerless, and surrounded by overwhelming threats. But there is another, more profound reason for why this part has prevailed within your subconscious. As you might have already guessed, that younger self—the source of your negative self-talk—and the inner protector are usually one and the same.

This younger subconscious protector develops specific strategies designed to keep you safe and protected. These protective strategies can take on very different forms. For some, it may be the hypervigilant search for potential danger, including ridicule, rejection, or failure. Others might feel safe by making themselves invisible in order to avoid hurtful judgment and criticism. Invisibility can be achieved through blending in, hiding, disengaging, or continuously putting oneself down before others can do the same. Some people become pleasers, working hard to ensure that nobody will be upset with them. Perfectionism, often regarded as a virtue, in the end is an extreme protective strategy to avoid rejection and failure. On the other hand, you can also achieve protection by adopting the role of the aggressor, the rebel, or the critic, all of whom push others away to avoid intimacy and, again, potentially hurtful rejection.

Here's an example from one of my clients. Mary, an attractive woman in her mid-thirties, grew up as the third of four sisters and always felt like an outsider within her family. When she was young and living at home, her siblings were outgoing and extroverted, but Mary felt timid and shy. As a typical form of dinnertime entertainment, the entire family teased Mary until she cried. Her tears prompted more mocking and laughter, which made family dinners absolute torture for her. At some point, after she had endured many of these painful meals, Mary told me that something inside her clicked. She decided it was much better for her to be invisible and disappear than play the role of the laughingstock of the family. From that moment on, she tried to disconnect from her family as much as possible by making herself small—by being quiet and unnoticeable.

This strategy worked during Mary's childhood; she was able to escape the family mockery by avoiding interaction with fellow family members or by hiding in her room.

WHEN PROTECTION LEADS TO CONFLICT

When Mary went to college, staying small no longer served her as it had in the past. Like all her peers, she wanted to go out, have fun, and meet other people. But whenever she felt a little bit expansive, bolder, and better about herself, an overwhelming sense of anxiety and worry immediately pulled her back down; she went on hyper-alert, on the lookout for the possibility of painful ridicule. Obsessively, Mary replayed casual conversations in her mind, analyzing every sentence to determine whether she'd said anything potentially upsetting or that could have been considered stupid. Then she'd burrow even deeper into her self-investigation, trying to recall times in the past when others had indicated their displeasure with her. What was wrong with her that people didn't like her? Over time, her bouts of anxiety could turn into full-blown panic attacks whenever she thought about going out to meet her friends.

During our first session, Mary told me about a deep-seated inner voice that ruined her social life by constantly questioning her appearance, doubting everything she did, and pointing out what negative opinion others must have of her. "Whenever I am with friends," she told me, "I feel as if I'm placing myself under a microscope that magnifies all my flaws and shortcomings. I'm so anxious that I can't really talk or be myself."

However, there was also a completely different side of Mary, one that came forth after she graduated and began her career. This new persona was fearless, strong, and competent. She called it her "professional me"—elegant, self-assured, and "very adult." Mary was very successful and accomplished in her career. While she pursued business projects, advocated for her company, and negotiated deals, she felt infused with confidence, clarity, and determination.

I can imagine you might be saying now: "Lucky Mary. I wish I had such a positive, encouraging subconscious part. At least she gets a break from her insecure self when she's at work. All I'm aware of is the devil inside of me, who doesn't like me, doesn't believe in me, and is afraid of everything. I wish I could get rid of it."

Because every struggle needs at least two sides, there must be a part of each one of us that possesses and wants to express the opposite of the anxious and negative part. If you're not well acquainted with that positive side, it's probably because your inner protector has regarded this opposite part as potentially harmful or too risky to acknowledge. In order to keep you safe, it may have temporarily pushed this part aside or muted it. But the fact that you decided to work with this book is already evidence that a part of you has higher aspirations than being stuck in anxiety.

Ideally, the various aspects of your subconscious, even if they have completely different opinions, tasks, and priorities, learn to collaborate by sharing their information and resources with each other. This allows, for example, parents to recall how it felt to be an "I-know-better-than-you" teenager and let their own teens express their opinions and individuality. Teachers can remember their own academic struggles and help their students with problems they're having. Doctors can empathize with the vulnerability of their patients. The greater the flexibility of our minds, the more easily we can shift even between the most opposite parts and effortlessly use their input and strengths. Subconscious parts support, enhance, and balance each other to accomplish their two primary tasks—avoiding danger and increasing pleasure.

The problems begin when our mind becomes rigid, out of balance, and eventually battles itself, engaging in a sort of internal war. This sounds dramatic and overwhelming, I know, but it's nothing you won't be able to change. A disproportionate negative, or even positive, outlook occurs when one aspect of our mind becomes too dominant and overshadows the other parts of our subconscious. The facet of a diamond that catches the most light shines the brightest, but while this facet casts an intense glow, it can also distract from the true, overall beauty of the entire stone. In this same manner, the part of us that receives the most energy and attention is the part we often identify with most strongly, sometimes to the extent of discounting our true brilliance.

Here's an example from my personal story. During the most stressful period of my residency, work occupied my entire life. The unhealthy mixture of intense pressure, the never-ending patient load, lack of sleep, and my own insecurity made the ego strokes that came with the white-coat status more and more important. Eventually, I was so caught up in being a physician that I almost forgot who else I was. When I introduced myself at parties with, "Hi, my name is Friedemann. I'm a doctor"—which looking back was a little embarrassing and not a great icebreaker—I started to realize that I'd given far too much attention to only one aspect of myself and that it was time to make a change.

Just as I was stuck in being a stressed doctor, you might be so caught up in fear and anxiety that you can't see anything else about yourself. The protective part of you, the facet of your subconscious mind whose job it is to deal with potential threats, occupies most of your attention and became your predominant identity. At the same time, it detracts from all the other amazing aspects that make you unique and valuable.

Let's return to Mary's story for a minute. Because her professional and her anxious side didn't get along or even communicate with each other, the conflict raged within her. When she was at work, Mary generally felt strong and good about herself. But as soon as she left the office and walked down the hall, the anxious, critical part was waiting for her by the elevators (at least it seemed that way to her—like a strong force outside of her), ready to wrestle the confident side for the reins to her mind.

Mary couldn't understand how she could be so completely incongruent, how in just a matter of minutes her whole mind-set could switch. All she wanted was to get rid of the critical and insecure voice, the part of her that scrutinized her every move outside of work, the part that stirred up crippling doubts and misgivings. However, the more Mary tried to focus on her confident side and ignore or angrily combat that negative voice, the more tormented she felt by the latter—and the greater her anxiety and insecurity became. "Sometimes when I'm battling with myself," she said, "it feels as though two people are yelling at me—one in my left ear and one in my right—while I'm trying to figure out what to do and who to be. It feels like I have a split personality or I'm going insane."

I assured Mary that she wasn't going insane and that, in many ways, all of us have different personalities. What she needed was a new understanding and a different relationship with her anxious, insecure part.

This is where you may want to have another look at chapter 6, where we explored negative self-talk and its subconscious source. As I explained there, ignoring, getting angry, or buying into the negative messages usually doesn't work and even aggravates the anxiety. Now you can understand why. When you attempt to dispose of that anxious, yet protective, younger self, it will resort to desperate attempts to grab your attention and make you realize how you're putting yourself in danger by trying to get rid of it. As a result of its efforts, which you may experience as panic attacks, the gap between the opposing "positive" and "negative" parts widens. Eventually, the protector may no longer trust the input from other parts of the subconscious that may focus on success, growth, relationships, and play. It becomes so engrossed in keeping you safe that it considers the input from other parts unnecessary, risky, or even threatening—a perspective that sets the stage for a growing inner conflict.

In the course of our work together, Mary recognized that her insecure, anxious, and worrying inner voice originated from her childhood when she was helplessly exposed to the upsetting, and for her, often frightening family dynamics. She finally understood that the deeper purpose for that negative side of her was to keep her out of harm's way. Until that point, Mary truly felt that being anxious and insecure was just a huge flaw and weakness of her personality, thus reinforcing her belief that she couldn't measure up and just wasn't as good, fun, or interesting as others. For the first time, Mary appreciated that this "negative" part of herself—the side that told her to stay unnoticed—had provided her with a sense of security and control during a time when even her own family didn't seem safe.

Mary finally made sense of her ongoing inner conflict. Subconsciously, she had associated work with being an adult and her career with something she'd built and was in charge of. So when she donned her ambitious, empowered, professional persona, she couldn't allow her nerves and anxiety to interfere with her work. If she did, she wouldn't be able to advance toward and reach her career goals. On the other hand, from the perspective of her younger, subconscious protector, Mary's professional persona appeared completely unsafe and irresponsible, because it often put her in what seemed to be high-risk, extremely visible situations such as business negotiations, presentations, and dinners with strangers—all of which exposed her to potential criticism, hurt, and rejection by others.

So how do you resolve a conflict between two sides that appear to follow such opposite agendas?

THE INNER CRITIC—A GOOD INTENTION GONE BAD

When resolving an inner conflict, the first critical step is to recognize that neither side is right or wrong and that both ultimately have your best interest in mind. It may seem difficult to accept that the anxious part you've been struggling with has far more to offer than just negativity. Or you may feel like you've been dealing with a conflict between two negative sides; for example, a fearful, insecure side is struggling with a much-resented inner critic who has beaten you up and worn you down, especially during the times when you could *really* use some reassurance and encouragement. I know you might wonder what positive aspects this inner fault-finder could possibly have. If helping you to avoid pain is one of the primary concerns of the subconscious mind, why would it cause you agony by berating, slapping, and kicking you—albeit "just" in your mind? This makes no sense. Or does it?

Sam had been asking himself that very question for many years. He'd been tormented by disturbing images inadvertently flashing across the inner screen of his mind for many years. Daily, he felt forced to watch himself being violently punished and beaten bloody by some unrecognizable person. He couldn't help it. No matter how hard he tried, these frightening thoughts pushed themselves relentlessly into the forefront of his mind, leaving him emotionally drained and depressed. He often wondered, "Why do I do this to myself? I must have some form of severe mental illness." Naturally, these thoughts didn't help his already low self-esteem and confidence.

Sam told me that as a child, he was regularly beaten and slapped around by his father. Almost every evening before dinner, he received his punishment, which was most often administered without Sam having done anything wrong. Sam's father responded to his desperate pleas for mercy by saying, "Don't cry, or I'll give you something to cry about." Sam's life as a boy was very confusing and unpredictable, and soon the only certainty he had was the daily dose of physical and emotional anguish.

At first glance, it may seem pretty obvious that the violent images that tortured Sam as an adult were nothing but vivid memories of his traumatic punishments. Yet every form of therapy he'd sought to relieve the effects of these traumas had failed, and a part of Sam continued to project these images onto the screen of his mind.

During one of our sessions, Sam recalled a day when he was in his early teens. He decided to beat his father at his own game by being the first one who caused himself pain. All he needed to do was to imagine how his father laid into him and how much it would hurt—before it actually happened. Sam figured that this way he would at least gain some control over the unavoidable torture. Can you imagine the desperation that led this young boy to such a survival strategy? Yet, at the same time, this was an ingenious method Sam's mind had developed to give him some sense of control during completely disempowering circumstances.

In the beginning, this strategy worked. His father's beatings weren't as unbearable anymore because, in Sam's mind, the punishment had already happened. Over time, Sam even gained some sense of self and personal power. Although he wasn't able to control his father, at least he could control himself and how much he would allow the punishments to affect him.

When Sam was sixteen years old and strong enough to fight back, his father stopped using him as a punching bag. However, Sam's self-inflicted internal beatings continued. While the images of being beaten to shreds relentlessly haunted him, Sam gradually forgot that they had once served a purpose. By this point, he was just irritated with this "cruel habit of his mind." Irritation grew into frustration and anger, until Sam was consumed with hatred for whatever was inside him that kept torturing him in such a sick and malicious way. The first time we met, Sam had just turned fifty-one. His internal struggle had raged more than twice as long as his external troubles with his father.

Although Sam's example may appear quite unusual and somewhat extreme, the theme of beating oneself up—for example, by using harsh, self-critical thoughts or self-defeating deflating comparisons with others—is rather common. The protective intention behind this internal critic can be to keep you small, so that you don't get in trouble with others, or to keep you on your toes, so that you don't fail or slack off. And similar to what Sam experienced, the part of you that berates you and beats you down may believe that you're better off rejecting and hurting yourself than having to endure receiving this pain from others.

Now you can see how our subconscious mind, including its negative parts—or I should say the parts we *perceive* as negative—operates, in general, with the intention of supporting us. As you may realize in the course of the following reintegration process, although some parts of our mind may appear completely anxious, insecure, and limiting, these aspects of ourselves are anything but expendable. In fact, the true strengths and abilities of the inner protector are usually extremely valuable resources that, when integrated, make us more whole, well-rounded human beings. The reintegration process provides us with the insights, leverage, and tools to not only resolve inner conflicts but also to align our subconscious with our goals and purpose, allowing us to access and utilize our full potential.

Maybe you're wondering why, if the source of negative self-talk and the inner protector are identical, you couldn't just use the negative-positive counterbalance self-talk exercise from chapter 6 to resolve the inner conflict. The goal of counterbalancing negative self-talk is to reassure and comfort your anxious and, most of the time, younger self and direct its attention toward a more positive and brighter perspective. However, reassurance and comfort in itself doesn't necessarily lead to a complete reintegration of that part, which may have been operating separately from the rest of your subconscious, fighting for its life to save yours.

REINTEGRATION: WHY IS IT SO IMPORTANT?

The rewards of this reintegration process are multilayered and, for many of my clients, nothing short of life changing.

Peace of mind. Reassuring your inner protector that there is no danger can quiet the voices and calm the anxiety. But reassurance alone doesn't make this part resign from its job of protecting you. As long as a part of your subconscious holds on to its role as a guarding entity that's separate from the rest of you, it won't officially retire, no matter how long you feel safe and confident. Over time, this guarding part may start to step back cautiously and not interfere as much with your life, but it will continue to be watchful, always waiting for that moment when the other shoe may drop or when your peace and safety could be exposed as just a deceptive illusion.

I'm always fascinated by the tenacity and dedication of this subconscious protector. I've seen many times that, when triggered, the inner protector not only kicks into full attack mode, but it also doubles its efforts to keep a person safe. It's as if the fearful side that continued to respond to the early instinct for self-preservation is saying, "See? I told you that it's not safe out there. I hope you'll believe me now and let me do my job." The reintegration process guides the inner protector back into the fold of your entire subconscious mind and also makes this younger self realize that it no longer has to be responsible for your safety and well-being, because as an adult you have developed other, more mature and resourceful parts, which can now take on this task. As a result, you will be left with a much greater sense of wholeness and peace within yourself.

Increased energy. As you probably can attest, the constant battle with yourself and your resulting incongruences are enormous energy drains and distractions. Just as in a tug-of-war, two parties are pulling (in this case, your negative and your positive sides) in opposite directions, using up a large amount of energy without really getting anywhere. As we saw with Mary, when she heard the opposing voices, one in each ear, she didn't have the energy or concentration to figure out who she was or what she should do.

A conflicted subconscious mind doesn't operate at full capacity. Like a fragmented computer drive, a conflicted, fragmented subconscious takes more effort, time, and energy to accomplish normal tasks. In the same way a defragmented hard drive runs much more smoothly, a reintegrated subconscious functions as a whole much more efficiently, going far beyond the sum of its parts.

Improved health. Wholeness and harmony are the foundation of health and well-being. It's well documented that the emotional charge of inner conflicts, whether they're caused by anxiety, anger, or depression, can impact your immune system. It's entirely possible that inner emotional conflicts can also result in the predisposition for autoimmune diseases and cancer, where parts of your physical body are literally battling each other.

Access to your true potential. The anxious or critical part has more to offer than it would appear. As you may discover in the following reintegration process, anxious or negative parts often possess great strengths and abilities. For example, the very traits that lead to hypervigilance and obsessive harping can empower you with such qualities as tenacity, analytical awareness, and sensitivity—which are huge gifts. However, only when you've reintegrated that part of yourself into your subconscious mind can you tap into its true potential.

THE PARTS REINTEGRATION PROCESS: SIX STEPS TO INNER PEACE

How can you establish wholeness and harmony when you've felt conflicted for most of your life? Is it really possible to understand and accept a negative part of you that has caused you nothing but pain, anxiety, or frustration? Yes, it is, and you can. In this six-step Parts Reintegration Process, we'll start by identifying which part of you is fighting another and then work through the steps until these two parts can reconcile, appreciate their mutual purpose, and reintegrate to work with you and each other.

Here is a brief summary of the following six steps.

Step 1: Who is fighting whom? In this step, you discern the major anxiety-driven conflict, its theme, and the views of its opposing sides.

Step 2: What is the true identity of these parts? Here you discover the deeper roots of the conflict and are able to connect to the subconscious parts that are involved in it.

Step 3: Is there a higher purpose? While each opposing part has pursued its own agenda, both have a greater objective in common, and they can strive for this objective together in the future.

Step 4: What are the true gifts and strengths of each part? Until now, you may have viewed one side as negative, anxious, insecure, or critical and the other as positive, confident, and motivated. However, in this step, you'll find out that each has far greater potential and abilities than you have assumed.

Step 5: How can these parts support and complement each other? Since both parts have recognized that they share a higher purpose and each possesses valuable resources for you, they are now able to consider specific ways to collaborate rather than pulling in opposite directions.

Step 6: Reintegration through love and appreciation. In this final step, you are, on a deep, subconscious level, reconnecting both parts with the wholeness of your being.

This process, as well as some of the exercises in chapters 9 and 10, requires you to enter a relaxed and introspective place that allows you to connect and work closely with your subconscious mind. To reach this place, I ask you to close your eyes during parts of the process, which is why you may want to familiarize yourself with the steps before you delve into them. You can read through the description several times until you have a grasp of what to do, record your own or somebody else's voice reading through the instructions aloud, or listen to abbreviated versions of the steps by streaming them online.[1] Before you begin this exercise, find a nice, quiet place where you won't be disturbed, and get a pencil and paper so you can write down some of your insights. Writing down your thoughts will help you work through this exercise now and give you an opportunity later on to review your responses. You'll be amazed at how far you've come.

STEP 1: WHO IS FIGHTING WHOM?

Resolving any conflict first requires becoming acquainted with the adversaries. Who are they? What does each of them want? When it comes to your inner conflict, you may know the answers to these questions right off the bat, yet you may also feel that your mind is an enormous battlefield and that no part of you is getting along and playing nicely.

Think about the *areas* of your life where you feel the most stuck, anxious, or stressed. Were there other times when you felt the same way despite completely different circumstances? Can you trace back to when these patterns started?

Here are a few examples:

- **Relationships.** You're feeling lonely, and you long for a committed relationship. But whenever you meet a potential partner, you keep yourself from sharing your thoughts and feelings. As a result, you might come across as cold and aloof. You recognize that a part of you has always been very hesitant to let anybody get close to you. Looking back at your childhood, you might realize that a disillusioned parent told you that you shouldn't trust anybody or truly rely on anyone but yourself.
- **Career/success.** You're ambitious and strive for success in your career. But no matter how great your achievements, a part of you believes that you could have done better or that you'll soon be exposed as a fraud. This pattern was already active in your childhood, when you may have

pushed yourself extremely hard academically or athletically because you wanted the approval of your parents or you were compensating for feeling left out by your peers. Yet despite all your accomplishments, you didn't receive the recognition you were longing for.

- **Weight loss.** You want to lose weight not only because none of your clothes fit, but because your joints have begun to hurt. Yet despite your efforts to diet, you still find yourself emptying a pint of ice cream at night. Looking back, you realize that in the times you did lose weight, you received too much attention or were hurt by someone who took advantage of you. As a result, a part of you believes that being in good shape is unsafe.

Although it is helpful to be able to pinpoint situations when the self-protecting, anxious thoughts were first set up, it isn't essential for the reintegration process to work. If you can't recall what may have prompted your inner conflict, just focus on how it shows up in your current day-to-day life.

How is this conflict reflected in your inner self-talk? Your opposing parts may be engaged in a constant back-and-forth argument, which can sound like a heated inner debate or a bickering couple firmly ensconced in the pattern of their arguments. Or you may notice one side of your subconscious only during the times when its counterpart has temporarily retreated into the background. For example, say you've just paid off your credit card, received a compliment from your boss, or fit into your favorite pants for the first time in a year. The world is a good place. Your protector seems to have gone fishing, and failure or rejection is the last thing on your mind. But then, a few days later, you're hit with an unexpected expense, find yourself struggling with a deadline at work, or hear your spouse lamenting that the two of you used to have much more fun together. Any of these things can trigger the voice of the worried protector, causing it to reappear in the forefront of your mind and push the confident part of you into the background.

How would you define each side of this conflict? Here are a few examples:

- "I want a relationship" versus "I don't want to get hurt again."
- "I have what it takes to be successful" versus "I am afraid to be found out as a fraud."
- "I want to lose weight to feel good about myself" versus "I want to eat and gain weight because I don't want to be noticed."

You goal is to recognize the larger themes of each of the conflicting facets, such as the desire to be successful and appreciated versus the fear of failure or rejection, or the beliefs that you're safe and that the world is a good place versus the beliefs that the other shoe will drop any minute and that nobody can be trusted.

What roles did each of the conflicting parts of you take on? Assuming that one part in this conflict is anxious and insecure, what label best describes the way it's behaving: the worrier, the invisible one, the chameleon, the pleaser, the critic, the saboteur, the rebel?

Also notice the opposite side—the side that might take more risks or reach for a larger life. When focusing on this side, do you view yourself and the world in a much more positive and empowering manner? Or is this risk-taking, positive part mainly angry, disapproving, or frustrated with the part that seems to be afraid or holds you back?

STEP 2: WHAT IS THE TRUE IDENTITY OF THESE PARTS?

After step 1, you probably have a pretty good idea about the part of your subconscious that works to protect you and its opposing counterpart. Now you're ready to connect directly and communicate with these subconscious parts to gain a deeper understanding about who they really are.

By the way, at the beginning of this process, you may wonder, "Am I doing this right? It feels like I'm making it all up." Don't worry. Yes, you're making it up—with the support of your creative imagination, whose source and inspiration is your subconscious mind. So whatever bubbles up from that source is exactly what you're aiming to work with. The less you think about getting the "correct" answer, and the more you allow the answers and sensations to come up, the easier it will flow. Ready?

Take a Moment to Prepare

Sit in a comfortable chair, feet on the ground. Rest your hands on your thighs, keeping a ten-inch gap between your hands. With your palms facing up, lift your hands a few inches above your thighs until your upper and lower arms are hinged to form a ninety-degree angle. Take three deep breaths, in and out, letting your eyes close as your breathe. Relax deeply and focus your attention within. If your arms begin to feel heavy and uncomfortable, you can bring your hands, palms facing up, back to your thighs. I will ask you at the end of this process to lift them back to their original, elevated position.

Externalize the Negative and Positive Parts

1. **Connect to the "negative" aspect of the inner conflict.** Ask yourself what this negative aspect feels like—anxious, insecure, hesitant, confused, irritated, impatient, or just somehow negative. How does your body usually react to these emotions? Do you notice tightness in your chest, heaviness on your shoulders, or heat in your face?

2. **Ask the negative part if it would be willing to communicate with you.** Wait for a yes or a no—which you may hear internally or feel as sensations—that tells you unequivocally whether this part is or is not willing to communicate with you. If you receive a no or just no answer at all, reassure this subconscious part that it's completely safe and that you don't want to punish, hurt, or get rid of it—even though you may have felt a lot of frustration with it in the past. You simply want to gain a better understanding of what this part is really about, and hopefully, in this way, better support it in the future. This reassurance will usually lead to a yes.

3. **When this part has agreed to communicate with you, ask if it would be willing to come out and stand, as if it were a tiny person, on the palm of one of your hands.** Invite this negative part to choose which hand it would like to stand on—the left or the right. (You can also ask the part to choose between the left and the right knee.) When you get a positive answer from this subconscious part, and it actually feels as though it's standing on your palm, thank and appreciate it for its willingness to communicate with you.

4. **Connect to the opposite part, the part of your subconscious mind that is in the most conflict with the anxious part standing on your palm.** Recall the feelings and behaviors you associate with this aspect of yourself. Ask this part if it would be willing to come out and talk to you. Invite it to choose which hand it prefers to stand on. Sometimes you might have both parts wanting to stand on the same hand. In this case, you might have to negotiate and ask which one would be willing to go to the opposite side.

Get to Know These Parts Better

1. **When one part is standing on each hand, turn your attention to the part of you that holds on to anxiety, and imagine in your mind's eye what this part looks like.** Sometimes this part may appear as a person—maybe you, the way you look now or when you were younger, or maybe somebody else you know. Or you may find that this negative/anxious part looks more abstract—like

a cartoon figure or amorphous, maybe a dark blob. Some of my clients have even described their negative part as looking like a little devil, which is quite a scary distortion.

2. Realize its true identity. Remember when you first experienced the feelings and patterns you associate with that part. For most people, this first experience will be some circumstance from their childhood. You may instantly recall situations from early in your life when you had already experienced these feelings of anxiety or insecurity. Imagine the negative part morphing into this younger self. Become aware of the posture, facial expressions, and the feelings this little self holds inside and holds onto.

3. What do you feel about this part now? For example, are you beginning to embrace this part, or are you rejecting it? Do you feel compassionate empathy for this part, or do you want simply to get rid of it? This may be the moment when you begin to change your mind about this aspect of your subconscious, because you realize that no matter how negative it has appeared, at its core, it's only a younger self who is still burdened and stuck with the events, emotions, and beliefs from the past. (If you don't yet feel differently about this aspect, don't worry. There are many more opportunities for you to heal the relationship with this part of your subconscious.)

4. When you've fully recognized and connected with this little negative/anxious part, shift your focus to the positive part standing on your opposite hand. Again, imagine what this part looks like. How old is it? Does it look like you at the present time or a version of a more empowered self? Does it stand, sit, or move around? What does its facial expression tell you? Try to get a sense for what this part feels inside. What emotions are contained within this part?

5. How do you relate to this positive part of yourself? Do you reject it or embrace it? Maybe you feel excited and hopeful, realizing that there is great potential inside you. Or do you envy it, or feel angry or sad because you haven't been able to embody this side of you more consistently?

STEP 3: IS THERE A HIGHER PURPOSE?

At this point, you have uncovered the sources of your inner conflict and hold both parts, literally and figuratively, in the palms of your hands. In a well-conducted mediation between two opposing sides, it's best to keep the focus away from the details of the disagreements and step back to look at the larger picture to determine the mutual aim and purpose. Gaining this higher perspective is the first goal for the third step of the reintegration process. Because both parts originate from the same source, your subconscious mind, it makes sense that they ultimately share the same intention and highest purpose for you—your purpose for living.

Are you intrigued? This common purpose may have been pushed to the background, especially for the negative and anxious part after it took on the role of the protector. As you already know, the root of the conflict stems from the anxious/negative part's separation, or dis-integration, from the rest of your subconscious, enabling it to become a separate and seemingly stronger voice than the other parts. Reminding the two conflicting parts of their original purposes and their common source builds the bridge that leads them both back into the wholeness of your subconscious mind.

Remind Both Parts of Their Original, Greater Purpose

1. **Ask the anxious part for its job description.** Turn to the "little you" that feels more negative and anxious and ask, "I know how you feel and how you've affected my life, but I wonder, what's the purpose of what you've been doing in the past? What is your job?" Listen carefully to its answer.

Here's an example of how such a conversation may sound:

Part: I'm anxious. I create this critical self-talk (or avoid social events or procrastinate or whatever this part does) because I don't want to feel hurt (or embarrassment or rejection).

You: What's the purpose of not getting hurt (or embarrassed or rejected)?

Part: To avoid pain.

You: So what's the purpose of avoiding pain?

(There may be a pause.)

Part: To not get hurt.

You: What is the purpose of making sure that you don't get hurt?

Part: To protect myself.

You: What does protection do for you?

Part: I will be safe. I will survive. (If this part, as an entity separate from the rest of your subconscious, is truly aware of its role as protector, you might hear, "We will be safe, survive . . .")

You: What's the purpose of being safe and surviving?

Part: To live.

At this point, you're lifting this part beyond the wall of protective thinking and reminding it that there is more to life than safety.

2. **Now it is time for this negative/anxious part to remember its higher, original purpose for living.** Say to it, "Let's assume that you and I are safe and protected. What would this allow me/you/us to do in life?"

Initially, this question may be followed by a pause or "I don't know." Be patient, because the answer *will* come. This younger self has long believed that life is dangerous, a war zone, or a prison and that without its protection you're in big trouble. There simply has been no time or opportunity for it to contemplate a new career.

Very often, the answers that surface will be things such as, "To grow and explore life," "To live my purpose and follow my dreams," or "To do whatever you choose to do." As you continue to ask questions that delve more deeply—for example, "What is the purpose of growing, exploring life, or doing whatever you choose to do?"—you'll eventually reach the greatest purpose of that part. This purpose could be to be happy, to love, to be free, to be whole, or to feel connected to everything.

The answers I've given you here are only examples. Keep an open mind and know that no response is right or wrong—whatever comes up is unique and perfect for you. Helping your anxious part to remember its higher purpose may take as few as two minutes to more than twenty. There's no rush, and you can go through this process several times. Just remember always to treat this negative/anxious part of you with kindness and appreciation for being open to the possibility that there is a higher purpose and another way of supporting you than what it had pursued in the past.

There may be a time when this negative/anxious part feels stuck. Either it will respond with the same answers repeatedly, running an internal loop, or it may actually not know the answer. Hesitation or giving no answer are actually good signs, because they mean that this negative/anxious part is now running against, and thus becoming aware of, its own boundaries and limitations of thinking. It is now forced to consider if there is anything more important than the purpose of safety and protection it has been focused on almost exclusively.

This is when it's crucial to be patient. With gentle persistence, ask in different ways about this part's higher purpose. It may help to switch your questions from "What is the purpose?" to "What is the intention?" or "What would this do for you?" or "What would this give us?" or "What would this allow you or me to do?" You can mix those questions up because they *all* will eventually lead to a higher purpose.

Working with a part whose protective strategy is to be highly critical and highly judgmental can also bring up answers such as, "I need to keep you on your toes; otherwise you will only screw up" or "I need to punish you so you will do better." Even answers that seem to be rather antagonistic or self-destructive usually come from a protective intention.

Simply ask, "What does hypervigilance and punishment do for me? What is the purpose of not screwing up? What will doing better give me?"

The answers may be, "You won't get hurt, criticized, or fall behind" or "You'll avoid painful failure by pushing yourself toward a better performance." As I mentioned before, this aspect of your subconscious may also believe that it needs to punish you, put you down, and make you small and invisible so that no one else will do that to you—which, again, is meant to protect you by preventing you from getting hurt by others. And the purpose of protection is survival and safety, which gives you the opportunity to remind this aspect of you of its higher purpose by asking, "If you would be safe and protected, what would this allow you to do?"

3. **Once you have reminded the inner protector of its higher purpose, thank this part and switch over to its counterpart on the other hand.** Proceed with the same kind of questioning you did with the negative/anxious/protective part, also trying to find out its higher purpose. What you will discover is that, eventually, this side will come to similar or even identical answers as the anxious part, which makes sense, because they both stem from that wholeness of who you are.

4. **As soon as you've reached the common higher purpose level for both, ask each part whether or not it has realized that it actually shares the same purpose with its opposite side.** At first, you may get a no from one part or from both. This is understandable, because who would have thought that the part of you that is negative or anxious actually has the same intentions as its counterpart, such as to enjoy life to the fullest or to become the best you? But after further reiterations with the necessary mix of kindness and tenacity, both sides will agree. At this point, the separating wall that was built on the differences in perspectives and priorities has been broken down.

• • •

You've already accomplished a lot and are well on your way to resolving this inner conflict. You've brought the two conflicting parts into a conversation with one another and taken on the role of a neutral mediator. You removed the masks of the emotions and behaviors and identified who is really behind this battle. And you helped both parts discover that they are like two branches of the same tree, two beams of the same light source, and two extensions of your core being. However, this process goes further, aiming for both sides to recognize that they're parts of a larger whole and that the best way to support all of you is through their integration and collaboration with each other and *all* the other parts that make up your subconscious mind.

At this point, there still may be distrust and suspicion keeping the parts at a distance.

The anxious-protective side may still deem itself the shepherd, in charge of your safety and survival. Asking to let your other parts at least take part in this responsibility may cause the protector to feel that he or she is letting the sheep watch over the flock. And the anxious-protective part may be reluctant to let go of its mission, because it fears that this would make its entire existence obsolete. After all, what's the use of a weapon or a shield when it's no longer needed for protection? What happens to the cocoon once the butterfly has emerged?

On the other hand, the positive side may drag its feet because it still holds onto resentment and a lack of understanding about the negative emotions and actions with which the protective side had burdened you.

The key to overcoming these hurdles is for each side to grow to trust and appreciate each other. Only then will the reintegration impact your entire being and become permanent, which is why steps 4 to 6 of this process are so crucial.

STEP 4: WHAT ARE THE TRUE GIFTS AND STRENGTHS OF EACH PART?

1. **Focus on the part that opposes the protector. Notice its special gifts, qualities, and resources. Ask yourself how these abilities support you.** This part could be good at finding solutions, trying something new, and not worrying about what other people think. You may find that its abilities instill you with confidence, strength, optimism, motivation, or wisdom. Find at least five positive, powerful attributes for this side.

2. **Turn to "little you," the anxious-protective part. Ask yourself what special gifts, resources, or strengths this part contributes.** Where does the anxious side excel? Where might the more confident side need help? This can be a very interesting challenge, because at first glance, your objective view can be obstructed by the attributes of the anxious part's old behavior. The terms

hypervigilant, insecure, and *judgmental* may come to mind—not exactly characteristics you'd call gifts and strengths. But with patience and the flexibility of your mind, you can pierce through the layers of old behavior and discover the true potential this protective part holds. At this point, you may find qualities such as tenacity, caution, and strong, practical analytical abilities.

Going even deeper, you'll realize that for this part to feel anxious or insecure, it must be very sensitive. How else could it take everyone's opinion personally or notice potential threats before anyone else does? Is sensitivity a gift and strength? Absolutely. In my opinion, there isn't such a thing as "too sensitive." Sensitivity is a special power—one that not everyone possesses. However, as with every power, the more you have, the more important it becomes for you to learn how to master and apply it. You wouldn't feel ashamed of having extraordinary physical or mental strength, so there's no need to feel ashamed for your power of sensitivity.

When well utilized, sensitivity leads to compassion and greater understanding for other people's pains and challenges. It can be the basis of deep and meaningful relationships and allow you to enjoy life more fully. Other expressions of sensitivity can be greater awareness, the ability to read people accurately, intuition, and even psychic abilities, which can help you make decisions with greater clarity and move through life with more ease and calmness.

3. **Ask yourself what it would be like if your life were completely controlled by the positive side. What would you be missing if you didn't possess at least a trace of the anxious part?** To your surprise, you may realize that the previously preferred positive side has its limitations, too. You may find that if you would only have that confident, motivated, self-reliant side, you would be too driven, maybe even reckless. Potentially, you would just focus on doing and striving for external rewards and undervalue internal qualities such as peace, contentment, and compassion.

You might rush through the days and never develop the emotional range and sensitivity to appreciate the precious subtleties in life, the seemingly unimportant moments in nature, with others, and with yourself—the gifts that give life meaning. Your relationships may be fun and light, but without depth and intimacy. Many people describe that vision of themselves as a sparkling facade without depth.

4. **Then ask yourself what kind of person you would be if you only possessed the protective side. How would having no influence from the positive side change your life?** "I'd be a complete mess," you might think. "I'd be depressed,

anxious, never reaching out or getting anything done." If you had only the anxious part at your disposal, you may believe that your list of successes would be painfully short or nonexistent and that your expectations and motivation for creating a better, more fulfilling life would be dramatically reduced. Or you may feel that you would be completely alone and isolated, because of an overwhelming fear of rejection or because, in that state of mind, you couldn't trust anybody.

• • •

Discovering the true potential and value of each conflicting part may be quite an eye-opening experience. Do you remember how, before you started the reintegration process, you might have believed that you would be better off without the anxious, negative, or critical part? Or how frustration with your own anxiety or lack of self-esteem made you want to get rid of this valuable side of yourself? I hope you've changed your mind and have come to realize that while each side has valuable gifts and potential, without the balancing influence of its counterpart, these powerful qualities can turn into self-defeating limitations. The wholeness of who you are is so much more than the sum of your parts, which leads to the next step.

STEP 5: HOW CAN THESE PARTS SUPPORT AND COMPLEMENT EACH OTHER?

As you've seen with the example of your inner conflict, our gifts are only as valuable as how we use them. Each conflicting part has amazing strengths and resources to offer you. However, in the past, rather than each part enhancing the other, each has restricted or even cancelled out the potency of the opposite side. In this step, you will further solidify your goal for them to actually collaborate with each other—not merely to coexist.

First, remind the positive side of the true gifts and potential of its opposing side (the negative side). Then turn to the negative part and explain the positive side's gifts and potential. Remind them of their common highest purpose for you (for example, finding happiness, finding fulfillment, sharing your gifts with the world). Now ask each part how it could support the opposite side so that you can reach your highest purpose in the future. To create a closer collaboration, each side will need to take the concerns and needs of the other more seriously. For example, the protective side, which will still need to know that you are safe, may find the positive side too outgoing, too careless, too busy, or too selfish. A collaborative effort could mean that the anxious part informs its counterpart about these concerns. In response, the positive side could slow down, choose to act with greater care, and take other people's feelings into account more often.

At the same time, the anxious side may have to let go of, or at least tone down, the old protective patterns that used to sabotage the efforts of the positive side. Often, the positive side will agree to take on the role of the mature protector, who listens to, encourages, and reassures its anxious counterpart and shields it with self-assured confidence from the opinions and judgments of others.

Some people I've worked with described the two parts as *horizontal and vertical forces* in their lives, which I find very poignant. The horizontal force, commonly the positive and confident part, focuses on expanding their life by striving for more success, prosperity, relationships, exciting experiences, and any positive possibilities that may unfold. The vertical force, which is commonly the sensitive/anxious part, is more interested in the deeper aspects of life. It often values close and meaningful relationships, feelings, stillness, and peace, as well as spirituality and creativity. Where the horizontal force propels you forward in life, the vertical force provides substance, depth, and grounding. It makes sense that, to move through life in a safe and successful way, both need to be in balance—your head with the stars and your feet on the ground.

STEP 6: REINTEGRATION THROUGH LOVE AND APPRECIATION

The previous five steps laid the foundation for this final resolution of the conflict. During this step, it's important to move through the process at a pace that's comfortable for you. Use your intellect and your conscious mind, but let your subconscious, your emotions, and your heart guide you.

1. **Bring your hands back up into the original position**. If your hands became too heavy or tired during the previous steps and you've been resting them on your lap, now is the time to lift them back up, with your elbows at about a ninety-degree angle. Make sure your palms are facing up, keeping them about ten inches apart from each other. In your mind's eye, look at your positive and negative parts and remind yourself of their true strengths and gifts.

2. **Send love and appreciation to the part of you that has been frightened and anxious.** Tell that part that you're sorry for all it had to go through in the past.

Tell it that you're sorry for having ignored or even rejected it for such a long time, for not realizing that it was just doing its best, and for not acknowledging and valuing its true gifts and resources. Imagine love, in the form of light beams, emanating directly from your heart, surrounding and enveloping the little person on your hand in a warm, loving, and secure blanket of energy. Take time to really connect with, embrace, and appreciate this part that, for so long, seemed to be the source of your fear and anxiety.

3. **Turn to the opposite, "positive" side.** Tell that part that you're also sorry for not paying more attention to it, that you haven't created more balance inside, and that you haven't been able to fully value its strength, gifts, and resources. And then, also from your heart, pour love and light over that part. Reconnect with it. Appreciate it. Embrace it.

4. **Get an agreement from both parts to reconnect and collaborate with each other.** Turn your attention back to the anxious part and ask it, "Realizing that you two have the same highest purpose, would you be willing to share your gifts and strengths and to work with the other side?"

When you've received its agreement, focus on the positive side and ask if it's willing to collaborate with the formerly anxious side to support your entire being and help you achieve your higher purpose more easily and effectively. Again, wait for its answer before proceeding.

Usually, the answers from both parts will be an instant yes. If not, ask for each part's objections to working with the opposite side and continue to remind each part of the higher purpose it shares with the other side. Negotiate in a kind but firm manner, making it clear that it's in the highest and best interest of the wholeness of your being for both parts to connect, communicate, and collaborate with each other.

5. **Reconnect.** Now something almost magical will happen. Once you've received a yes from both sides, you'll sense a magnetic energy developing between your hands. As you visualize, with your eyes still closed, the two parts walking toward each other, your hands will move on their own accord, inch by inch, until your palms are touching, which is a sign that the subconscious mind has been reconnecting these two parts. It's an amazing feeling to realize that your subconscious mind is bringing your hands together without your conscious control.

When your hands are touching, notice what the parts are doing now that they are together. Are they holding hands? Are they giving each other a hug?

Are they merging with each other to form a "super part" with the gifts and qualities of both sides unified? Let your imagination guide you.

Take your time with this reconnection process. It may take from one to ten minutes. The subconscious strives naturally for wholeness. The movement of your hands symbolizes that your subconscious mind has overcome old blocks and boundaries that had separated the two conflicting parts and is now mending the gap between them. The ongoing struggle and separation of the "positive" and "negative" parts required and ultimately drained tremendous amounts of energy from the subconscious mind. Once you've resolved the conflict, the energy that was necessary to keep the parts separate switches its orientation to bring them back together. It's like switching the poles of two magnets from repelling to attracting each other. This is why you may feel not only quite relieved but also a bit exhausted after this reintegration process, because you realize how much you were depleted by living in a state of subconscious conflict.

6. Reintegrate. Focus on your heart, and visualize it as a pool of brilliant light, the seat of your wholeness and your true essence. Start gently lifting your hands toward that light and visualize these two parts entering into your heart, fully integrating inside your wholeness, coming home again.

During this reintegration, you may feel a tremendous amount of energy, warmth, or a tingling that starts from your heart and radiates out into your entire body. Spend several minutes simply allowing this healing energy to flow through all levels of your being. Enjoy the sense of peace and wholeness that is gently wrapping itself around you, leaving you with a greater understanding of your resources and true potential.

After this reintegration process, it's a good idea simply to rest and let the process complete itself without consciously trying to influence it.

HOW TO PROCEED FROM HERE

After completing the Parts Reintegration Process, you will feel immediately more relaxed, harmonious, and whole. However, this new, integrated state of being will require further attention to become completely solidified. Although the subconscious is a fast learner, it also requires repetition and consistency to achieve mastery.

To further consolidate the reintegration process, think about the following questions:

- What were the two parts of this inner conflict?
- What did they discover their common highest purpose to be?
- What are the special gifts and strengths of each part?
- What does each part need, and how can the two parts support each other in the future?
- How will you know that the conflict is resolved? How will you think, feel, and act differently?
- Who are you now that you've reintegrated two very important parts of your subconscious?

Revisit these questions and your answers as often as you can to remind yourself of the fundamental insights you gained during this process. I also recommend using a journal to record the ensuing emotional and behavioral changes and the potential challenges you notice.

As a direct result of the Parts Reintegration Process, most clients notice a significant difference and are quite impressed with their ability to deal with previously anxiety-triggering situations with much greater calmness and confidence. Based on my experience, it is possible that sometime after you've gone through this process, old thoughts of worry, anxiety, or frustration with yourself may return to the forefront of your awareness. Why? You can look at these thoughts as echoes from the past or old grooves that your mind has slipped back into. However, there is another explanation, as we'll see from the next example.

Andrew was hit especially hard by a resurgence of anxiety after the reintegration process. Initially he had, for the first time in his life, felt a great sense of self-worth and security. But then, a few weeks later, the familiar dark cloud of fear and sadness seemed to completely envelop him again. What had happened? Did his subconscious change its mind again? After a few days of dragging himself through his life, he suddenly remembered that I'd told him about the importance of staying in touch with his younger, sensitive, subconscious part. A light bulb went on. He took a deep breath and started visualizing Little Andrew inside, gently asking him how he was doing.

"This part of me was not only anxious," Andrew recalled, "he was really distraught. It was as if Little Andrew had just started to gain some trust in the whole me, and I completely forgot about him again. No wonder I felt so bad." What astounded Andrew the most was that within just a few minutes of communicating with his younger self, all the worry and anxiety lifted, and he felt empowered again.

To stay in touch with your younger, inner protector, you could write a heartfelt letter reinforcing your commitment to support and care for that more vulnerable side of you. Another effective way of staying connected to that part is the negative-positive self-talk exercise you already know from chapter 6. Because you met and worked with this part of you during the Parts Reintegration Process, it may now be even easier to address its anxious and insecure messages with kindness, compassion, and reassurance. Paying a little bit of attention every day to these formerly conflicting parts is a very small price, considering the rewards.

Now that you have established greater congruency and wholeness, you are ready to address and resolve the second subconscious root cause of fear and anxiety: the emotional baggage of the past.

CHAPTER 8

Time to Let Go

HOW TO RELEASE EMOTIONAL BAGGAGE FROM THE SUBCONSCIOUS MIND

"I KNOW IT DOESN'T make sense, but whenever I talk to my employees, I get really tense and stressed," said my client John with a sigh. "Recently it's getting worse—I start feeling anxious even when I'm talking to my friends. There's absolutely no reason that I should feel this way."

Mandy shared, "I'm fifty-three years old, and I'm still afraid of my father, who's almost ninety and bound to a wheelchair. He only has to say something negative about my weight or my clothes and I become paralyzed with anxiety and shame. I want to tell him to stop, but I can't get a word out. It feels as if I'm twelve years old again—going on five."

Another client, Alice, said she felt anxious as soon as she left her house for more than an hour. No matter where she was or what she was doing—shopping at the mall, attending a party, or visiting her adult children—and no matter how much fun she seemed to be having, as soon as an hour had passed, the anxiety started to creep up on her. Her body felt increasingly heavy, her movements sluggish, and her mind foggy. The only thought that continuously flashed through this fog was, "You have to go home *now!* This place is no longer safe." Most of the time, Alice gave in to the panic and bolted as fast as possible to the safety of her home. Over time, these symptoms worsened, and it became difficult for her to leave her house at all. "Eventually my world shrank to the size of my living room," she admitted.

You likely have made the same scary observation John, Mandy, and Alice have: the longer you struggle with fear and anxiety, the worse it becomes. You're triggered more easily, the emotions appear more intense, and they show up more often—at inopportune moments in inappropriate ways. You jump when a fork drops, freeze when asked a question, or yell at someone for just saying your name—all of which causes you to feel overwhelmed and out of control.

Why do the intensity and frequency of our anxiety and our unreasonable reactions to it increase over time? Why can't we just get over it or at least become more used to being a bit on the jittery side?

By now I'm probably preaching to the choir, but as you recall, to heal fear and anxiety we must identify and attend to its root causes. Remember the three subconscious root causes of fear and anxiety introduced at the beginning of the book: inner conflicts, emotional baggage, and unsupportive core beliefs. In chapter 7, I showed you how to resolve inner conflicts. Now in this chapter, you will learn how to persuade your subconscious mind to lighten its—and your—load by letting go of the emotional baggage of the past.

Emotional baggage is the subconscious accumulation of unresolved anxieties. As you try to ignore and suppress your fears and insecurities in an attempt to fit in and appear confident, capable, or at least "normal," your subconscious storage space is filling to capacity with these unaddressed emotions. As a result, a harmless situation can turn into the proverbial drop that causes the water to spill over the edge of the cup or the last bit of steam that causes the pressure cooker to explode. The reaction to such a situation presents as panic attacks, unexpected free-floating anxiety, or a constant undercurrent of worry and doubt. As you become increasingly susceptible to these feelings you've tried to avoid, the heavy burden of unresolved fear and anxiety drains your energy, clogs your mind, and can even lead to severe physical problems.

"But wait a second," you may be thinking. "Aren't the two highest intentions of the subconscious mind to preserve our body and increase our happiness? If so, why does our subconscious hold on to fear and anxiety if doing so causes so many problems? Is it possible that our subconscious isn't that smart, after all?"

WHY DO WE HOLD ON TO UNRESOLVED FEAR AND ANXIETY?

There are three good reasons our subconscious mind hangs on to emotions from past events. I've already touched on the first reason in chapter 4: we all are provided with an innate ability to free ourselves immediately from "negative" feelings. As infants and toddlers, we don't hesitate to strain our little vocal cords and vehemently express our discontent. As we grow up and learn that we're more accepted and appreciated when we control, suppress, or at least hide our feelings, we gradually "unlearn" the natural instinct to release emotional pressure. By the time we enter adulthood, most of us have lost sight of how to handle these feelings, other than shoving unpleasant emotions under the subconscious rug. Because our subconscious supports us like a faithful servant, it patiently continues to execute our conscious decision to suppress and store emotions until we instruct it differently—or until we have stuffed it to capacity and the subconscious forces us to address those emotions.

Another reason the subconscious mind holds on to fear and anxiety, along with other uncomfortable emotions, is to protect us. It securely stows away and safeguards memories that appear emotionally overwhelming or damaging, such as recollections of being molested during childhood, serious accidents, or other significant traumas. These traumatic memories can be reawakened when we're confronted with certain situations that are somehow similar or connected to the frightening past. Or we might spontaneously remember suppressed memories during the most stable and comfortable times in our lives, as if our subconscious mind had been waiting until the circumstances were just right to address and heal these past wounds. Only when the subconscious is convinced that we're ready and it's safe for us to remember the trauma does it open the lock to the information and present it to our conscious. We may then remember these events in quick flashes of memory, in our dreams, or as strong emotional surges that arise either spontaneously, without any external trigger, or in situations we subconsciously associate with the trauma.

You may wonder why, if the subconscious mind can suppress traumatic memories, it doesn't simply erase and eliminate potentially harmful and debilitating emotions. Good question. The answer is connected to the third and maybe most important reason: the subconscious mind is holding on to "negative" emotions.

LEADING, LEARNING, LETTING GO

It's a basic evolutionary principle: only when we continue to learn and grow can we survive and thrive. We learn best from the events that have the most meaning for us, those that we feel most strongly about. An interesting phenomenon we've all observed is that the lessons we learn from a negative event can be more profound than those learned from a pleasant or neutral encounter. From an evolutionary perspective, this makes sense. When it comes to sheer survival, experiences that cause us to feel anxious or hurt are simply more important for our subconscious to store, process, and learn from.

So what has felt like emotional baggage from the past actually has a much more important purpose than just haunting us or weighing us down. Unresolved fear and anxiety serve as signals—red flags that mark the memories that still require our attention. Our subconscious mind holds on to these emotions until it's safe and we are ready to remember and learn from these events. Then we can understand the lessons and claim the growth potential that has been enclosed within these memories. Doesn't this perspective turn your views about fear and anxiety upside down?

Taking this notion further, you'll come to a very empowering conclusion: the more unresolved fear and anxiety you've stored in your subconscious, the more untapped potential awaits you.

Confirming this notion is the fact that as soon as you've retrieved the insights and learned from these anxiety-charged memories, your subconscious mind is more than willing to let go of the emotional attachments. Sound too good to be true? Well, here's an example showing you that you probably have, without even realizing it, experienced this fundamental principle of "leading back, learning, and letting go" many times.

Let's say one of your best friends doesn't call you on your birthday. You wonder what happened; how could she forget your birthday? Who does she think she is? Is she upset with you? Was it something you said or did? Days pass, and you can't stop thinking about the snub. Maybe you vacillate between hurt, resentment, and insecurity. But one thing's for sure—you're not about to call *her.* Then you find out that her father was rushed to the hospital, or that she had a very challenging time at work, or that she felt so bad she'd forgotten your birthday that she was hesitant to call you afterward. When you learn the true reason behind the perceived slight, your hurt, resentment, and insecurity change to compassion, forgiveness—and possibly a bit of embarrassment that you made such a big deal out of the incident.

What have you learned from this experience? Perhaps that, until you know the truth, it doesn't pay to react to assumptions. Or maybe you ask yourself why you allowed the missed call to spoil your birthday. Or maybe you explore why, on *your* day, you made your friend more important than yourself. Whatever you take away, you know that this incident has presented you with the opportunity to examine your self-worth and your tendency to give your power to others.

Learning and letting go of past anxiety works relatively smoothly if you only have to deal with one or two events. But what if you've been shoving down countless anxiety-ridden memories throughout several decades—maybe as long as you can remember? How can you address all these unresolved emotions and learn what you need to without becoming completely overwhelmed? Trust your subconscious to offer an elegant and effective solution for this problem. It all begins with the way the subconscious stores memories.

HOW DOES THE SUBCONSCIOUS MIND STORE MEMORIES?

The smell of cigars takes me right back to the seemingly endless hours of studying with my grandfather and his heroic but ultimately futile attempts to teach me the spelling rules of the German language. I can still hear his exasperated voice through a cloud of smoke, calling me an *Armleuchter*—which literally means "chandelier," but I'm pretty sure he meant "bonehead"—after I had made the same mistake for the umpteenth time. It was all about the use of the triple *s*, which, in my defense, has been almost abolished since then by the German spelling reform. Isn't it interesting how simple things, such as the smell of cigars, a song on the radio, an old photograph, or the taste of your mom's favorite dish can bring back old memories? Where do these memories come from?

Memories are sorted and filed by the subconscious in a linear fashion and relative to the time when they occurred. This allows us to distinguish events that occurred last week from those that took place when we were ten years old and from those we imagine could happen in the future. It continues to fascinate me that everyone, regardless of gender, age, background, or walk of life, subconsciously codes time and memories in this linear, sequential way—from the past to the present to the future. This subconscious filing system is referred to as "the time line" in the field of Neuro-Linguistic Programming (NLP) and by Tad James, founder of Time Line Therapy. I prefer to call this collection of experiences and memories of a person's life journey "the life line."

One of the great features of this subconscious storage system is that it's easy to access. As you'll experience in a moment, all you need to do is enter into a relaxed, light trance state and imagine that you're floating out of your body. Looking down onto yourself, you'll notice that your subconscious mind projects your life line with all its memories in a distinct relationship to your body.

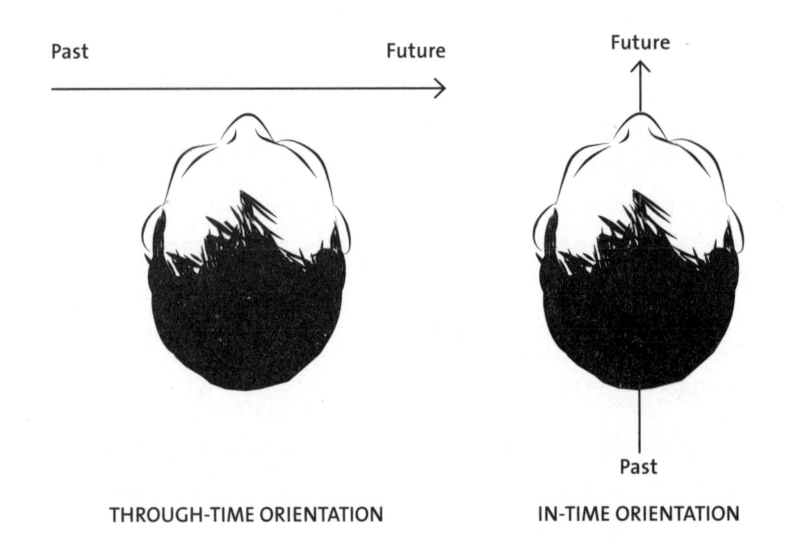

FIGURE 3: How our subconscious mind stores memories

Most people perceive their life line in one of two ways, which Tad James called *through-time* and *in-time orientations.* With a through-time orientation, people see their life line running horizontally in front of them. Some see the past to the right and the future to their left. Some see the reverse. People who view their life line with an in-time orientation picture the past behind and the future in front of them, or vice versa, while the present is inside of them (see figure 3).

In addition to these two major orientations, the life lines of a small percentage of people are organized in other creative ways, such as a mixture of both orientations, or as a line running diagonally or vertically. The direction of your life line can give you a great deal of information about your subconscious mind's relationship to time in general and to your life in particular.

Dr. James found that those who see their life line in a through-time orientation are usually punctual and expect others to be, as well. They're good at staying on task, meeting deadlines, and organizing their time in the most efficient way possible. However, since their entire life is laid out in front of them, they perceive past, present, and future simultaneously, which can make it more difficult for them to be flexible and open-minded, to leave the past behind and make a fresh start. People who store time and memories in an in-time way, with the future straight in front of them and the past behind them, tend to more easily let go of the past and focus on what's ahead of them. They can be rather loose about being on time for their own appointments. On the other hand, they're not put off if somebody else is late. In-time people often appear more spontaneous and easy going; at the same time they may be more flakey and unreliable.[1]

These are generalizations and certainly will not apply to everybody. However, once you've found the orientation of your own life line, notice whether some of these tendencies are also true for you. And if you should choose to change the orientation of your life line, it can be even more interesting to see whether one or the other propensity shifts, as well.

For my client Lydia, changing the direction of her life line was truly life altering. Fifteen years before she came to see me, she had lost her husband of ten years. Since then, she'd battled with often paralyzing depression and anxiety. When we talked about how she'd been dealing with the sudden death of her husband, she told me that she felt incapable of letting go. Even his clothes and shoes were still occupying the wardrobe, as if she expected that he might come back one day. Lydia hadn't been interested in dating or creating a new life for herself. For fifteen years, all she could think about was how much she missed her husband.

When Lydia discovered the orientation of her life line, she realized why she had been so stuck in the past. Her subconscious mind projected the past in front of her and the future behind her. So all she could focus on were the years gone by, while the future was hidden behind her. After she went through the Pattern Resolution Process, which you'll learn in this chapter, and was able to resolve residual grief and anxiety, I suggested she turn her life line around, leaving the past behind and placing the future in front of her. Immediately her face lit up, and her energy shifted. "It was as if a door that had been shut for a long time finally opened and let my life back in," she said.

Within the next few months, Lydia donated all her husband's belongings, redecorated her house, and started traveling again. A simple change of perspective can make all the difference.

Let's have a look at your life line and find out how your subconscious relates to your past, present, and future. All you have to do is to follow the simple instructions that follow.

One quick note before we start: if you find it difficult visualizing, that's most likely because you prefer to process information kinesthetically, which means you feel rather than see with your mind's eye. If this is the case, simply focus on the feelings and sensations that are described in this process and get a sense for the orientation of your life line that way, rather than trying to picture it.

DISCOVERING YOUR LIFE LINE

This technique is the second step in the Pattern Resolution Process described later in this chapter, but it is also valuable when done on its own. As with the Parts Reintegration Process in the last chapter, you may either read through this exercise to familiarize yourself with the steps before you do it or record your own or somebody else's voice reading through the instructions aloud.

Find a quiet place and sit in a comfortable chair. Close your eyes. Take slow, deep breaths. Imagine that you're inhaling peace and light and exhaling all the tension, worry, and stress of the day. As you fill your lungs with peace and light, you'll notice a weight gradually lifting from your body.

After a few minutes of relaxing and unwinding, visualize yourself standing in front of a beautiful door with your name on it. You know that you have the key to unlock this door. As you turn the key, the door swings open easily, and you enter a very special room, one that is deep inside yourself. A light at the center of this space immediately catches your attention. As you approach this light, you realize that it emanates from the bottom of a large, round basin that is filled with shimmering, crystal-clear water. This pool of water and light is the place from which you can travel beyond the limits of time and space and connect to your life line.

Gently sloping steps lead you into the basin. As you begin to immerse yourself in the warm and comfortable liquid, you experience a growing sense of ease and contentment. When you're completely submerged in these soothing, healing waters, you lean back and realize that you can lie on the surface and float. As if you are held and embraced by a safe and supportive invisible force, you can remain completely still and motionless and simply let yourself drift. With every breath, you feel lighter and lighter and lighter—weightless and still. Soon you feel so light that you can actually float out of your body into the air, like a feather in the wind.

You are floating out of time and space, right up in the air—higher and higher, higher and higher—until you reach a very special place, all the way up. From there, you look down on your own body and detect your life line, the continuum of past, present, and future. As soon as you see your life line, you know that you are now consciously connected to your subconscious mind.

All memories and events of the past, present, and future are stored in your life line. Notice its orientation in relation to your physical body, which is comfortably resting in the basin of water below you. Does your life line pass through your body or extend horizontally in front of it? Is your past behind or in front of you? Does it originate from your left or your right side? Or does it point up toward the sky or reach all the way down into the floor? And what about the future?

Now notice whether the past or the future appears brighter and has more energy than the other.

If it turns out that the future is less bright or as bright as the past, find on the side of your future a dimmer light switch. Is it a round or a vertical switch? Go to that light switch and turn up the brightness of the future, so that the glow expands, becomes more vibrant and inviting. Increase the brightness of the future until it is at least two or three times brighter than the past.

If your past is much darker than your future, it will be more difficult to orient yourself during the Pattern Resolution Process. In this case, you use the dimmer switch on the side of the past to increase its brightness, keeping in mind that you want to have the future at least twice as bright as the past.

Take one more look at your life line before you gently float back, right into your body and right into the present moment.

• • •

Changing the brightness of your life line can make a huge difference. Some of my clients haven't been able to see their future. There was just nothing there. Their initial shock, the realization that their subconscious mind had no concept or relationship to the future, was quickly replaced by their relief of finally understanding why they'd felt so hopeless and stuck in the past. By turning up the light of their future and making this part of their life line longer and wider, they signaled to their subconscious mind that from now on their focus is directed toward the infinitely greater possibilities and opportunities to come. This small adjustment is often all that's needed for someone to gain more hope and optimism.

Now that you have established direct access to the subconscious storage space of all your memories, you are able to work consciously with your subconscious to clean up the emotional baggage from your past.

THE PRINCIPLES OF THE PATTERN RESOLUTION PROCESS

The prospect of finally letting go of fear and anxiety may be exciting—or daunting. You may ask, "What if I can't let it go?" "What if letting go means I'm no longer safe?" or "Who will I be without fear and anxiety?" Staying stuck on the fence may appear safer than taking a leap of faith into the unknowns of change.

It's said that change only happens when the pain of holding on is greater than the fear of letting go. What if we don't have to wait for the pain to become unbearable but instead could make letting go easy, comfortable, and effective? And what if letting go wouldn't leave you empty, but would instead provide you with valuable new insights, understanding, and self-empowerment?

I developed the Pattern Resolution Process on the basis of the time-line work of NLP and Tad James's Time Line Therapy, which are both extremely potent methods of addressing negative emotions and limiting beliefs. The Pattern Resolution Process incorporates additional aspects that I've found to be especially powerful for releasing subconsciously stored fear and anxiety. As you'll see, this approach is as effective as it is gentle and safe because it doesn't require you to relive the past, which could potentially lead to retraumatization. And its steps are so easy to learn that you can work with this process right away.

So what is the Pattern Resolution Process and how does it work? Let me start with explaining some of its major principles.

FEAR AND ANXIETY ARE STORED IN MEMORY PATTERNS

Discovering your life line showed you how the subconscious mind files memories in a sequential and linear manner. In addition to the time factor, memories are also processed and sorted by the emotions they have in common. As you have probably noticed for yourself, you haven't been incredibly creative when it comes to experiencing and responding to fear and anxiety. Most of the time you've repeated the same patterns over and over again. Imagine that all these fear- and anxiety-charged events are linked together on your subconscious life line like beads on a chain (see figure 4). Such a chain of memories, all of which fall under the same pattern, can span across decades, from the very first time you experienced anxiety all the way to the present.

Some of the memories may stand out, and you're able to remember them easily because they are related events that happened just recently or are the

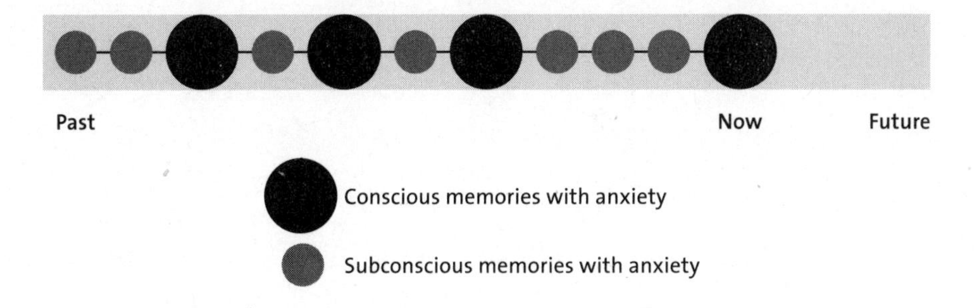

FIGURE 4: Conscious and subconscious memory patterns

biggies you often think or talk about. Yet most anxiety-charged memories that are chained together according to their emotional pattern will stay in your subconscious, unnoticed by your conscious mind. This is often because there were just too many similar events to keep separate or these events occurred before the age of three, which for most people is too early to remember. And, as I mentioned before, your subconscious suppresses the more intense and traumatic experiences to protect you from becoming overwhelmed and retraumatized.

So why stir things up? Wouldn't it be easier to simply keep all those "forgotten" events swept under the subconscious rug and deal only with those you can actually recall? However tempting that may seem, it's far better to unpack and address those stored memories, because there are, as you'll see, significant disadvantages to ignoring them.

THE PATTERN RESOLUTION PROCESS ADDRESSES BOTH CONSCIOUS AND SUBCONSCIOUS ANXIETY

You may have had the same experience as many of my clients: after years of therapy, there remains an anxiety and weariness that doesn't seem to release. One client described this to me: "I'm still left with that unspeakable, untouchable part of my anxiety. There's nothing to talk about or analyze. It's just always there."

This intangible anxiety stems from those subconscious memories that you couldn't access with your conscious mind. Emotional charges from those subconsciously stored events can also bleed back into memories you thought you had resolved previously. Although this can be quite frustrating, it's nothing but a nudge from your subconscious telling you there's more work to do and more for you to learn and grow from—just on a deeper level. After all, if you address only those few events you consciously remember, you wouldn't take full advantage of all the untapped growth potential the past can offer you.

To find completion and resolution with the past, you need to learn from and release the anxiety of all the events that share the same emotional pattern. Sounds pretty daunting, right? Don't worry. There's no need to recall and work through each individual memory. This would be much too time- and energy-consuming. The Pattern Resolution Process utilizes the fact that anxiety-charged memories are chained together. As you consciously instruct your subconscious how to release anxiety from one event, it extrapolates these instructions and applies them to all previous and subsequent memories that fall into the same chain of patterns. So you can unload decades of emotional baggage—and outgrow the past—in a matter of minutes.

How do you resolve an event that has already happened? Everyone knows that time flows only in one direction—toward the future—right? Your subconscious mind, as well as Albert Einstein and his theory of the fabric of time, would beg to differ; both say that the past, present, and future exist simultaneously. For the subconscious, the past is not written in stone and can be changed as much as the present or future. And as you'll see, neither magic nor insanity is required to do so.

THE RELATIVITY OF TIME AND REALITY

Napoleon Bonaparte once said, "History is the version of past events that most people have decided to agree upon." I can imagine that, in true emperor fashion, Napoleon would decisively disagree with the ways some historians have decided to portray him. Who likes to be remembered as an egomaniac gone wild or have his name associated with a syndrome (in his case, the "short man's complex")?

Even our own history lies in the eyes of the beholder. How many times have you and your siblings or lifelong friends disagreed on certain facts of your childhood, from the size of that enormous fish you caught in grade school to whether your first dog died or ran away or, in the case of siblings, who was Mom's or Dad's favorite. It sometimes appears as if you grew up in completely different families or groups of friends. Wouldn't it be great if you had a time machine and could go back to find out what really happened? Actually, you can.

Take a moment and think about one of your favorite vacation spots—maybe a beach in Hawai'i or a lush green meadow somewhere in the Rocky Mountains. When you close your eyes, try to remember how it feels to be there. Inhale the salty smell of the ocean or the spicy scent of pine trees. Feel the sun warming your skin and a light breeze brushing your face. Notice your feet in the wet sand or your hands digging lightly into the earth. Listen to the sounds of the waves splashing on the shore or the melodic songs of the birds in the trees. Are you there yet? When you're completely engaged in this memory and have forgotten everything else around you, your subconscious believes that you are actually there, which makes this little exercise the world's cheapest vacation.

Here is another impressive example of this ability of the subconscious to travel to different realities. "Snow World" is a 3-D virtual-reality game that helps burn victims deal with the excruciating pain of their recovery. Originally designed for children, it is now also successfully employed with combat burn victims. While the patients focus on the playful challenges they're facing in this cold and calm virtual world, they're able to temporarily forget the extreme physical discomfort from their burn wounds. The results of this form of pain therapy are impressive. The patients require significantly less pain medication, and they develop a greater range of motion in their burned limbs, as their muscles are able to relax more.[2]

Whether you take an imaginary trip to a snowy mountaintop or lose yourself in an exhilarating movie or an engrossing book, your subconscious does not differentiate between fantasy and reality. Think of all the adventures you have experienced in your life. How many times have you explored different worlds, taken on new identities, and traveled through time and space—all from the comfort of your own sofa? I heard Laura Simms, an internationally renowned storyteller, talk about how most cultures throughout history had revered storytelling as a powerful healing tool. She explained that as we're captivated by a story, we temporarily detach from our fixation on our own story and its current challenges. This allows our minds and hearts to open up and create more space for our innate wisdom and true healing potential to emerge. We return from the land of fiction with an expanded consciousness and a calmer and more relaxed mind and body, and we're able to perceive the problems of our own story from a wider angle and address them with a renewed sense of confidence. I believe that the famous Dr. Norman Cousins tapped into the healing power of storytelling when he successfully treated a life-threatening form of arthritis with a self-prescribed laughter therapy by watching hours of Marx Brothers movies.

Now, you're probably already a proficient time traveler and storyteller. Fear and anxiety may have led you to spend ample time rehashing and regretting the past and worrying about or dreading the future. But making your life into a drama or horror movie didn't help ease your fears. So how can you use these natural abilities of your subconscious to overcome fear and anxiety? Can you turn back time, rewrite history, and thus create a brighter future?

Yes, you can.

THE PLACE OF LEARNING

When it comes to memories filled with fear and anxiety, the idea of rewriting history may seem preposterous. You just *know* that in the past you've been bad, guilty, wronged, hurt, or broken. The damage has been done and can't be repaired.

Well, this may have been the limiting perspective of your inner critic and protector, whom you met and worked with in the previous chapter, but it's certainly not the truth. We can always make the choice to change our perception of ourselves and what has happened to us. Once we accept this simple fact, we accept that we have the power to create our own reality.

A new perception requires a new perspective. Trying to resolve anxiety-filled memories by talking about and analyzing them may make sense to our conscious mind; however, this method often doesn't reach the subconscious. The Pattern Resolution Process makes use of the subconscious mind's innate ability to transcend time and space and guides you back in time to gain a fresh look and deeper understanding of the events of the past. Instead of having you relive the memory, which could potentially aggravate the fear and anxiety already associated with this event, the Pattern Resolution Process leads to a new vantage point high above your life line—a point I call *the place of learning.* From this perspective, you are no longer a part of the space-time continuum, and you have access to the infinite wisdom of your higher consciousness. As you look down from this safe and comfortable place onto the memory you want to resolve, you're free from any emotional attachments to this event and untethered from other people's input and imprints, and you're able to calmly examine what happened.

The place of learning allows you to gain insights about your life and yourself that go beyond one-dimensional conscious analysis. You learn with your conscious, subconscious, and higher consciousness (or your mind, heart, and spirit). When you work with all these aspects of your whole consciousness, you are able to obtain the teachings and growth potential of this memory, and you also gain a deeper understanding of yourself, which some people have described as a shift in consciousness that defies words and explanations.

LEARNING THE TRUTH

At the beginning of the Pattern Resolution Process, I'll ask you to remember some of the earliest events that you associate with fear and anxiety and that may be at the root of the emergence of your inner protector. Then, with my guidance, you'll go back and safely revisit and address those memories from the place of learning.

You'll probably find that it wasn't only anxiety you felt at that time, but also an overwhelming amount of confusion—confusion about why those you should have been able to trust hurt or betrayed you, or about what you did that led you to be punished or ignored, or why life was harder for you than for others. You may even discover that already at this early stage of your life you didn't understand that how people treated or saw you wasn't a true reflection of who you were or that people were simply acting out their own issues, which had nothing to do with you.

The Danish philosopher Søren Kierkegaard believed that we lose our innocence as a result of the punishments and traumatic experiences that occur in our early childhood. He considered the confusing contrast between realizing what we're *capable* of doing and the fear of getting punished for what we're *actually* doing as the loss of innocence and the source of anxiety.[3]

Inspired by the writings of Kierkegaard, Rollo May, one of the most influential psychologists of the twentieth century, examines the role of confusion in the development of anxiety in his book *The Meaning of Anxiety*.[4] For example, Dr. May's studies found that unmarried women who had been rejected by their mothers during childhood were more likely to suffer from anxiety as adults if the rejection had been "covered over by pretenses of love and concern." In my opinion, because these women were never sure whether they could expect the "good" or "bad" mom, their subconscious protector was on constant alert, thus leaving them frequently anxious. Another layer of confusion I have observed in clients with such upbringings pertains to the questions of whether or not their mothers' reactions were their fault and whether they're flawed, not good enough, or not loveable.

On the other hand, Rollo May found that women who had experienced constant overt abuse and rejection by their mothers were less susceptible to feeling trapped in fear and anxiety. He quoted one of these women, who lived in a shelter and was pregnant by her own father, saying, "We have troubles, but we don't worry." As children, they learned quickly that they couldn't expect love, kindness, and safety from their mothers, and therefore they didn't feel conflicted or confused about this relationship. This clear view of their world, even though it didn't appear safe or supportive, allowed them to accept that they needed to mainly rely on themselves to survive in it.

In my experience, this view of life doesn't mean that these survivors aren't burdened by emotional baggage and wounds of the past. However, in their quest to somehow carry on, pushing fear and anxiety out of their minds—and out of the way—appears to be the only viable option. They often continue to hold on to their survivalist view of the world until the pain of living this way makes them realize that a part of them is still trapped in the traumas of their childhood. (Although May's study focused only on mother-daughter relationships, from my viewpoint, his findings could also be applied to abusive and neglectful fathers and their role in the development of fear and anxiety in their children.)

As you review your childhood from the place of learning during the Pattern Resolution Process, you go beyond the consciousness of the confused, anxious, and powerless child. Instead, you become a powerful source of healing, compassion, and love. By asking yourself a series of questions that will help you to clarify, reframe, and learn from the memory, you can peel off and release the layers of anxiety and confusion that concealed the true essence of who you were at that time. As a result, you'll feel complete and at peace with what occurred in the past, and you'll also have gained a deeper awareness and appreciation of your true self.

Rollo May says in *The Courage to Create,* "Anxiety comes from not being able to know the world you are in, not being able to orient yourself in your own existence."[5] In *The Concept of Anxiety,* Kiekergaard called anxiety "the dizziness of freedom," because it can lead us to remember the gift of free will and our true identity.[6] When we merge both viewpoints, anxiety becomes the catalyst, the springboard, that can bring us from a state of confusion and unawareness of who we truly are to a state of clarity and self-conscious reflection. The Pattern Resolution Process makes this journey from anxiety to remembering our truth, with all its innate potential, so much easier. Are you ready to discover who you truly are?

THE SEVEN STEPS OF THE PATTERN RESOLUTION PROCESS

Before we start, it's worth mentioning again that especially at the beginning of this process, some of you may feel that you aren't doing it right or you're just making it up. Guess what? You're right. You *are* making it up, in a sense. As you're floating above your life line and gaining a new perspective on your past, your conscious is working with the part of your mind that's in charge of creativity and imagination—your subconscious. So whatever images or insights you're consciously receiving in the process, no matter how made-up they appear, stem directly from your subconscious. So you're right on target. If you just allow the process to unfold rather than overthinking or forcing it, there's really nothing you can do wrong. To reassure yourself, you can always go back and repeat some or all of the steps as often as you wish.

Here is a brief summary of the following seven steps:

Step 1: Preparation. In this step, you determine the memories and emotional patterns you want to let go of and prepare your subconscious mind for the Pattern Resolution Process.

Step 2: Lining up your past, present, and future. Here you connect to the subconscious storage place of all your memories and emotional baggage—your life line.

Step 3: Going back to the past. Hovering above your life line, you have transcended time and space and are now able to travel back to one of your earliest memories that still holds fear and anxiety.

Step 4: Learning from a higher perspective. From the place of learning, you are able to access the insights and growth opportunities that are associated with this early memory and thus gain a new perspective on the event.

Step 5: Uncovering the truth. In this step, you peel away the layers of emotional baggage and confusion and remember the light of your true essence.

Step 6: Resolving the patterns of the past. Now that you've taught your subconscious how to learn from and let go of past fear and anxiety, it can extrapolate this process to all previous and subsequent events of the same emotional pattern, thus releasing decades of stored emotional charge within minutes.

Step 7: Healing the present. Here you focus on your present self and release any remaining fear and anxiety from your subconscious and cellular memory.

Since you will have your eyes closed during most of the Pattern Resolution Process, it is best if you read through the steps several times before embarking on this journey. Alternatively, you may want to guide yourself through this process by recording the instructions with your own voice. Or you can stream an abbreviated recording of the exercise online.[7]

STEP 1: PREPARATION

The preparation step connects you with the memories and emotional patterns you want to release and gets your subconscious on board with the process. A word of caution: if you have a history of severe trauma or abuse, it's advisable to avoid focusing on these events the first time you work with the Pattern Resolution Process. It's best to first become familiar and comfortable with the method, so you can then use it more effectively as you dig into these events.

a. Take a piece of paper and list six or seven events, situations, and people from your past that caused you to be anxious and afraid. Ideally these memories span across your lifetime—from your early childhood to the last time you felt frightened, worried, or insecure.

b. Notice what these situations have in common. Were you confused or paralyzed by fear and anxiety? Did you use the same coping mechanisms or protective strategies, such as trying to be invisible, running away, fighting, pleasing others, or trying to be perfect? Did you feel disempowered and, if so, who had the power?

c. Check to see if these memories are still charged with fear and anxiety. How do you know? Close your eyes, and as you delve in to each event, notice how your body responds. Do you start feeling dizzy or ungrounded? Does your heart pound, your breathing become shallow and accelerated? Do you detect a weight pressing down on any part of your body? Do you feel tension or heat? Any kind of physical response indicates that your subconscious has held on to at least some of the fear and anxiety you experienced at that time.

d. Determine whether it's worth holding onto the fear and anxiety connected with this memory. Ask yourself the following questions:

- Do I like the way this old fear and anxiety feels?
- Does holding on to these emotions serve me or help me to reach my goals?
- Does it keep me safe?
- Is any part of me resistant to releasing this emotional baggage?

Ideally, your answers will be no, unless your inner protector still believes, possibly out of habit, that letting go of past anxiety will inadvertently put you in danger.

If you detect such resistance, you'll need to convince that part of your subconscious that it's safe and beneficial for you to release the fear of the past. For example, you could use these arguments:

- Does the fear of a deer trapped in the headlights of an oncoming car keep it safe, or does its fear paralyze it and thus increase its risk of getting hit?
- The weight of these old emotions drains my energy, overloads my mind, and negatively impacts my immune system. Do a lack of energy and a clouded mind really make me safe?
- When I burn myself on a hot stove, do I have to hold on to the pain to remember that I shouldn't touch a stove once it has been turned on? Or can I learn this lesson and let go of the discomfort?
- Wouldn't it be more beneficial if I could learn from the past and then let go of the old fear and anxiety?

These arguments are usually sufficient to convince your inner protector that it's in your best interest to resolve and release your emotional baggage—and to help you to get ready for step 2.

In addition to preparing your subconscious mind for the Pattern Resolution Process, this first step also serves as a reference point that allows you to compare the emotional intensity of these memories before you start the process to the intensity after you finish.

STEP 2: LINING UP YOUR PAST, PRESENT, AND FUTURE

Now that you're prepared, it's time to connect to the place where all your memories and emotional baggage are stored—your life line.

Turn off your phone and go to a quiet, comfortable place where you won't be disturbed for the next thirty to forty-five minutes. Sit or lie down, relax, and close your eyes.

Set your intention for this process by focusing on what you want to accomplish with it: to free yourself from the emotional baggage of fear and anxiety, to learn from and outgrow the challenges of the past, and to return to the present moment with greater peace, clarity, and access to your true potential.

Follow the steps about how to discover your life line from earlier in this chapter (see pages 130 to 131). Then adjust the brightness of the past and future portions of your life line, so that the future is at least two to three times brighter than the past. Also make sure that the past is clearly visible and not hidden in the dark. You don't have to spot the individual events on your life line; you just want to gain a sense of where and how your subconscious stores your memories.

STEP 3: GOING BACK TO THE PAST

When you see or sense your life line, you've established a conscious connection with your subconscious mind, which provides you with the most powerful leverage for change. You can now direct, collaborate with, and observe the healing potential of your entire consciousness.

As you're floating above the present moment, turn your full awareness toward the past portion of your life line.

Tell your subconscious mind to guide you to the earliest event on your list of fear- and anxiety-charged memories from step 1. Allow your subconscious to take you by your hand and lead you quickly across time and space—all the way back to that earliest experience, so you're watching it from above.

When you're hovering above the event, observe from this higher, outside perspective what took place at that time. Who were the people involved, and what were the circumstances that caused your younger self to feel frightened or afraid? If you still can't see the event, descend slowly until you're floating closer above it. Imagine that you're breaking through the clouds of subconscious obscurity and gradually gaining a better view of and more information about this event.

If you feel that you're being pulled too deeply into this memory or becoming too emotionally involved, inhale deeply. On the exhale, quickly rise at least ten times higher than you are at the moment, watching the event become smaller until you see it as nothing but a tiny speck on your life line. Stay at this altitude, far above your life line, until you're feeling calm and unattached to the memory. At this point, you can either go back down to gain more insights or proceed to step 4.

STEP 4: LEARNING FROM A HIGHER PERSPECTIVE

By viewing your past from the place of learning, you're claiming the role of the empowered observer, one who is no longer attached to the emotions that were associated with the memory, but who is now ready and eager to learn from and grow beyond it.

Still floating above your life line, go back to a point before the memory you want to resolve actually occurred. As you drift further into the past, your subconscious loses its emotional attachments to this memory simply because, from its point of view, the event hasn't happened yet.

As soon as you no longer detect the emotions of the memory, float straight up, high above your life line, toward a space that's imbued with peace and light. As you approach this very special place, the place of learning, imagine that you're becoming lighter and more relaxed. Once you've arrived there, take a few moments to bask in its soothing energy. (This state of consciousness may be similar to one you've experienced in a deep meditation.)

From the higher vantage point of the place of learning—outside the time and space continuum—your heart and mind are wide open. In this empowered state, reflect on what happened during the event you just visited. The following questions and contemplations allow you to dismantle the memory from its confusing elements and emotions and obtain the insights and growth potential for which your subconscious wanted you to return.

Because it's important that you remain associated with the observer position, the following questions are formulated to inquire about your younger self, the person you were at that time. The questions are phrased in the third person (referring to your younger self as *he* or *she*), which allows you to stay dissociated from the event and thus prevents you from being drawn back into the memory and reliving the painful experience.

Ask yourself the following questions and wait for the answers to arise from deep within.

What is your younger self afraid of or confused by? For example, being bullied by kids in school, being yelled at by a parent, or feeling alone.

Was whatever happened your younger self's fault? Does he or she deserve to be treated this way? Usually the answer is no, especially if you're starting with an event from your childhood. The place of learning allows you to recognize and remember your innocence at that time.

If it was his or her fault, what were the intentions of the younger self? Maybe in the past you blamed yourself for what happened during that time. You told yourself it was your fault that you were bullied because you were a "pathetic" kid; it was your fault your mom yelled at you because you broke something or received a bad grade; it was your fault you were abandoned because you were sent to your room as a form of punishment for being bad. Even if you saw your younger self as being at fault, you'll now find, from the place of learning, that his or her intentions were innocent. Maybe instead of pathetic, you were awkward because you were trying so hard to make friends or because your parents didn't have the money to buy you cool clothes. Maybe you broke something because you got too excited and didn't pay enough attention. Maybe you received poor grades because you believed that you weren't smart enough and therefore didn't apply yourself in school.

No matter what the situations were, observe your younger self with compassion, and assume that you can gain a deeper understanding of the goodness and innocence of who you were.

Did your younger self pick up on other people's negative emotions or limiting beliefs? If so, whose emotions and beliefs were they? This question provides you with greater insights about the feelings and motives of others involved in the event and how you might have taken on those feelings, without even noticing. The bullies probably didn't feel only angry or cocky. When you look beneath their emotions, you may detect that these bullies had their own fears and insecurities. The parent who punished you may have felt overwhelmed, frightened, pained, or consumed with self-loathing. Did these people project their feelings on to you? Did you subconsciously soak them up as though you were a sponge? It can be quite illuminating when you realize that potentially a large portion of the emotions and limiting beliefs you have held on to weren't even yours in the first place.

How would a person who dearly loves and cares about this younger self interpret this situation differently than you may have in the past? No matter how alone and misunderstood you felt, there was probably one person—a grandmother, sibling, friend, teacher, or neighbor—who loved and appreciated you for who you were. If not, can you look at your younger self with love and compassion? Through the eyes of kindness, you may see that the bullied kid was actually stronger than the bullies because he or she didn't choose to put others down to feel better about him- or herself. You might recognize that the younger self should not have been punished for a bad grade but instead should have been supported and reassured by Mom and Dad, who might have regarded themselves as underachievers. And maybe you can assess that the kid who felt abandoned and alone was, in fact, loved—or at least had many reasons to love him- or herself.

What other empowering and liberating lessons can I learn from this memory before I find resolution and completion with it? This question invites your subconscious and your higher consciousness to provide any additional clarifying insights about this event. You may recognize more aspects of your younger self that you're able to appreciate now. You may be able to look at those who hurt you with greater understanding and compassion because you can understand the pain or fears they struggled with. And you may be even grateful for those who did make mistakes because they taught you how not to be or act. It's also perfectly fine if you don't receive earth-shattering realizations and all that's bubbling up from the subconscious are words, images, or sensations.

If you don't seem to get any answers at all, don't be concerned. Some teachings and insights will take time to reach your conscious awareness, and you may be unable to verbalize them for a while. By conveying to your subconscious that you're ready and open to learn from the past, you've already set the most important part of the process into motion. Even after you've completed this process, you may receive additional information about this event and its patterns. These pieces of the puzzle can appear during your dream time or in the form of a spontaneous revelation, where suddenly the event makes total sense. And sometimes you may just feel more neutral and at ease about your past and more comfortable and confident with yourself without really knowing why, which demonstrates that the healing work of your subconscious doesn't require input from your conscious mind.

STEP 5: UNCOVERING THE TRUTH

Step 4 provided a new perspective about what happened, enabled you to set the record straight, and helped you rewrite your story. Now that your subconscious has provided you with all the information it wanted you to retrieve, you can peel away the layers of emotional baggage and confusion and remember the truth of who you are.

From the place of learning, kindly gaze at your younger self and share with him or her all the teachings and insights you've gained so far. What does this self need to hear from you to resolve the event? What advice would you like to offer?

Then imagine that you're sending a brilliant light beam of compassion and love directly from your heart to this young person, enveloping him or her with the soft blanket of your love and appreciation. The light from your heart infuses the little self with healing energy, which gently penetrates into each and every cell, circulating throughout his or her body. While this healing energy is gradually filling his or her entire being, it easily pushes out all fear, anxiety, and emotional imprints that your younger self experienced or took on from others. Imagine the emotional charge releasing; for example, you might see it as dark smoke, dust, or clouds rising out of your younger self, out of the event, out of your life line, completely dissolving.

As the compassionate light from your heart continues to release and replace the emotional baggage, it soon overflows and expands beyond the physical form, creating a sphere-shaped field of energy all around your younger self. This sphere functions as a protective shield, within which your younger self can safely be, grow, and expand while all negative outside influences simply bounce off it.

While this field of shielding energy grows wider and brighter, the people or circumstances in this memory, which may have scared this little self, become much smaller, two-dimensional, translucent, and eventually insignificant.

Now that all the layers of emotional baggage have lifted and disappeared, and your love and compassion have safely enveloped your younger self, softly gaze into his or her heart and become aware of the brilliant light at its core—the essence of its being. How does this core light appear to you? What are its qualities, and what are its powers?

At this point, you may not be able to put into words what you experience. The essence of who we are goes far beyond our vocabulary and our conscious understanding. People I've worked with described feeling a strong sense of purity, joy, compassion, and love radiating from this inner light. But more frequently, they were simply in awe of the indefinable brilliance and power of their true essence, which most of them were completely unaware of until they gazed into the heart of their younger self.

Once you feel complete, at peace, or simply neutral about the remembered event, gauge whether or not the feelings of your younger self have also transformed. If you find that the anxiety charge hasn't completely resolved (a rare occurrence), repeat steps 4 and 5 of the Pattern Resolution Process. Make sure that your inner protector understands that it is in your best interest to let go of this draining, emotional burden.

STEP 6: RESOLVING THE PATTERNS OF THE PAST

Now that you've taught your subconscious how to learn from and let go of past fear and anxiety (and, by doing so, created the space for the light of your true essence to emerge and expand), it can extrapolate this process to all previous and subsequent events of the same emotional pattern, creating a domino-like effect. Your subconscious mind is a very quick learner and can easily implement this process after the resolution of just one memory. However, your more skeptical conscious mind may want to work through this process with one or two more events before you place the process in the capable hands of your subconscious. If this is the case, repeat steps 3, 4, and 5 with events that happened either before or after the one you just resolved. When you're satisfied and convinced that your subconscious is sufficiently trained to take over, continue the process with the following step.

From the place of learning, high above your life line, it's evident that the same anxiety-driven emotional and behavioral patterns repeated themselves. Some of these events may have happened before the event you started with, but most of them occurred after. Instruct your subconscious to retrieve more knowledge from the remaining unresolved events and store them in a special place where you can easily retrieve them at the appropriate time. *At this point, you don't need to be consciously aware of the specifics of these insights.*

While your subconscious provides you with the innate wisdom and growth potential of your past, send beams of light, compassion, and love from your heart to the younger selves in each event. Fill them with this healing energy, and allow the clouds of fear and anxiety to lift out of your life line and disseminate.

As your younger selves are liberated from the emotional baggage, you can see how the bright lights of each of their core essences emerge and expand—all across the past section of your life line. From your comfortable higher perspective, watch how your subconscious releases—within just minutes—decades of old fears and anxieties, making room for the brilliant light of your core energy to come forth.

STEP 7: HEALING THE PRESENT

In the final step of this process, you can concentrate on your present self and release any remaining fear and anxiety from its subconscious (and cellular) storage places.

Still viewing your life line from the place of learning, slowly move back until you end up floating above the present moment and your current physical form, which is comfortably propped in a chair or lying flat on a bed. With a tender smile of compassion and appreciation, take a moment to contemplate and appreciate the positive choices you've made throughout your life and ask yourself these three questions:

- **With all the fear and anxiety I've experienced in the past, did I give up on believing in kindness, compassion, goodness, and love?** The answer is no, because you've just proven to yourself that you can utilize the love from your heart to heal your past.
- **Is my inner light, my core essence, still strong and intact?** From all you've experienced so far, the answer is, of course, yes.
- **Looking across my past, what have I learned about who I truly am?** This is a big question, one that has been pondered by the greatest minds throughout history. So once again, resist the temptation to let your analytical (and maybe philosophical) mind take over. Instead, allow the response to this question to come to you in whatever form it needs to—as words, images, sensations, or simply the comforting realization that the potential of your true essence is and always has been far more powerful than your fears.

Radiate the light of compassion and love from above into the body of your present self, where it expands and fills up the head, torso, arms, abdomen, pelvis, and legs. As this healing force ripples throughout your entire body, it forces out and clears away any residual fear and anxiety that was trapped in your subconscious and your cellular memory. Pay special attention to the parts of your body that became tense or felt heavy when you recalled anxiety-charged memories. Imagine that you are releasing any remaining vestiges of stored fear and anxiety as dark smoke or clouds, which rise out of your body and completely dissolve.

Once your entire physical body appears filled with light and in a complete state of peace and harmony, gaze down from above into your heart and recognize the familiar light of your core essence emanating from there. Take a moment to bask in its radiance and appreciate that it still comprises the same qualities of beauty, purity, and power that you've witnessed within your younger self.

Take one more glance at your now "enlightened" past, then gently float down toward the light of your essence, where you can reenter your physical body. Anchor yourself in your heart, your spine, your legs, your feet, and then all the way up to the top of your head.

Take three slow breaths in and out. Welcome back!

• • •

I know you may feel a bit overwhelmed by all these details and information, but I told you this was an easy process—and it is. And it's much easier to follow when someone else guides you through it, which is why, as I mentioned before, I have made available a summary of this process as an mp3 download. To help you feel even more comfortable taking this journey on your own, here is an example of a client I worked with.

Gerry was in her late fifties when she contacted me after listening to one of my radio shows. Although Gerry had been a very successful, award-winning saleswoman for many years, when her company was sold to a new owner, her insecurities and anxieties reached a new high. "I've been with this company for eight years, and I now have to prove myself all over again," she told me. "The new management wants me to take on more and more tasks, and I'm already overwhelmed. I think they don't like me and are trying to get rid of me."

Company meetings became tortuous for her. Every time Gerry said anything, she felt incompetent and stupid. She was sure that her peers looked at her with a mixture of disapproval and pity. On top of that, she felt confused about a long-distance relationship with a man who seemed kind and interested in her during the brief times they could see each other, but who became cold and distant as soon as she returned home. In the last six months, all her old fears about not being good enough, smart enough, or even loveable enough had come rushing back to the surface. Feeling trapped and powerless, she was finally ready to face and resolve her past.

Gerry's childhood was anything but easy. Her mother was emotionally unstable and usually vacillated between outbursts of rage—during which she once almost drowned Gerry's little sister—and deep, dark depression. Because her mother was unfit to be a mom, and her father—a weak man, who avoided any confrontation with his wife—was busy working to make ends meet, young Gerry had to take on the role of housekeeper and parent for her sister. It was extremely difficult for her, a young girl, to cook, clean, and keep up with all the chores and responsibilities that come with taking care of a toddler. But no matter how hard she worked, her mother always found a reason to berate her. Nothing she did was ever good enough.

One early morning when Gerry was about twelve years old, her mother tried to commit suicide and was rushed to the hospital. As Gerry shared this story with me, she could still feel the shock and panic that had overcome her when she saw her mom carried out of the house on a stretcher. "What will happen to us?" she thought. "Who will take care of us?" Her father's response was nothing but a blank stare; then he turned toward the door to leave for work. Gerry remembered that despite all her anxiety, she knew exactly what she was supposed to do: feed her little sister. Her mother didn't return for several months, and Gerry had to skip school to take care of everything at home, which was extremely hard for her because she liked to learn. Her home life was overwhelming—both physically and emotionally. She had no help. And all she could expect from her father was his silence or his absence.

Gerry's troubles didn't end when she entered adulthood. She married a man who continued to reinforce her beliefs about not being good enough and not being safe in the world. Although he couldn't keep a steady job, gambled away their money, and had an affair with another woman, Gerry stayed with him.

"During the twenty years of this marriage, I had to constantly put out fires, cover for my husband, and make sure that we didn't go bankrupt or lose our house. Every year that went by, my shame and self-loathing grew. If I hadn't been so concerned for my son, I would never have mustered the strength to leave my ex."

Gerry's life line showed the past to the left and her future to the right. Because her future line looked rather dim, we increased its brightness, so that her subconscious would feel more drawn to the possibilities of what *could* happen, rather than what *already had* happened.

Then Gerry went back to the morning her mother tried to end her life. Floating above the tragic event, observing her younger self, Gerry could feel the anxiety and powerlessness that was still stored in the memory. However, as soon as she reached the place of learning, positioned before and high above that memory, she felt relaxed and actually eager to gain a deeper understanding of what had taken place. I began to ask questions to help lead her through the experience.

Me: What is your younger self afraid of or confused by?

Gerry: She is all alone. Her mother is gone, and her father is useless. She is confused and doesn't know what to do. Nobody talks to her. How can she and her sister survive without their mother?

Me: Was whatever happened that day her fault? Does she deserve to be treated this way?

Gerry: Absolutely not. She's just a kid and didn't do anything wrong. It wasn't her fault that her mother was mentally ill. I wish I could help this girl.

Me: Did your younger self pick up on other people's negative emotions or limiting beliefs? If so, whose emotions and beliefs were they?

Gerry: I can see how she picked up how anxious and overwhelmed her father was. He didn't know how to deal with this situation, so he just escaped to work. I also feel that he didn't like himself very much; he didn't really believe in himself. So there's some self-loathing, I sense. My mother feels like a big, dark energy of sadness, self-hatred, and shame. She didn't want to leave us alone, but she also felt unable to provide for us. Her emotions feel very strong, although she was at that time more or less out of commission. This is so interesting. A lot of what I have been feeling weren't even my emotions. Now I know where a huge piece of my anxiety and insecurity comes from.

Me: How would someone who dearly loves and cares about this child interpret this situation differently than you may have in the past?

Gerry: I can imagine that a loving grandmother—whom I never had—would say, "I'm so sorry for what this child had to go through. She's so little and yet has to be so strong." I am also feeling sorry for the parents. They seemed to be in a great deal of pain themselves. It's amazing how this little girl is the strongest and healthiest person in the family. She's willing to put her needs last and is sacrificing so much to take care of her sister—and everybody else. What a powerful spirit she has.

Me: What other empowering and liberating lessons can you learn from this memory?

Gerry *(after a few minutes of silence):* I can clearly see that my younger self was a very sensitive, beautiful being who didn't want anybody to suffer or be in pain. So to take care of those in need, she did whatever she could, no matter how hard it was for her. All she wanted for herself was a little bit of acknowledgment and love. Her parents, who were stuck in their own problems, weren't capable of giving her what she needed. This little girl was so desperate for some kind of connection that she was open to feeling and taking on her parents' fears and pains. Maybe she thought that she could help them if she would carry some of their load. Wow, I can't believe how much love and kindness this tiny person has.

(After a few more moments, tears started to stream down Gerry's face.) It just occurred to me that Little Gerry always received support and protection from other sources. I don't know what it is, but it feels as if a higher power, God, was always looking out for her.

After these realizations, it was very easy for Gerry to find love and compassion for her younger self, release the emotional baggage of the past, and recognize the light of her essence. When Gerry was back above the present moment and able to review her entire past, she shared more information.

Gerry: I never was able to see myself that clearly before. I always believed I was weak, flawed, and unlovable. I was always ashamed of my past and myself. Now I realize how wrong I was. *(Pause.)* My essence is so pure, loving, and innocent. And at the same time, I can sense so much strength and vibrancy pulsing from this core. I can understand now what gave me the courage and determination to keep on going—and never give up. I'm a strong person. I was strong during my childhood and also during my marriage; although I had no self-esteem, I was still the one who kept us above water. Without my strength and resilience, who knows what could have happened.

What really amazes me is that despite all the negativity, lies, and anger that I was constantly surrounded with since my childhood, for some reason, I never became bitter or contentious myself. Instead of becoming like my mother or father, something inside made me choose to remain open and sensitive to the needs of others and treat them with compassion and kindness. The only person I wasn't very nice to was myself. That'll change from now on. I have reasons to feel good about myself, and I will stand up for myself with pride for who I am.

I'm happy to report that these revelations were the beginning of Gerry's self-transformation. She stopped worrying about her peers at work and decided that she no longer would try to fit into a company whose energy and values she didn't agree with. With her newfound confidence and self-esteem, she quickly landed a new, much better-fitting job—the type of work she had previously believed would be impossible to attain at her age. In the past she would have made her new position the main focus in her life and constantly been afraid that she would be criticized or even fired. Instead, she committed to making balance and impeccable self-care her highest priority. "What still surprises me the most," she told me one year after her Pattern Resolution Process session, "is that I still wake up most mornings with a smile, feeling happy for no reason."

Once you have gone through the Pattern Resolution Process yourself, you may find yourself wondering, "How do I know that it worked?" Here is one way to tell: Right after you reenter your body, briefly think about some of the events on your anxiety list (the one you created in step 1, the preparation step) and notice how you feel now about them. There's a difference between remembering that you used to be anxious or scared and still having these emotions. So pay attention to how your body reacts when you briefly revisit these past events. If you don't notice any physical responses as you recall the memories, you have successfully released the emotional charge from your subconscious mind and cellular memory.

You may find that you're now perceiving those memories in a much more positive and empowered light. However, you may also feel nothing about them. While it can appear a bit puzzling to have no emotion about a past that used to make your hair stand up straight, it is actually a very good sign; it means you've reached a resolution with this event and can consider it from a place of peaceful neutrality.

After you've checked on those events, you may want to refrain from digging into the past for at least a couple of days. Your subconscious healing is still progressing, and you don't want to disturb the process. The pattern resolution doesn't end when you open your eyes. You've provided your subconscious with distinct guidelines for releasing emotional baggage, and it will continue to work with those guidelines even without your conscious awareness, while you're sleeping or daydreaming, for instance.

Working with your subconscious mind to release emotional baggage is an extremely liberating experience. The good news is that once the past is resolved, it stays that way; the old emotions are gone, and they won't come back. However, just releasing old patterns and limiting identities without replacing them with new, supportive and empowering ones can also leave you with a subconscious vacuum or void. If you stay in this void for too long and don't create a new foundation of self, your subconscious may gradually slip back into old, familiar grooves of thinking and feeling. This is why the final chapters of this book are so critical for you.

PART IV

Readjustment

CHAPTER 9

Core Alignment

IT'S TIME FOR you to pat yourself on the back. You've come far and accomplished a lot. Think about all you've done so far:

- Demystified fear and anxiety
- Greatly increased your understanding about how and why you create fear and anxiety in your subconscious mind
- Learned to communicate with your subconscious and work consciously with this incredibly powerful inner resource
- Discovered and connected to your subconscious inner protector, which has been at the root of your anxious, negative self-talk and your "self-conflicted" behavior
- Learned to appreciate the valuable strengths and talents of this subconscious part and its "positive" counterpart and, through the Parts Reintegration Process, brought them back into alignment with your wholeness and greater purpose
- Understood, grown from, and released the emotional baggage of fear and anxiety from your subconscious storage

Now that you have a clean slate and are ready for a fresh start, what's left to do? In some ways, the most important work begins now. As I mentioned, it takes more than letting go of what no longer serves you to create permanent change and healing. As you've peeled away the different layers of fear and anxiety from your conscious and subconscious, you've also disconnected from the ways you used to see yourself. As liberating as this may appear at first glance, it also invites a rather nagging question, "Who am I now?"

We all need a sense of self, a foundation to stand on and to move forward from. Without this foundation, we feel ungrounded. You probably know people who fell into a depression after they graduated, retired, or their kids left for college. These people had been focusing so predominantly on one aspect of their lives that when their identity as a student, professional, or parental provider was "lost," they felt completely lost.

You can argue that by letting go of fear and anxiety you've retired from an old identity; therefore, you might be prone to facing a similar crisis. So this chapter and the next provide you with all you need to establish a solid foundation for your new you. Rebuilding is actually the fun part, because you can choose who and how you want to be now that you've grown up—or maybe, more aptly put: now that you've outgrown your self-limiting identity.

This chapter guides you through the first step of this rebuilding process. You'll reconnect and realign yourself with the part of you that has always been solid and perfect by nature—your essence. For this alignment to become the strong foundation of your new you, you need to anchor it consciously and subconsciously until it becomes your cellular identity.

CELLULAR IDENTITY

As I mentioned earlier, emotions and beliefs are stored not only in our subconscious but also in our cells. For 2,000 years, the concept of *cellular memory* has been an essential part of traditional Chinese medicine.[1] Recently, cellular memory has also received greater recognition in allopathic medicine and Western science.[2] The role of cellular memory was studied in heart-transplant recipients. In several documented cases, patients experienced puzzling changes in their tastes, preferences, behaviors, emotions, and habits after waking up from surgery; the new traits turned out to be distinctive characteristics of the organ donors. Strikingly, none of the recipients knew anything about the donors prior to noticing changes in themselves, which suggests that those traits were remembered and encoded by the cells of the transplanted organs.[3, 4]

The exact means by which cells store emotions and memories are still unknown. In his book *The Biology of Belief*, cell biologist Bruce Lipton provides evidence suggesting that the behavior and identity of a cell is to a large extent determined by the interactions between neurotransmitters and cell receptors, specialized proteins in the cell membrane.[5] Neurotransmitters function as messengers between the nervous system and the rest of our body and are released by neurons and some glands, such as the adrenal and pituitary glands. Fear and anxiety cause the secretion of stress hormones—a special group of neurotransmitters that includes epinephrine, norepinephrine, and cortisol—into the bloodstream, where they are able to reach most cells in our bodies. As they bind to specific membrane receptors like keys fitting into their corresponding locks, they initiate distinctive responses and chemical changes within the cells.

Stress hormones mobilize the body's energy reserves and increase breathing, heart rate, and blood pressure, which allows oxygen-enriched blood to move more rapidly to the brain and muscles. The body is getting ready to manage the source of anxiety by fighting it, running away from it, or as a last resort, playing dead. Stress hormones also stimulate so-called transcription factors that migrate to the cell nucleus and activate specific genes.[6] Gene activation leads to the increased production of certain proteins that are required for the cells to respond adequately to the ongoing stress. So when stress hormones travel through the body and activate the cells' stress responses over and over again, as they do in cases of chronic anxiety, the results can be long-term changes in metabolism, structure, and behavior of cells.[7] The cells take on a new identity: "I am stressed and anxious."

These adaptations to stress and anxiety cannot be sustained without harming the delicate homeostasis of the individual cells and the balance of the entire body. For example, the resulting increase in oxidative stress leads to accumulation of free radicals, which cause stress-related cell damage. Free radicals can injure all components of a cell, including telomeres, which are specific DNA sequences on the end of chromosomes. Telomeres are designed to protect chromosomes from degradation and prevent them from fusing with each other. Research has shown that cells of people suffering from chronic stress have significantly shortened telomeres, which means that these people are at higher risk for accelerated aging, cancer, and autoimmune and heart diseases.[8]

Another significant way anxiety can affect us on a cellular level is when our cells literally become addicted to it. As cells adapt to the constant stimulation caused by chronic stress, fear, and anxiety, they change their dietary habits. They become so used to being activated and fueled by stress hormones that they may crave these neurotransmitters after we've reverted to a calm and relaxed state of mind.

If you think it's impossible for the body to become addicted to its own hormones and their effects, consider self-proclaimed "stress junkies"—those people who love living on the edge and thrive on such activities as race-car driving, bungee jumping, rock climbing, and then relax with a few hours of "special ops" video gaming. These people often say they need adrenaline rushes (*adrenaline* is another word for epinephrine) to feel alive. Or take avid runners, of which I am one, who can become so dependent on the release of endorphins they experience while running (the "runner's high") that they'll start nervously tapping their feet on the days they can't get their ten-mile fix.[9]

If we can develop a physical addiction to drugs, such as alcohol, nicotine, and pain medication, or to the neurotransmitters that are released by thrill-seeking and running, why shouldn't it be possible for us to also become addicted to anxiety? It's perfectly conceivable that chronic fear and anxiety make our cells demand their daily dose of stress hormones, as well as endorphins and opioids, which are also released in response to these emotions. There is no scientific proof for this hypothesis, but to my knowledge, it's never been thoroughly investigated either.

You may have experienced firsthand the effects of these cellular cravings. Everything is stable and peaceful in your life, and then an inner restlessness arises, causing you to search for something to worry about—the devastation of the rainforest or the little bump on your skin that you've had for years but now wonder if it might be cancer after all.

This brings me back to my original point. Releasing fear and anxiety in and of itself cannot create *permanent* change on a subconscious and cellular level. You might feel great for a while, but at some point, your subconscious and your cells might undergo an identity crisis or experience drastic withdrawal symptoms because they are still craving stress hormones. Both have been conditioned by fear and anxiety and, therefore, are uncomfortable without these emotions.

So it's important to replace the old anxiety-driven identity with a new foundation of self at the subconscious and cellular level. This new foundation needs to elicit powerful and positive emotions that prompt the release of other neurotransmitters, such as dopamine and serotonin, which stimulate and recondition your cells to a feeling of calmness and confidence. This way, you will transfer your new identity from your conscious mind to the subconscious and cellular level and thus truly embody it. What better place to start building your new foundation than with that aspect of you that is already solid and perfect by nature—your essence.

THE TRUTH IN YOUR ESSENCE

Let's talk about your essence, the core energy you've already gotten in touch with during the Pattern Resolution Process. How do you know that what you've seen and felt in your heart is real? This idea of a core essence may appear a bit esoteric and "woo woo." Believe me, my scientific mind was ruffled by this concept when I first got in touch with my own essence. However, what truly astounded me and confirmed my own experiences was that no matter how open-minded or skeptical my clients were, when I guided them to connect to their essence, the overwhelming majority described sensing it in the same way—as a brilliant light in their heart.

People commonly associate qualities such as love, compassion, goodness, strength, joy, and passion with this core energy. Although some of the news these days might lead you to believe that human behavior is largely defined by greed, self-righteousness, and a disregard of the greater good, there is at least as much evidence testifying to an inherent goodness in all of us. It's that powerful force that makes us jump into the freezing river to save another human being, or even an animal, from drowning. It's that natural instinct that drives us to reach out and support each other when disaster strikes, as countless stories described people doing after the events on September 11, Hurricane Katrina, the tsunami in the South Pacific, or the earthquake in Japan. It's that inner source that rewards selfless service with a deep sense of joy and fulfillment. It's a place from which we can draw love, compassion, and forgiveness, even for those we don't know or who hurt us the most. This is our core essence.

The Dalai Lama has pointed out that love and compassion aren't limited to human beings; they're also well established in animals. I've heard many times from people that the only unconditional love and acceptance they've ever known came from their beloved dogs or cats. It was through the adoring gaze of their dogs or the snuggling of their cats that they could pierce through their own lack of self-worth and see themselves as fundamentally good and loveable. There are different degrees and expressions of love and compassion. However, in their purest form—in the form that is unconditional, selfless, and giving—love and compassion generate from a place that goes beyond the conscious and subconscious.

OK, so maybe you still aren't sure about the goodness of your essence because you haven't saved anybody's life, you don't volunteer, you don't like pets, and you still can't forgive your ex. I am sure that you're being far too hard on yourself. Here's a way to recognize that you've actually been in touch with your pure essence more often than you previously realized.

Take a pen and paper, and write down events of the present and past where you have:

- Accepted and loved a person or animal without expectations or conditions
- Forgiven someone out of a sense of kindness and compassion
- Put your own needs and desires aside and focused solely on another person's well-being
- Been completely open and willing to listen, consider, and understand a different point of view
- Admitted with humility (not shame) that you were wrong
- Felt touched and inspired by another person's generosity, patience, acceptance, or selflessness
- Embraced and appreciated the beauty and the gifts of your life
- Awakened feeling happy and light for no reason
- Been in complete peace and harmony with yourself—and the world and people all around you

While you're revisiting your past, make sure that you're gentle with yourself. Focus on your potential, and keep in mind that even if these experiences of compassion, love, or peace passed rather quickly, they can still help you find your way back to a deeper connection with the source of those emotions and energies—your essence. The question is, how can you create a closer relationship with your essence and its powerful resources and make it your foundation of self on a subconscious and cellular level?

MEDITATION: THE BRIDGE TO YOUR ESSENCE

Numerous scientific studies have demonstrated that meditation is very beneficial for your health and well-being. Meditation has been shown to support the healing of physical conditions such as high blood pressure, high cholesterol, and chronic pain.[10] Meditating has also proven to be helpful for alleviating anxiety and depression.[11] People who meditate daily generally enjoy a higher quality of life with an increased sense of health and well-being.

Sounds promising. But if you're like me, you've probably also struggled with learning how to meditate. When I first tried meditating at age eighteen, I thought there was nothing to it. All I needed to do was lie down, close my eyes, and after a few moments I would float into that blissful nirvana I'd heard others talk about. Unfortunately, one of two things seemed to get in the way: either I fell asleep after a few minutes or my mind insisted on presenting me with a long list of things I hadn't done yet, the miserable failures of the past, or the unsolvable problems ahead of me. How can you reach that state of inner peace that meditation is supposed to give you when the moment you close your eyes, the very thoughts you want to let go of start popping up like firecrackers on the Fourth of July? Since my meditations only led to frustration, I decided that I was just one of those people who wasn't meant to meditate.

Then, when I started practicing kundalini yoga in my early thirties, I changed my mind and made peace with meditation. Like all forms of yoga, kundalini yoga engages the mind, body, and spirit. What appealed to me was that this practice doesn't focus so much on shaping your body into a perfect pretzel, but more on your relationship with yourself. Your eyes remain closed during the exercises—which allows you to stay aware of your thoughts, emotions, and your essence—while your body goes through the different movements. My yoga teacher said that it is a misconception to believe that we can completely turn off our minds. The illusion that we can only sets us up for failure. That sure took a load off my mind. He made me feel even better when he said that if we could still our minds for only one second, we would have mastered the art of meditating.

With the pressure off, I delved into meditation without great expectations, and I got so much out it that I even started teaching classes on how to meditate. For me, one of the most fascinating outcomes of meditating was that I didn't get sick anymore. Whenever I felt a cold coming on, I simply meditated for fifteen minutes, focusing on vibrant health and well-being and knowing that my immune system could now handle whatever bug had invaded my body. It worked like a charm every time.

Many people shy away from even attempting to meditate because they believe they don't have enough time, it's too difficult to learn, or they don't know what form of meditation to choose. The truth is, meditating is not rocket science, and you can learn it in a short amount of time. Since meditation is such a powerful tool for helping you connect to your essence—as the upcoming exercise will show you—I'd like to go over some of the most common questions and concerns students have asked during my meditation classes.

What is meditation? Meditation isn't a religion or magic; it's a technology that facilitates the communication between your mind, body, and spirit. Through concentration and awareness, meditation creates the stillness and space that allows you to realign yourself with your core essence so that you gain a more centered and balanced perspective of yourself and your life.

There are countless forms of meditation. Mindfulness meditation, where you're simply present and aware of your breath, your body, and your thoughts, is the form used the most in clinical studies. In transcendental meditation you concentrate silently on mantras, sacred sounds that often stem from Vedic or Tantric traditions. There is walking meditation, in which you focus on the experience of moving forward, one step at a time. During breathing meditations, you notice your breath or build up to inhaling for twenty seconds, holding your breath for twenty seconds, and exhaling for twenty seconds. You can practice writing meditations, such as free-form writing or asking a question about something you're troubled over, struggling with, or just curious about and then letting the answers flow through your pen. Guided meditations and visualizations usually take you on an inner journey and, thus, focus your mind on a mental path to a destination, such as inner peace or confidence. There are even laughing meditations, where you imagine a funny situation, remember hilarious jokes, or simply think about how kooky it is to be laughing by yourself.

Do some research, try out those forms that sound appealing, and see what works best for you at specific points in time. Each form has its unique benefits, but all of them have the potential to bring clarity, balance, and harmony into your life.

When is the best time to meditate? The ideal times to meditate are early in the morning or in the evening before you go to bed. I believe it's more important to meditate once a day whenever you can, rather than only once a week when you can find a break in your schedule to meditate at the perfect time. You don't have to spend hours in a contemplative space to reap the benefits of meditating. If you can commit to just ten to fifteen minutes per day, you'll notice amazing changes within a few weeks. One study showed that eight weeks of meditation were more effective than cognitive-behavioral stress reduction for lowering stress and pain levels.[12] You can even meditate while you're doing the dishes or sitting in a traffic jam (with your eyes open, of course).

Ultimately, the goal is to live your life as a continuous meditation. That doesn't mean you're constantly spacey or off in your own world; in fact, it means exactly the opposite. Your focus intensifies, and you increase your ability to be in the "now," aware of your surroundings and at the same time centered within your mind, body, and essence.

Why does my mind start racing when I meditate? Yogi Bhajan, who brought kundalini yoga to the West, called meditating "taking a mental shower" or "housecleaning for our subconscious mind." Knowing this is how meditation works, doesn't it make sense that when you start practicing, the mind races, thoughts fly in from seemingly nowhere, and repetitive thinking patterns become more apparent? Dust flies when you start cleaning up. In other words, it's normal and OK to have your mind freak out a bit while you're trying to find peace and harmony. When you realize that every thought that bubbles up is actually a thought that is on its way out of your subconscious (as long as you don't hold onto it), you can begin to enjoy watching these thoughts surface and then float away.

Now, watching and releasing these thoughts as they arise from the subconscious doesn't mean that from now on you should devalue or ignore the input from your subconscious mind. Continue to use the tools you've learned over the course of this book to communicate with and address your subconscious. However, while you're meditating, make it your intention to realign yourself with your essence, your true self, and to detach from the potentially limiting ways your subconscious perceives you.

How can I stay focused during my meditation? Some believe that meditating is about learning how to control your mind. I prefer to see meditating as creating the sacred space that allows your conscious, subconscious, and higher consciousness to come into balance. The challenge is for your conscious mind to set the course, stay present, and avoid getting distracted by or attached to whatever happens during the meditation. In my experience, gentle discipline is the most effective approach to keeping your mind focused and engaged. One of my meditation teachers once suggested thinking of the mind as a puppy that needs to be house-trained. You understand that your adorable puppy is learning and that it can't do so without your guidance, so you don't judge it for not understanding what to do right away. So if the puppy starts to relieve itself somewhere other than on the newspaper you've set out for that purpose, you patiently and gently bring it back to the paper.

You can do the same with your mind while you're meditating. If it wanders, just bring it gently back to your breath, your inner focus, or to the sensations in your body in the present moment, without judgment. Every time you're able to refocus your mind on the meditation, you add another piece to the foundation that you're building through this practice. Soon this foundation will serve you very well, enabling you to stay calm and centered no matter what storms brew around you.

Throughout the process of learning to meditate, be consistent and kind with yourself. Discipline doesn't mean punishing yourself; it means being your own disciple—a faithful servant for your greater good.

How should I meditate? It is said that to master any specific meditation exercise, you should practice it for at least 120 consecutive days. However, I believe that if you can stick with meditation for forty consecutive days, you can feel quite proud of yourself. To successfully establish a daily meditation routine, I recommend making your practice as easy and as comfortable as possible. Although there are benefits to sitting in the traditional cross-legged position, if the discomfort of your knees or legs becomes a distracting obstacle, it defies the meditation's purpose of finding inner peace and stillness.

Start with sitting in a chair, with your feet placed on the ground. Ideally your spine should be straight, but once again, if this position feels too difficult, don't let this get in the way of your daily commitment to meditate. You can also lie down on your back. Just make sure you don't find yourself falling asleep.

The classic meditation hand position, or *mudra,* asks for the thumb and forefinger on each hand to join, while the rest of the fingers are extended. The hands are placed palms-down on the thighs. Alternatively, you can keep your hands relaxed by your side, fold them in your lap, or place the palms together in front of your chest as you would to pray. Experiment and find out what feels most comfortable and doable for you.

There are only two other guidelines I would suggest that you follow: First, keep your eyes closed during the meditation, so that the focus is turned inward. Second, to avoid having to peek at your watch, use some sort of timer, which will signal when the time you set aside to mediate is up.

In chapter 11, I introduce two basic breathing exercises, which I highly recommend practicing for forty days. However, at this point in your journey to break through fear and anxiety, I would like you to delve into the following guided meditation.

REALIGN WITH YOUR ESSENCE: A GUIDED MEDITATION

This guided meditation will help you to align yourself with your essence and build a strong foundation for your new, empowered identity on a conscious, subconscious, and cellular level. But how, you may wonder, can you reach your cells through meditation or visualization?

As I mentioned in chapter 4, our subconscious oversees and regulates all the functions of our body, including the processes on a cellular level. One way our subconscious communicates with us is through metaphoric dreams, which need to be interpreted to understand their deeper meaning. The reverse is also true: we can use metaphors to communicate consciously with our subconscious and, by extension, our cells. Bernie Siegel, MD, pioneered the use of metaphors and visualizations to activate the mind-body connection to support the healing of chronic illnesses. For example, he teaches his patients to visualize sheep, fish, or vacuum cleaners removing and destroying cancer cells in their bodies. Although the precise processes involved are unclear, the successes Siegel has reported show that somehow these images are deciphered and translated to the cellular level, causing cancers to shrink and patients to heal faster. (For more information on Siegel's work, see his books *Peace, Love, and Healing* and *Love, Medicine, and Miracles.*)

When one of my friends and colleagues was diagnosed with breast cancer, she spent the two weeks before her surgery, visualizing little fish chewing away the tumor every day. She wasn't very surprised when, after the operation, the surgeon reported that the tumor had shrunk by 50 percent between the time the cancer was originally diagnosed and the time it was removed.

The following guided meditation makes use of healing metaphors to consciously communicate to your subconscious and to your cells that you are now creating a new foundation of self, which replaces your old, anxiety-based, self-limiting identity.

As with previous processes, you can either memorize the steps of this meditation or record your own or someone else's voice reading the description. A recording of an abbreviated version of this process is also available to stream online.[13]

For this meditation you can sit in a chair, lie on your bed, or float in a bathtub—any position works, as long as you're comfortable.

• • •

Close your eyes and take five or six deep breaths. At the same time, allow your mind to slow down and your body to relax and unwind. Focus on your eyelids, and let them become so relaxed and heavy that it would take a great effort to try to open them. So don't even try. Instead, let the relaxation of your eyelids spread across your face and, from there, all across your body. Then focus on your intention to connect to and realign your mind and body with your essence at the core of your being, to become more grounded and in harmony with yourself, and to access your untapped potential.

Now turn your focus inward to your heart, and for a few minutes, tune in to its faithful, life-sustaining beat. Draw your attention closer to your heart, and zoom in on its lower tip, the apex. Move in closer, and notice one particular cell—let's call it the *master cell.* As each breath brings you closer to it, increasingly appreciate this cell's beauty, complexity, and perfection.

Soon you reach the cell membrane with its layers, channels, and gateways shuttling nourishment and information in and out of the cell. The complexity and perfection of this magnificent cell is awe inspiring. Within the layers of its membrane float thousands of receptors, all eager and ready to listen to and communicate with neighboring cells and their environment. You now understand that your cells are actively listening to you. It is through these receptors that your thoughts and feelings are able to communicate with and affect the workings of the cell. You can see how your mind and body are intricately connected with each other.

Continue your journey by floating easily through one of the gateways of the membrane and into the cell plasma. Here you're surrounded by countless organelles, ribosomes, vesicles, and the life-force-generating mitochondria. It gives you great comfort to know that you have such an abundance of energy, vitality, and vibrant life residing within your cells.

Yet your journey takes you deeper, all the way into the center of the cell, into the nucleus, the sphere-shaped storage place for your genetic coding, your DNA. Inside the nucleus, you marvel at the sheer, unlimited amount of information your DNA holds. Someone once said that if every piece of information in your DNA were a star, you'd hold an entire galaxy of knowledge. You are in the halls of your inner library, where all the wisdom of life is preserved. Here, all questions can be answered, all problems solved.

However, your journey to your essence guides you further, beyond the molecules of the DNA down to the level of the atoms. As you approach a single atom with its solid core of neutrons and protons and a number of small electrons circling in distinct orbits around it, it strikes you that this configuration looks just like our solar system. The saying, "As above, so below, and as below, so above," takes on a new dimension and meaning for you. You are a reflection of the universe, and the universe mirrors your unlimited nature back to you.

Now float down into the atomic nucleus to the level of the subatomic particles, the smallest elements of your being. What you find there truly astonishes you. All there seems to be at the deepest level of your existence is an infinite amount of energy. The tiny subatomic particles are almost undetectable within the vastness of this powerful energy field. You clearly understand now that you consist predominantly of this energy and not the small amounts of matter you're accustomed to identifying yourself with. So change, healing, and growth are, at their core, nothing but changes in your energy field. This realization gives you a great sense of empowerment, because you know that your thoughts, beliefs, and feelings can shift your energy—and therefore your entire being.

As you are drawn into the core of this energetic field, you become aware of a brilliant light—the light of your essence. Delve into this light and become aware of its magnificent qualities and unlimited potential. Bask in the glow of your essence and allow peace and serenity to envelop you. All your worries, tension, and perceived limitations can dissolve here. Your old identities and outdated beliefs disintegrate and vanish in this light, while you recalibrate to the perfect blueprint of your true self.

Through the light of your essence, you have permanent access to all your inner gifts, resources, and powers. Focus on one or two specific qualities of your essence that seem to be the most pertinent for your life right now. These could be peace, strength, clarity, compassion, love, or awareness of your own worthiness. Then inhale and feed the light of your essence with love and appreciation, and notice how its brightness and brilliance increase. As you exhale, simply think, "I am . . . ," adding the quality or qualities of your essence you want to focus on. As you do this, watch how the light at your core begins to expand and radiate outward.

Continue to breathe in and out, fueling your essence with love and appreciation and allowing its light to intensify and spread out. Soon your essence envelops the atoms and molecules of your DNA and expands inside your cell's nucleus, restoring peace and harmony to your genetic coding. Those genes that have been overused by fear and anxiety are turned down, while others that are crucial for your healing and growth are activated.

After a few more breaths and silent "I am" declarations, the radiant light of your essence overflows into the cell plasma, revitalizing and rejuvenating all the organelles within it. At last your essence infuses the cell membrane, restoring all its elements and receptors to complete balance and harmony.

Now that your entire master cell is glowing brightly with the light of your essence, notice that this light can ignite the core energy that resides within each cell of your body. Continue to affirm internally your "I am" statement on the exhalation, and see how the cells around the master cell begin to shine brightly in the light of who you are.

With every breath, this brilliant energy expands to the millions of cells in your heart. Once your heart is completely illuminated and appears like an internal sun, its countless rays pulsate gently through your body. Each ray further ignites the light of all the cells in your chest, your abdomen, your arms and legs, your neck and head. Notice the waves of this harmonizing energy expanding throughout your entire body. Pay special attention to the areas that used to feel tense or tight when you experienced fear and anxiety. Each of your body's trillions of cells, the spaces between the cells, every cavity, and every vessel becomes infused and filled with the light of your brilliant essence.

Let the light of your truth overflow and expand beyond the confines of your body and illuminate your electromagnetic field in all directions. This field of energy around you also functions as your protective shield and deflects any negative influences or projections from the outside, keeping you in a comfortable space of peace and self-reliance.

Allow this energy field to expand to a size that honors who you truly are. For the next several minutes, completely relax in the softly pulsating light, and let your mind and body recalibrate and come into harmonic resonance with the essence of your being. Be one with yourself.

To end, simply take three breaths in and out.

• • •

Know that every time you go through this process, realigning with your essence becomes easier and more natural, until soon your essence is the foundation of your identity. Through this realignment process, you're building a solid foundation of self-worth and inner peace, and you're also restoring your mind and body to its original energetic blueprint of health and well-being.

The process worked beautifully for a client of mine. Claire had been struggling with anxiety and low self-esteem her entire life. When I first met her, she was barely thirty-eight years old, but she felt and moved like a woman twice her age. She'd recently lost a lot of weight. Her joints and back increasingly ached, her skin had started to break out with acne, and her menstrual bleeding hadn't stopped for five weeks. She told me that at night she couldn't rest, and if she did fall asleep, she was tormented by violent nightmares. In the mornings she barely crawled out of bed and had to drag herself through the already limited activities of the day.

"I've always taken care of myself," she told me in dismay. "I eat well. I don't drink or smoke. I meditate every day. And still my body is breaking down from the constant stress and anxiety."

Since medical treatments and herbal supplements hadn't provided significant improvement, Claire was certain that she needed to find and heal the deeper root cause of her challenges. During our work, she quickly realized that her foundation of self had been defined by lack and fragility. She grew up in extreme poverty and had spent many nights awake, hungry, and freezing. At school, she was often teased because of her old and ragged clothes, so she preferred staying alone and invisible to her peers. Despite her challenging childhood, Claire had managed to provide for herself pretty well as an adult. However, most of her choices, including those contributing to her healthy lifestyle, were still motivated by fear and anxiety. In her mind, she was simply too small, too sensitive, and too weak to fit into a highly demanding, rather unforgiving, fast-paced world.

The first time Claire practiced the realignment process, she noticed a dramatic shift. "My essence is so much stronger and more solid than I expected," she said. "There's such an abundance of energy and potency. Just looking at it makes me feel safe, as if nothing bad can ever happen to me."

During the following days, she was able to remain calm and centered, even when her coworkers were stressing out. Their frequent bouts of stress usually zapped her into high-anxiety mode. But now, every time Claire meditated on her essence, her positive feelings solidified while the familiar undercurrent of stress and anxiety dwindled. Soon she noticed that her body started to adjust as well. After only three months, her pain was gone, her menstrual cycle was regular, her skin cleared, and she'd even put on some weight. Claire had so much freed-up energy that she decided to practice ballet again, something she hadn't been able to do for years. Most of all, Claire appreciated that her sense of being was now founded on her genuine trust in the amazing potential and strength of her essence.

When you align yourself with your core essence on a regular basis, you can approach your life—with all its opportunities and potential challenges—from a self-empowered place of balance and neutrality. It still amazes me how the simple act of turning inward and reconnecting to the light of who we are can transform our entire perspective about life and ourselves.

For me, this meditation changed my life. Micromanaging and overachieving used to be my normal mode. My days consisted of too much to do, too little time, and subpar (in my mind) accomplishments. The alignment with my essence made me understand that rather than trying to constantly prove myself and force life to happen, I could choose to flow with it and let the gifts of life come to me. This realization didn't turn me into a couch potato (although I now actually allow myself to enjoy sitting on the couch from time to time). But it helped me, in a profound way, to shift my attitude of overachieving and underappreciating myself into an attitude of gratitude for the core of who I am.

By being in alignment with your essence and, thus, in a place of integrity with yourself, you're no longer as affected by or attached to outer circumstances. You simply know that you have all the powers and inner resources you may need and want at your disposal. This doesn't mean that your foundation of confidence and self-reliance will make you cold, calculating, or arrogant. Remember that your essence is also the source of love and compassion. Therefore, when you align with your core, you have greater access to these energies and can share them more easily with others. You may also find that you have much more love and compassion for yourself.

Through this realignment process you are building, on a mental, emotional, cellular, and energetic level, the essential foundation upon which you can create anything and anyone you want to be. Which brings us to the topic of our next chapter: who do you want to be?

CHAPTER 10

Breaking Through to Self-Empowerment

YOU CAN ONLY keep a change when you own it. In other words, for change to become truly meaningful and permanent, it needs to affect deeply how you perceive and relate to yourself at your very core. The work you've done so far through this book has prepared you to own your changes. So take a deep breath, get ready to redefine how you see yourself—your inner identity—and own it.

Keep in mind that no matter how hard we try, we can never fully appreciate and comprehend all of who we truly are, simply because we're too complex, multilayered, and vast. This is why our subconscious applies filters to condense and simplify the otherwise overwhelming amount of information about ourselves into more comprehensible formats—our inner identities. Some of the strongest subconscious filters that shape how we see ourselves and the world around us are our core beliefs.

There's a common saying, "What holds us back is not who we really are, but who we think we are." In other words, we're always more than who we believe and imagine ourselves to be. The truth of who you are goes far beyond your old fear-and-anxiety-based identity, which may have been defined by limiting core beliefs, such as "I'm not good enough," "I don't have what it takes," or "The world isn't a safe place." As we've discussed, no matter how much emotional baggage we release from the past, fear and anxiety will start to rebuild quickly if we continue to identify ourselves fundamentally with such limiting beliefs. Even more than the actions we take, our beliefs determine the results we achieve and, therefore, how we feel. Albert Einstein defined insanity as "doing the same thing over and over again and expecting different results." Haven't you also found that despite trying many different approaches, your results often haven't improved? Why is that? Because you haven't changed your mind-set and beliefs. Changing behavior without changing beliefs is like buying a new car to become a better driver.

In the previous chapters, you've forged a closer connection to the essence of who you are. In doing so, you've built a stronger foundation of self. In this chapter, that strength will help you delve more deeply into your limiting core beliefs, eliminate them from your subconscious, and then replace them with a new, self-empowered identity.

TRAPPED IN A LIMITING BELIEF

In the circus, elephant handlers train their animals to remain calm and obedient when tied to a post. The method they use is rather sad. When the elephants are young, handlers take heavy chains and tether the animals to large tree trunks. No matter how hard the little elephants tug on the huge chains, they can't break free. At some point, completely exhausted, the animals stop trying. Over time, handlers replace the chains with increasingly smaller ropes until it would be easy for the elephants to tear away the flimsy cords and escape to freedom. Still, the animals don't even try to pull on the cords, because since their youth, they have associated the idea of being tied with the inability to move.

We humans too develop many of our limiting beliefs during childhood and adolescence, when the subconscious is most susceptible to outside influences. These beliefs aren't usually our original ideas. Instead, they're based on the beliefs and behaviors of our parents, peers, teachers, and other influences in our environment. To acquire a limiting core belief, we have to hear its message or experience its ramifications many times, each time feeling a relatively strong emotional response to it.

Shirley had been suffering from anxiety, guilt, and lack of self-worth for most of her life. Because she'd been adopted at birth, she dealt with feelings of sorrow about being abandoned by her biological mother. Her adoptive mother exacerbated the wound Shirley felt. The woman was extremely controlling, judgmental, and at times violent. For as long as Shirley remembered, no matter what she did, it was never good enough for her mother. She told me that when she was four years old, she decided that the only way to survive and someday have a chance to leave home and be free was to fully obey and please her mom.

However, as the years went by, the insults and judgments from her mother gradually erased Shirley's sense of self. Even as she became an adult, with a successful career and her own family, Shirley's identity remained defined by guilt, anxiety, and almost nonexistent self-worth. Still, dutifully, she continued to call her mother daily, wincing through the screaming accusations and petty insults.

Even as her mother grew extremely ill and Shirley became her caregiver, the dying woman continued to berate and criticize her. The last words Shirley heard as she sat by her mom's deathbed were, "What do *you* want?" Then her mother deliberately turned her head away from her daughter and passed away.

Shirley's husband, friends, and children saw clearly that she was a victim of her mother's anger and abusive behavior. But no matter how much others supported and adored her, Shirley continued, even after her mother's death, to hold on to the belief that there was nothing good or loveable about herself. Finally, when she was well into her fifties, the anxiety and the pain of believing that she was so seriously flawed sparked the courage and determination she needed to address the root cause of her limiting identity.

During the Pattern Resolution Process, Shirley tapped into a memory of when she was just one or two years old. She recalled her mother placing her on the kitchen table, gently tickling her, and speaking to her very sweetly. Shirley was delighted and responded with a big smile. At that very moment, her mother's demeanor completely changed. She pointed her index finger at Shirley's tiny face and yelled, "No! You're a bad child."

Struck with disbelief and confusion, the little girl felt her eyes widen and her body become tense and stiff. Immediately her mother's behavior changed again. Once more she was sweet and loving—until Shirley smiled again, then her mother snapped back with angry words and threats until Shirley squirmed and cried. This bizarre and cruel behavior went on for quite some time, until finally Shirley's adoptive father intervened. Looking back at this event from the place of learning, the adult Shirley finally understood that it must have been her mother's fear of being powerless and out of control that made her want to control the one person she could—her daughter. It now made sense to her that when her mother faced her death, the ultimate loss of control, she still tightly held on to what had always given her a sense of power: control over Shirley.

Once she could release the patterns of anxiety and guilt from her subconscious, Shirley could accept that she was truly innocent and had taken on the self-hatred and limiting beliefs her mother had projected onto her. What amazed me about Shirley was that despite these realizations, she didn't turn toward hatred or resentment for her mother. Instead, she felt compassion for the suffering and pain her mother's heart must have been tormented by for her to be so cruel to a little child.

WHY LIMITING BELIEFS ARE SO "STICKY"

Shirley's story shows why limiting beliefs are so difficult to change and, at the same time, so important to change. One of the challenges with limiting core beliefs is that they're accepted as reality rather than questioned for their validity. This is because these beliefs tend to turn into strong self-fulfilling prophecies.

To quote Henry Ford, "If you believe you can or cannot, you're always right." It's a fact of life that what you believe and expect to take place is likely to occur just because you believe and expect it to. A study researching the likelihood of older people falling showed that those who'd stumbled in the past and believed they'd fall again actually fell more often than those who'd never stumbled and had no fear of falling. The study revealed that because of their limiting, fear-based belief, people changed the way they walked and held their bodies, which consequently increased their likelihood of tripping and falling again.[1]

Even if your negative expectations don't turn out to be true, limiting beliefs still continuously reinforce themselves. You might be like Shirley—or know people like her—who continue to see themselves as flawed and undeserving despite all the successes, love, and admiration they receive in their lives. Let's say you believe that you're not good enough and that most people around you are more capable, more successful, more likeable—you name it. No matter what you're planning to do, you assume, at least subconsciously, that the outcomes of your actions will only confirm that you're not good enough. Not only will you pursue your plans with less energy, confidence, and focus, but your subconscious mind will also filter and interpret the results of your actions according to the limiting belief that you are, once again, inadequate. Consequently, you will feel even more insecure, anxious, and deflated, which further drives the "I'm not good enough" belief and so increases its validity and realness to you. Through this self-reinforcing cycle, a limiting belief becomes your identity.

Just like in Shirley's case, limiting beliefs are fueled and kept alive by anxiety, guilt, shame, sadness, and anger. This is why trying to "program" a new belief into our minds—by only visualizing or repeating affirmations, for example—doesn't work that well. For limiting beliefs to lose their hold on our subconscious mind, we need to first release the associated negative emotions. You've already accomplished that part by working through the previous chapters, so now you're ready to examine your limiting beliefs from a detached and more neutral vantage point—and thus pave the road to a new, empowered identity.

WHO DO YOU THINK YOU ARE?

As I said in the second chapter, identifying limiting beliefs, especially those that have been driving fear and anxiety, can be challenging. These beliefs can become so engrained in the fabric of our identities that we don't even recognize them as limiting beliefs. Instead, we accept as fact that we don't measure up, that we can't get what we want, or that we're not safe. No matter how often in the past these beliefs proved to be true, when it comes to the future, they still remain nothing but generalizations and assumptions.

Imagine how you'd respond if your partner, your child, or your best friend saw themselves or their lives the way you see yours. Would you concur and encourage your loved ones to accept those limitations as their reality? Definitely not. Instead you would vehemently contradict him or her because you wouldn't want this dear person to be stuck with such self-restricting presumptions.

The following process helps you examine carefully whether your views about yourself and your world confine you, disempower you, or provide fertile ground for further anxiety and insecurity.

Take a piece of paper, and answer the following questions.

What limiting beliefs were you surrounded with in your childhood? Think about what your parents, teachers, or other important people surrounding you during your early years told you about money, work, health, others, or life in general. What do you recall they believed about you? How did they view and treat themselves? Did anything you heard or experienced in those relationships make you feel anxious, smaller, or unsafe?

Which of those limiting beliefs have you adopted and still hold on to? There are different ways you may have assimilated anxiety-triggering beliefs from your childhood. The most obvious is that, at one point, you accepted what you were told as the truth, even though it might have hurt you. It might have been someone's judgment that you were not smart enough, too sensitive, or fundamentally flawed.

Another way someone else's limiting beliefs may have infiltrated your subconscious matrix is by example. Perhaps one of your parents was a worrier and was also very critical of him- or herself. Because our parents or guardians are our role models, we subconsciously internalize their views and beliefs as our own. Several clients have told me that, looking back, they realized that they had so much empathy for their anxious and insecure mother or father that they became like them.

A third, more subtle way of incorporating limiting beliefs during childhood is through your interpretation of their meaning. Your parents may have told you that you have the potential to reach any goal you set your mind to. Sounds very encouraging, right? You, however, may have felt burdened by the pressure to succeed and ultimately become *deflated.* Because your parents' expectations seemed to be so extraordinarily high, you started to believe you could never measure up to them and perceived yourself as a failure.

Which aspects of your life cause you to feel the most anxious, insecure, or trapped? Ask yourself, "Why do I feel this way?" When you have an answer, ask yourself, "Why?" or "Why not?" When you receive the answer to the question of "Why?" or "Why not?" dig four to five levels deeper until you uncover the limiting core belief. Don't overthink—just go with the first answers you get. As I've said before, the subconscious mind processes information much more quickly than the conscious mind, and for this exercise you're interested in the views of this deeper part of your mind.

Here's an example of how your inner discussion might take place.

"I'm stuck. I don't like my job."
"Why do I feel this way?"
"Because I've been job hunting for a long time and couldn't get anything better."
"Why not?"
"Because my education is lacking."
"Why?"
"Because I didn't go to college."
"Why not?"
"Because I thought I would fail."
"Why?"
"Because I'm not smart enough."

And there it is: one of your limiting core beliefs. Here's another example:

"My kids don't listen to me."
"Why do I feel this way?"

"Because they never do what I tell them to do."
"Why not?"
"Because they don't respect me."
"Why?"
"Because I don't enforce boundaries."
"Why not?"
"Because I don't like conflict."
"Why?"
"Because I'm afraid that they won't like me."
"Why?"
"Because I don't really like myself."

Bingo. One more example:

"I don't have the energy to date."
"Why do I feel this way?"
"Because I have done it many times before and was disappointed each time."
"Why?"
"Because no one asked me for a second date."
"Why not?"
"Because they didn't want a relationship with me."
"Why not?"
"Because I am not interesting enough."

What are the common denominators and themes of your negative, anxiety-driven self-talk? Notice how your daily thoughts may be connected by and revolve around common themes such as failure, judgment, lack, safety, and loneliness. The associated core beliefs might be any of the following: "I don't have what it takes," "I can't have what I want," "I am not safe," "I don't belong anywhere."

Even beliefs that ostensibly seem to be about others or external circumstances—"People don't like me," "Nobody can be trusted," "There isn't enough money to go around"—are ultimately based upon limiting assumptions and perceptions of yourself. From the perspective of your subconscious, you may appear too weak and too vulnerable to deal with this dangerous world, too flawed and too unattractive for people to like you, or unable or not talented enough to create financial prosperity. Since we often can't control or change our outer circumstances, externally focused limiting beliefs can appear especially untouchable and defeating. However, just by asking yourself what you need to believe about yourself to have those beliefs and make those assumptions, you bring your awareness and your power back to what you have control over: yourself.

By the way, if your negative self-talk has improved to the point of being almost nonexistent, revisit your notes from chapter 6 so that you can explore the limiting beliefs in which your negative thoughts used to be rooted.

A quick note to your inner perfectionist: there's nothing you can do wrong in this process. Most likely you'll find that you've subscribed to more than one limiting belief and then wonder on which one you should focus first or how you can let go of them all. Beliefs are stacked together and support each other like a house of cards. If you remove one of the deeper core beliefs, then the entire belief structure collapses. So no matter which core belief you choose to eliminate, it will inadvertently change and expand your inner identity.

To test whether or not you've found a core limiting belief, ask yourself what would potentially change if you stopped believing it. Would your thoughts change? Would you break out of the constricting mold of your childhood? Would you find the motivation to take action, to move from being stuck to moving toward what you want? But most important, would you see yourself differently? You've clearly uncovered a limiting core belief if letting go of it would change your image of yourself—in other words, if it would change your inner identity. But exactly what does your limiting identity look like?

THE LIMITED EDITION OF SELF

Whenever I think about my time in grammar school, I immediately picture my first-grade teacher. All I see is a dark beard (no face) and a knuckled fist swiftly whipping across the top of my head. This image is then directly linked to a rather painful cellular memory, one located at the exact spot where the knuckles landed on my skull. By the way, at that time, in our small rural school in the Black Forest, rapping on students' heads was a common practice, a discipline applied for even small transgressions (at least I like to believe that I wasn't *that* naughty). Other than this picture or internal interpretation, I have no other recollection or impression of that teacher in (or on!) my head.

Our subconscious has an internal interpretation for every facet and context of our lives. Similar to anxiety-triggering thoughts, some of those interpretations may float through our minds without us even consciously noticing them.

For example, let's say every time you go to the dentist you feel the same inexplicable nervousness and sense of doom. It doesn't make sense—your dentist is famous for her gentle touch, your experiences there have been nothing but positive (thank God for the men and women who developed local anesthetics). So what is this anxiety about? You're probably unaware of how your subconscious interprets and anticipates the idea of dental appointments. When you think about your upcoming visit at the dentist, your subconscious may visualize you strapped down in a completely powerless position and your dentist towering over you with a menacing frown and a high-powered drill. It certainly looks like horror movie material. However, as soon as you've become aware of this subconscious interpretation, you've gained the leverage to change and adjust its intensity—and even its qualities—within just a few minutes. I will show you how later in this chapter.

When you mentally and emotionally identify yourself with a limiting belief, your subconscious crafts an inner picture of you embodying this belief. This subconscious interpretation of you in the context of that belief is your limiting inner identity.

Jane, an attractive and very talented forty-five-year-old woman, felt for a long time that her relationship with her husband was unfulfilling and that he was stifling her. All her efforts to motivate him to pursue couple's counseling and to find ways they could connect with each other on a deeper and more intimate level came to nothing. After several years of frustration and disappointments, Jane realized that her husband's willingness to change, improve, or even save the relationship was pretty much nonexistent. However, whenever she was close to deciding to leave the marriage and move on, Jane became very afraid of how her husband, who was known to have a temper, would react to that news. "Typical me," she told me. "I'm just not strong enough to follow through with my decision."

When I asked Jane to remember an argument with her husband that left her feeling afraid and powerless, the image that popped up on her internal screen showed him to be significantly larger and taller than she was, which in reality wasn't the case. While her husband stood in the foreground, his face stern and angry, she saw herself farther away in the dark, her face frozen in a tense and anxious stare.

"Wow," she blurted. "I see myself really shrunken—as if he has all my power." Realizing how her subconscious mind "saw" her when she believed that she wasn't strong enough helped Jane better understand why she'd felt so paralyzed when it came to telling her husband she wanted a separation. As a successful businesswoman and active participant in her community, Jane considered herself a very confident and capable person. However, her husband's presence and demeanor triggered the old limiting belief of being weak and powerless—a belief that had been originally "installed" by her domineering father. Whenever her husband raised his voice, just like her father did so many times, her power and self-worth vanished because her inner identity reverted back to that of a small, vulnerable child unable to fend for herself.

I'm sure you're now curious to find out how your limiting identity is portrayed by your subconscious. So let's see.

Sit comfortably in a chair, close your eyes, and take a few deep breaths in and out. Then either think about the core limiting belief you just identified and want to let go of, or focus on a specific person, event, or situation that usually triggers this belief and its affiliated emotions.

When you get in touch with the limiting belief and the accompanying emotions, look at your internal screen and watch how you visualize yourself. Don't try to conjure a picture; instead let it just appear.

Focus mainly on your inner identity and not so much on the people or surroundings. First notice whether, in the image, you're looking through your own eyes (an associated point of view) or whether you're watching yourself from a vantage outside your own body (a dissociated point of view). Next notice whether the image is:

- In black and white or in color
- Small, life sized, or larger than life
- Bright, dim, or in between
- Focused or unfocused
- A still picture or more like a movie
- Right in front of you or five to ten feet away—or even farther

You can gain more vivid insights about your limiting identity by determining if there are any sounds, smells, tastes, or sensations associated with it—such as the temperature or the position of your body. Notice how you feel now or how you used to feel when you were previously steeped in this limiting belief.

Taking note of these visual and sensual qualities of your internal picture is important for the process of replacing the old identity with a new one, which I will introduce later in this chapter. Now you have your starting point. You may not have really appreciated what you were seeing because the image showed an insecure or powerless version of yourself. Or it's possible that this image of yourself is very familiar—and therefore somewhat comforting. In any case, I am sure you agree that this inner identity doesn't reflect all of who you are and that it prevents you from expressing your true potential and purpose. But as you already know, just letting go of what no longer serves you isn't enough. You need to replace your old beliefs and identity with a new, empowered version of self. So let's define what and who this *new you* can be.

THE BLUEPRINT OF EMPOWERMENT

Every day, TV commercials try to convince us that the best way to find confidence, happiness, and fulfillment is to improve our external conditions. We're told that a new car, a younger partner, bigger biceps, or fewer wrinkles will make us feel more worthy and at ease. During one of his talks, I heard Neale Donald Walsch, the author of *Conversations with God,* say that he used to identify himself with his hair. (Admittedly, his hair is quite voluminous.) Similarly, I tried to boost my self-worth in my midtwenties with expensive, handmade leather shoes. Well, as Neale and I did, you've probably found out that defining yourself by *what you own* and *how you look* instead of *who you are* only leads to big disappointments. All it does is put our real change and growth on hold because we continue to give our attention and power to something on the surface or outside ourselves and avoid addressing the deeper, subconscious root causes of our fears and insecurities.

My client Dan provides an excellent example. He wanted nothing more than to advance in his career. However, for more than six years, he'd been consistently overlooked and undervalued by the company he was working for. While others were receiving promotions, he went nowhere, even though he had worked the hardest and had continuously demonstrated great loyalty and reliability. Over the years, Dan's stress and anxiety about his work situation built to such an extent that it seemed to overtake his entire life. It wasn't until he suffered from severe chronic back pain, which didn't improve despite extensive orthopedic and chiropractic treatments, that he was ready to admit that his stress and anxiety had gotten out of hand.

When I asked Dan about his goals, he told me that he really would like to be more successful at his job, have greater financial stability, and, of course, rid himself of physical pain. However, as soon as Dan shared these objectives with me, he became very anxious and almost deflated. "Who am I kidding?" he asked. "I'll never be able to have what I want. I just don't have what it takes." There they were—the limiting core beliefs he'd been reciting to himself like a daily mantra since early childhood.

Dan grew up with a very strict and demanding father for whom he never seemed to measure up. And although his father had completely turned around in his old age, Dan's self-image was still conditioned by the emotional baggage and subconscious limiting imprints from his childhood. After Dan realized that he needed to address these deeper root causes of his challenges, he changed his goals to being at peace with himself, trusting and feeling confident about who he was, and being able to act from a place of self-worth and inner strength. Through consciously redefining and rebuilding his inner identity, Dan felt more empowered, content, and self-assured. For the first time in his life, he could truly appreciate and value himself. Because his chronic back pain had also disappeared, he truly felt that he'd reached his goals, despite the fact that nothing regarding his job or finances had changed.

A few months after our last session, Dan called to tell me that his boss had just notified him that he would be receiving the long-awaited promotion. "Isn't it interesting that I got promoted at a time when I didn't really care that much?" he asked. "All those years when I was striving and giving my all to work, nothing happened. And now that I'm more balanced and happier with myself and I put myself and my family first, I receive the validation I was waiting for. I guess first I had to know in myself that I am worthy—and then my life could catch up."

PARAMETERS FOR A NEW, EMPOWERING BELIEF

The core of the new you will be anchored in a new, empowering belief, which replaces your old, limiting belief. But how do you define a new core belief? How do you choose one that inspires you and makes you want to embody and live up to it? Here are some guidelines that will help you easily and effectively develop a new, custom-tailored belief.

For starters, there are three requirements a new core belief needs to fulfill.

The new belief needs to expand you. I've seen it many times. People come up with a new, empowering belief only to quickly dismiss it, because "It isn't me." Well, it isn't supposed to be you—yet—because you're aiming to grow beyond your old, limiting identity. If you feel that the new belief already fits you, it may not be expansive enough. So it's perfectly OK to be a little apprehensive at the beginning when your new belief may sound more like a fantasy or wishful thinking than reality.

The new belief needs to motivate you. This seems like a no-brainer, but it is still important to mention. Let's say you used to feel that you were "a failure." An obvious choice for a new, empowering belief could be, "I have all it takes to have success." However, you may feel ambivalent about the word "success," because it triggers negative associations with competition and failure. So better options could be, "I have the ability and drive to live up to my potential" or "I'm smart, capable, and resourceful." Make sure that the new core belief makes you feel excited and eager to grow into it.

The new belief needs to be realistic. If your new belief brings up some resistance inside of you, it probably appears too difficult to reach. Let's say you struggle with low self-esteem because you've been dealing with debt and unemployment for quite some time. Which belief could you more easily accept and continuously focus?—"I'm successful and prosperous" or "I have the power to make positive changes now." If your new belief appears too challenging or impossible to live up to, you'll quickly lose your focus. So choose a belief that propels you toward that next desirable level of your personal evolution but doesn't allow you to underestimate your potential or make you play it safe. Once you've fully accepted your new identity, you may feel inclined to aim for an even higher level of success, happiness, and fulfillment. What you'll find is that our boundless inner resources always offer more untapped power for us to harness.

So you want a new core belief that is exciting, motivating, challenging, and attainable. Easier said than done, right? Many of my clients experienced an instant brain-cramp when they were asked to formulate a new, self-empowering core belief. "I don't even know where to start," they'd say, or, "What if I don't find a belief that's right for me?"

These and similar concerns may have also started to occupy your mind. The key is simple: don't overthink or overanalyze the question, "What do I want to believe about myself?" Instead, trust your subconscious to give you the answers. This advice stems from a very unlikely source—*Science,* a prestigious, much-referenced research journal.

In 2006, *Science* published a study that attempted to tackle a question that has been pondered throughout the history of humankind: what is the best way to make a decision? Should we consciously deliberate the facts or trust our gut feelings?

In one of the trials, the investigators asked participants to choose the best of four hypothetical cars. Participants were introduced to either four or twelve different attributes of the vehicles. One group was asked to analyze the data for four minutes before making a decision. The other one was distracted for four minutes (by solving anagrams) and then asked to pick the best car on the spot.

The results were quite surprising. When given only four attributes on which to base their decision, the group that had time to carefully deliberate and analyze the data more frequently chose the best car. However, when twelve attributes about each car needed to be considered, the group that was asked to make their decisions spontaneously performed better and picked the best car with significantly greater frequency. In this scenario, spontaneous subconscious decision-making was far superior to intellectual analysis. After further tests with different products and endpoints, the authors came to the conclusion that it is best "to think consciously about simple matters and delegate thinking about more complex matters to the unconscious."[2]

So what does selecting a car—through conscious or unconscious analysis—have to do with choosing your new core belief and identity? Since you, as a human being, are a "complex matter"—and I mean this in the best sense of the phrase—you're better off letting your subconscious guide you to find the best-fitting belief for you rather than agonizing over it.

THREE STEPS FOR ESTABLISHING YOUR NEW CORE BELIEF

I find that when it comes to fear and anxiety, common limiting core beliefs are "I'm not good enough," "I'm not safe," and "I'm anxious." I use these as examples to explain the following process for defining a new belief and creating the basis for the new, empowered you.

STEP 1: DEFINE A NEW CORE BELIEF

A few general guidelines:

- The new belief needs to be stated positively. "I don't have anxiety" doesn't work as a new belief, because it still directs your mind toward the anxiety you want to overcome.
- At the same time, defaulting to the opposite, "I am good enough," or "I am safe," can turn out to be rather flat. It may sound too similar to your

old belief, and it may, at least subconsciously, bring up questions such as "Good enough? In what regard and for whom?" or "Safe from what?"

- A new belief is best stated in the present tense rather than in the future tense. Telling yourself, "I will be calm and confident," postpones the realization of this belief to the indefinite future. "I *am* calm and confident," places the belief here and now.
- Make the belief short and succinct. Long, drawn-out sentences often lack punch and are hard to remember.

1. **Take a pen and paper and write down at least ten to fifteen feelings, qualities, and attributes that describe the opposite of what you associated with the old limiting belief.** For example:

- The opposite of feeling "not good enough" could be feeling confident, empowered, capable, competent, strong, resourceful, motivated, smart, intelligent, wise, kind, loveable, passionate, valuable, or worthy.
- The opposite of feeling "unsafe" could be feeling trusting, supported, taken care of, secure, guided, confident, empowered, or strong.
- The opposite of feeling anxious could be feeling calm, centered, at peace, in the flow, relaxed, at ease, balanced, resourceful, capable, or powerful.

You may find additional inspirations by revisiting your answers to the goal-defining questions of chapter 5.

2. **Without analyzing extensively, circle three or four words that appear the most important, desirable, and enticing to you.** Let your subconscious make the choice. Notice which words trigger positive feelings and a sense of openness or expansiveness in your body—even if those sensations may appear rather subtle.

3. **Using these key words, frame your new core belief as a statement.** Begin your new belief by saying "I am" or "I have."

- Through an **"I am"** statement, you identify yourself with the attributes of the new belief: "I am confident, capable, and resourceful." "I am calm, centered, and secure." "I am at peace and in the flow." You affirm that this is who you are—or at least who you want to be. The only caveat with an "I am" belief is that it may at some point feel a bit limiting because it focuses only on a small subset of all the qualities of who you are.

- You may prefer an **"I have"** statement, in which you *own* your new belief versus *being* it: "I have powerful resources to create the life I want." "I have confidence in my abilities to keep myself safe and well." "I have inner peace and calmness." The downside here can be that you may still see these qualities as separate from you and that you may, at least subconsciously, worry that you could lose them.

Try different variations beginning with "I am" and "I have." To figure out which one works best for you, close your eyes and say each one out loud three times. Choose the statement you feel the most energized by and excited about.

4. If neither the "I am" nor the "I have" variation feels quite right to you, try these statements: "I love and appreciate myself" and "I trust and believe in myself."

Although it's very powerful when your new belief specifically addresses the limitations and shortcomings of the old one, it can be even more empowering to shift the focus to how you want to relate to yourself. Your relationship with yourself is ultimately the most important relationship in your life. When you declare, "I love and appreciate myself," or "I trust and believe in myself," you are free from other people's judgments and you no longer try to live up to their standards. Once you've truly accepted such a belief as your new identity, you can stay in your power and at peace with yourself, no matter what the circumstances.

Saying you love, appreciate, and believe in yourself may sound rather self-absorbed, complacent, or antisocial. But by loving, appreciating, and believing in yourself, you fill yourself with these positive qualities, which you can then share with others from the fullness of your heart.

Keep in mind that if the wording "I love and appreciate myself" doesn't quite suit you, you can always change it. A client of mine told me once that loving herself didn't sound authentic or appealing to her. As a fellow German, she wasn't used to the more liberal way the word *love* is used in the English language. The German "I love you" *(Ich liebe dich)* is usually reserved for the romantic partner, which is why, to her ear, "I love myself" sounded rather odd. "I appreciate and care about myself" worked much better for my client.

You can also create a combination of the "I am ____," "I have ____," "I love and appreciate myself," and "I trust and believe in myself" statements. For example, "I love and trust in myself. I am calm and confident and have all the resources I need to be happy and well."

Remember, at this point you don't have to fully buy into this new belief. Right now it's just important to clearly define the new belief you want to focus on and to feel excited, or at least hopeful, about its promise and potential.

STEP 2: SEE IT, FEEL IT, BELIEVE IT

Until now, your new belief and identity are mainly good ideas and positive intentions. To be able to use them as replacements for the old, limited belief, you need to translate the words into the language of your subconscious mind—images, feelings, sounds, and other sensations.

1. **Create a picture of the new you.** Imagine yourself as the person who embodies the qualities of the new belief—for example, someone who is peaceful, confident, energized, and empowered.

Make sure you can see *yourself.* If instead of seeing yourself, you're looking through your own eyes at the imagined world around you, the subconscious will focus on those external circumstances, which right now are of secondary importance. In fact, you want to imagine the new you independent from any outside context. For example, you might picture your future self in a new office, on a Hawai'ian beach, or at an award ceremony surrounded by friends cheering you on. You might want to see yourself as confident and cheerful, seventy-five pounds thinner, and driving a brand-new red Porsche. But when you make specific people, outer circumstances, or significant physical changes a part of your internal identity, you're adding certain conditions to your goals. Your subconscious could interpret these conditional images this way: only when you're in that new office, on the beach, surrounded by effusive friends, have the perfect body, or are driving a new red Porsche can you feel confident and at ease. Your subconscious might consider the external details as unrealistic or even unachievable outcomes and therefore generate very little motivation to change, because it doesn't want to set you up for failure. Including these conditions can also distract from the primary goal, which is to feel empowered and self-actualized regardless of outer circumstances.

Now notice whether the picture of the new you is:

- In black and white or in color
- Small, life sized, or larger than life
- Bright, dim, or as it would normally appear
- Focused or unfocused
- A still picture or more like a movie

2. **Entice the senses.** What will you see, sense, hear, smell, and taste when you are your empowered self? What about your body posture and facial expression?

Let's say your new belief is "I'm confident and excited about all my possibilities." Imagine looking into the mirror and seeing your face lit up with a big smile. You're standing tall and straight, but at the same time you're relaxed and comfortable in your own skin. You may have an upbeat and joyful song playing in the background; smell clear, refreshing air; and taste delicious, fresh-squeezed juice or invigorating sparkly water. By including the senses, you enrich and enliven the vision of the new you, which makes this goal for your subconscious even more exciting and palpable.

3. **Energize the new you with emotions.** How will you feel when you're the person you see on your inner screen? This step may appear redundant considering that you just decided that you want to feel confident, at peace, and energized. Nevertheless, I've seen what happens when my clients create wonderful internal images of their new selves but forget to link them with positive emotions. You can't fly a kite without a breeze or plant a garden without warmth and light, and you can't pursue an amazing new identity without enticing emotional charge. No matter how great your intentions, if you don't feel anything about them they'll never become your reality. A positive emotional connection to your desired outcome provides you with the subconscious energy you need to commit to and motivate yourself to follow your dream.

So how do you look? Are you excited about who you're about to grow into? Or are you still not seeing or feeling it? If the latter is the case, here's what you can do.

If You Can't See or Feel the New You

You may argue that you've never felt confident or powerful. Even after scanning carefully through the highlights of your life—graduations, athletic accomplishments, your first kiss, your wedding, the birth of your kids—you're still convinced that confidence and empowerment are completely foreign to you. Well, there's another very effective approach to connecting yourself to a desired emotion or state of being—even though you may never have experienced that emotion or state yourself. Neuro-Linguistic Programming calls this approach *modeling.*

We all have a natural ability to learn and acquire certain skills by simply mirroring someone who has already mastered them. In fact, many of our behaviors originate from modeling and imitating someone else. For example, pay attention to how you speak: the words you use, your intonation, gestures, and facial expressions. Do you recognize similarities to your mother or father? There's a reason many of us come at some point to the same, rather shocking realization: "I am becoming my parents."

As a child, you modeled not only your parents' manners and behavior, but also that of the heroes and heroines you read about or watched in movies. While you reenacted the adventures of Superman or Wonder Woman, using "superpowers" to fight against the dark and evil forces, you became these heroes. Sure, flying and stopping trains with your bare hands or roping a villain with a lasso of truth was rather tricky, but your attitude, energy, and confidence matched those of the idols you were impersonating.

You can still flex these modeling muscles even though it may seem a long time since you last used them. If you don't know what it feels like to be confident or empowered, mirror a person who embodies confidence in a way that you admire and aspire toward. This can be someone you personally know or a celebrity, humanitarian, or historical figure. Take some time to observe and study this person. Notice the characteristics that make him or her appear confident. Pay attention to this person's posture, body language, facial expression, tone of voice, way of breathing, or—to quote the famous anthropologist Gregory Bateson—look for "the difference that makes the difference." Then practice these characteristics on yourself and notice how your energy changes when you're adjusting your own breathing, facial expression, and body posture to match what you have observed.

It often takes only an open mind and a few of these adjustments to understand how it feels to be as confident as the person you're using as a model. It's even more effective to model the characteristics of a variety of people and thus find out which adjustments evoke the most powerful sense of confidence for you. Over time, you'll establish your own specific ways to feel and express this emotion. Although modeling is not as straightforward as drawing upon your own memories and experiences, it's the bridge that can lead you to an empowered state of being, one you previously believed was impossible to attain.

STEP 3: COLLECT SUPPORTIVE EVIDENCE

The greatest obstacle between an idea and its execution is doubt. As the architect of your inner identity, you've designed, in the previous two steps, a clear and exciting blueprint of your new concept of self. However, you may doubt the validity of the new belief, while the familiar, limiting perspective of yourself still appears more realistic. How can you alleviate the doubt and leverage your subconscious to release and replace your old belief and identity? The best way is to collect convincing evidence that shows you that you possess the potential and resources to truly become the empowered self you envision.

For the first twenty years of my life, I was very insecure about being clumsy. For as far back as I could remember, whenever I dropped or spilled something, my family burst into comments such as "Here he goes again!" or "That's typical," or "How can one person be such a klutz?" The belief was further reinforced by my grade-school teacher, who during each arts and crafts class sent me out to run his errands so that I wouldn't injure myself, he said. As a consequence, I became more and more insecure about my motor skills. Even simple things like bringing a tray to the dinner table or wearing nice clothes during festive meals made me shake and sweat in anticipation of another clumsy accident followed by painful mockery, which was usually exactly what happened.

But one day I decided that the old belief was no longer true. I remembered the many times during medical school and my residency when I had proven to myself that my manual skills were much more proficient than I had believed. As a waiter at the Oktoberfest in Munich, I'd balanced hundreds of food trays on one hand while wading through the crowds—and I hadn't dropped one chicken. I also realized that my college friends didn't view me as clumsy, so why should I any longer? In light of all the evidence that I was quite handy, the old clumsy identity didn't feel appropriate any longer. And because I was more confident and at ease with myself—even when I spilled or dropped something—my family started to acknowledge that my eye-hand coordination was more developed than they had given me credit for.

Anthony Robbins compares beliefs to tables. The pieces of evidence supporting the beliefs are the legs of the table. In other words, the more supporting data you have that your new belief is true, the more solid and stable the table becomes.

Here are three ways to find the supporting evidence that will prove you have what it takes to fully grow into and live up to your empowered self:

- **Write down ten things you've accomplished in your life, ten skills and talents that you have, and ten times when you solved a problem or overcame adversity.** If listing ten things in each category seems like too many, you're probably being far too critical and harsh with yourself. Be as generous and open minded as you would be with the people you love and care about.

- **Ask the people who care about you what they appreciate about you.** What reasons do they have to believe that your new, empowered identity is a reflection of your true potential? Don't be too shy to ask. You aren't fishing for compliments—you're looking for objective outside input. The fact is that most people take their best qualities for granted while they're busy focusing on their few shortcomings. Chances are that you won't believe all the great things you're getting to hear about yourself. However, give yourself permission to consider that the people who love you the most can often more clearly see your light because you're shining it more onto them than onto yourself.
- **Meditate and connect with your inner essence** (for example, by doing the guided meditation to realign with your essence, from chapter 9 on page 167). Contemplate where and in what form the qualities of your essence have been shining through in your daily life.

Remember, what defines you and your potential aren't only your accomplishments and successes but the choices you're making during the so-called normal and ordinary times of your day-to-day life.

In looking for your supporting evidence, you will likely gain a broader, kinder, and more complete perspective of yourself and your potential. You still don't have to subscribe fully to your new, empowering belief. But just by realizing that you actually have the inner resources to grow into a new and more expanded self, you've accepted that nothing but yourself can hold you back from taking the next, final transformational step on this journey. I'm sure you're ready for it.

TRANSFORMING INTO THE EMPOWERED SELF

The skeptical part of your mind might wonder how you could possibly take on a new, empowered version of yourself and let go of the limiting beliefs you've been stuck with for decades. First, as you've already experienced, when you work on the level of the subconscious, time is relative and rather irrelevant. Also, you've already met all four requirements for dislodging, releasing, and replacing your old identity. Just think, you have:

- Eliminated the emotional glue and attachments that held the limiting belief in place
- Identified the beliefs at the core of your self-limiting identity
- Defined a new belief and image of the empowered self
- Recognized that you have the potential to become the new you

You've prepared your subconscious to transform your inner identity, which is what you will accomplish with the following process.

SUBCONSCIOUS IDENTITY CONVERSION

Close your eyes and center yourself with a few slow, relaxed breaths. Then think about the limiting belief and the image of your old, inner identity. Place this image on the left side of your internal movie screen. Try to get in touch with any residual feelings and sensations that you might still associate with this version of yourself.

Now connect to the new, empowering core belief and identity. Place that picture of yourself on the right side of your screen. Become aware of the positive emotions that you equate with the empowered self.

Notice the contrast between the left and the right picture—the old and the new self. Do they already look visually different—one being bigger, brighter, or more colorful than the other? To which of the subconscious interpretations of self do you feel more drawn?

Modulate the images of the old and new you to increase the contrast. Just as you'd adjust the screen of your TV or computer monitor, change the visual aspects of each image. By modulating the color, size, brightness, and distance of the old and new self, you're telling your subconscious how you choose to relate to each of these inner identities.

Deactivate the image of the old self by:

- Switching it to black and white
- Shrinking its size
- Reducing its brightness
- Placing it farther away from you

Play with the "settings" and choose the combination that makes the image appear the least emotionally charged and real.

Now enhance the image of the new self by:

- Improving its color
- Increasing its size
- Turning up it brightness
- Bringing it closer to you

Modify the visual aspects of the image so that it appears the most exciting and alive to you.

Add the light of your essence to the image of your new self. Use the visualization from chapter 9 as inspiration. Imagine beams of bright light radiating from your core or a glowing field of energy surrounding and extending beyond your physical form. Although most of us can't see energy that clearly, this visual indicates for your subconscious that you're committed to letting your true and authentic self emerge.

Compare the two pictures and notice which one draws you in and motivates you the most. By now the new picture should definitely look much more enticing than the old one. By appreciating the enormous contrast, you're clearly instructing your subconscious that you've made your choice.

Now is the time to expel the old identity and adopt the new one. To exchange the old for the new:

1. Place both images in the center of your inner screen, with the new self on top of the old one.
2. Condense the image of the empowered you to the size of a postage stamp and place it on the left lower corner of the old picture.
3. Count "one, two, and *switch*," and watch the old picture quickly implode and shrink to the size of a dust speck. At the same time, the new image rapidly expands until it covers the entire screen.
4. Feel the positive energy emanating from the image of the empowered self and think or declare out loud three times the new core belief associated with it.
5. Quickly open and close your eyes. Take a breath and then try to bring the old picture back, placing the postage-sized new image at its lower left corner. Repeat steps 2 through 5 at least five to ten times—until it's almost impossible for you to bring back the old self.

This simple but powerful process highlights the transformational potential of the subconscious. It always amazes me how after the third or fourth time the old image starts to fade, appearing darker or more granulated until it seems impossible to bring it back. What a great visual demonstration of how the subconscious can erase beliefs that no longer serve or fit you! At the same time, you'll notice that your new, empowered self becomes increasingly easy and natural to access, until it remains all you can see and feel.

TAKE YOUR NEW IDENTITY ON A WALK THROUGH YOUR LIFE

How do you know that this transformation will really make a difference for you? How do you know that you won't fall back into the old anxiety and insecurity? You don't, until you take your new, empowered identity for a test run. As you're already well aware, your subconscious mind doesn't bother to distinguish between what is real and what is imagined. So let's take advantage of this phenomenon and create your future reality by rehearsing it.

Take your new identity on a walk through your life. Place your empowered self in different situations and circumstances and imagine how you, as that self, would act and feel. Move from one area of your life to another, one circumstance to the next. Don't let this vision get stuck anywhere. Just picture and observe how your new identity enables you to respond to common anxiety triggers and pitfalls in very different ways.

By moving through those future events, you establish and strengthen the neurological pathways and patterns that will lead you to think and conduct yourself from a place of true empowerment. And even if you find yourself tempted to slip into the deep grooves of the old, limiting patterns, at the very least you've given your mind two scenarios to choose from—the old, limiting one and the new, empowering one. Having different options about how you can view and respond to a situation, to others, or to yourself already gives you a greater sense of choice, power, and peace.

Remember Jane, the woman who wanted out of her marriage but was too afraid to leave? When we finished our work together, Jane's vision of her empowered, confident self was significantly different from the earlier image. She saw herself as tall and beautiful, smiling serenely, surrounded by a bright light. In this picture, she looked as though she had all the inner strength she needed to face any challenges and overcome any difficult situations with ease and grace. The moment she imagined her empowered self standing next to her husband, the proverbial light bulb went on. Grinning brightly, she told me, "He's much smaller now, and I'm so much brighter. And there's this energy surrounding me, like a protective light shield. I can really imagine how all his negativity, anger, and judgments just bounce off it." After this transformation, she felt much more confident that she could clearly communicate to her husband what her decisions were and what she needed to do to move on. While she was talking to me, her entire body relaxed. She sat upright, breathing slowly, even wearing that same serene smile that she'd observed in the internal portrait of her confident self.

Jane had taken back her power—and now, so have you. The question is, how can you keep your power, no matter what the circumstances? In chapter 11, you'll learn how to do just that.

CHAPTER 11

Keep Moving Forward

HOW TO STAY EMPOWERED AND IN BALANCE

DO YOU REALIZE how much you've grown beyond the person who opened this book for the first time? You've utilized fear and anxiety to transform the fabric of your subconscious. Although your outer circumstances may have remained unchanged, you've evolved and can now approach your life and the challenges that used to trigger fear and anxiety with calmness, clarity, and confidence.

However, at the risk of sounding like a party pooper or a German taskmaster, this isn't the time to rest on your laurels and stop working on yourself. Let's face it, the grooves created by years of fear and anxiety are well worn and deep. At this time, after all your work, these old patterns may appear outdated and irrelevant, but chances are you haven't completely eliminated them all yet. To maintain the positive results you've accomplished and avoid accidently slipping back into familiar, self-limiting emotional and behavioral patterns, you need to further solidify and expand on your new ones. The forty-day commitment program in this chapter helps you to integrate your new insights, tools, and self-empowering beliefs into your daily life. By following this program, you'll deepen the meaning and enhance the significance of all you've learned. In other words, this last chapter will get you ready for the next chapters in your life.

THE CONSISTENCY CHALLENGE

Isn't it interesting that it's often easier to make a change than to maintain one? If you've ever tried to lose those extra pounds or get into better shape through exercise, you may have had this experience. Once you've reached your goal, amnesia sets in. Somehow, all the knowledge and positive habits you acquired through hard work are pushed aside, making room for a pint of ice cream in the shopping cart or excuses for why you can't work out that day. Lo and behold, the pounds reappear, the muscle tone disappears, and you find yourself right back where you started.

Or you work through an empowering self-improvement program such as the one you're completing right now. At first, you're energized, motivated, and committed to diligently applying all the insights and tools you've learned. But a couple of weeks later, you have a bad day, your energy dips, and your thoughts grow negative. This is completely normal and very human, but because you've been feeling so much more positive, it feels like a huge letdown. In that moment, you may start believing that you're even worse off than you were before and that nothing ever works for you, which prompts you to drop all your previous efforts and intentions.

Yes, change can be difficult to maintain. Why do we stop using the tools and proven strategies that helped us reach our goals and made us feel better? I've already mentioned how we can fall back into the deep grooves of old, self-sabotaging behavior patterns. But another—possibly even greater—challenge is to avoid shifting into complacency mode.

A few years ago I started learning and loving glassblowing. Like all glass-blowing students, I had to learn first and foremost how to stay committed to the piece I was working on. The glassblower needs to work patiently and consistently through many processes—from heating the glass to make it soft and malleable to stabilizing the desired shape with specific tools—until the piece is finally solid enough to place in the annealing oven. Our minds and glass are very similar. They both range from clear to cloudy, strong to fragile, whole to cracked. Likewise, working with our minds and working with glass have a lot in common. By applying energy and structured guidance, we can shape both into countless forms. However, only through patient care and consistent attention can their forms become stable and solid enough to last.

One of the most common mistakes beginning glassblowers make is to start strong and focused but then, once the glass piece is close to the desired shape, to become a bit lax and neglect applying enough heat. This makes the glass rigid, impossible to work with, and stabilize—therefore more likely to break. When it comes to self-improvement, many people operate in a similar fashion. They're "all in," completely dedicated to the goals and changes they want to create. Once they reach the finish line, however, they crash like a first-time marathon runner and switch their minds from "all" mode to "nothing" mode. As a result, they can no longer muster the energy and motivation to continue working on themselves.

Some give up because they feel overwhelmed and believe that, considering how much effort it took to reach their goals in the first place, it will be impossible for them to maintain the positive changes. Others become complacent or bored with the idea of a maintenance routine and succumb to the illusion that they've already done everything they need to do to keep their changes and improvements permanently. In both cases, excuses, such as, "I don't have time," "I don't know how," or "I'm fine" crowd out their good intentions to stay with the program.

Another common glassblowing mistake is applying too much heat and manual pressure, which makes the piece "floppy" and unstable. In such a state, the glass cannot hold the shape the blower desires. When it comes to shaping their minds, some people also approach their personal growth with too much ambition and force. Rather than appreciating and solidifying the positive changes they've accomplished, they become impatient or easily discouraged by small setbacks. As they prematurely jump to the next goal or self-improvement program, hoping that this new one will provide them with the breakthrough success they long for, they destabilize and dilute the results of their previous efforts.

When it comes to firmly integrating your empowerment, how can you keep yourself on track, motivated, and engaged without becoming overwhelmed, bored, or worn out? How do you switch into consistency mode? As with glassblowing, the answer is to stay committed to what you have started.

COMMITMENT: THE FERTILE GROUND FOR CONFIDENCE AND SELF-LOVE

The word *commitment* may give you night sweats or cold feet. Although you understand the need to commit to maintaining and expanding your growth and empowerment work, you have a hard time subscribing to a specific routine. Your plate is already too full, and you can't imagine adding one more chore to the have-to-do list. I completely understand. However, by staying committed to your inner work, you solidify and strengthen what you've accomplished and you also deepen your level of trust in and love for yourself.

You've turned the tables. You no longer stay on the sidelines, watching your subconscious spinning in old patterns of fear and anxiety. Instead, you've established a collaborative and mutually supportive relationship between your conscious and subconscious mind. However, as is true for every relationship, this connection can only deepen and flourish with trust. The best ways to build trust are through consistency and commitment.

Let's say you want to remodel your home. After a diligent search, you entrust your house to a contractor, who assures you that the costs will not exceed X number of dollars, and he'll easily complete the job in X amount of time. Along the way, however, your contractor tells you with a shrug that somehow unforeseeable complications arose and that the job will cost more and take longer than estimated. Then maybe one day the workers don't show up, and the contractor doesn't return your inquiring phone calls. How quickly would you lose trust and confidence in the person you've hired?

Now think about how many times you've treated yourself in a similar way. How often did you discard your plans, not show up for yourself, and abandon your good intentions?

Don't feel too bad; most of us have been guilty of letting ourselves down, but we need to realize the damage we cause by doing so. Every time we go back on our word and break our self-commitment, we lose trust and faith in ourselves—consciously and subconsciously. Our word holds no power. Since we don't appear reliable and trustworthy to our subconscious mind, it may reactivate old, protective patterns, which consequently lead to more fear and insecurity. Now the good news is that the opposite is also true. Consistency and commitment are some of the most potent healing forces for the subconscious mind. They allow us to fortify our foundation of confidence rather quickly. After all, confidence comes from the Latin word *confidere,* which means "to trust and have faith in." And who better to trust and have faith in than ourselves?

One of my clients, Lisa, struggled with commitment to her self-growth. Overall, her drive and motivation in life had been nothing short of extreme. She was a very successful entrepreneur, and she had completed several Ironman triathlons, each consisting of a 2.4-mile swim, a 112-mile bike ride, and, for dessert, a 26-mile run. Despite all her accomplishments, she was plagued by a deep-seated anxiety and insecurity, which she, like most overachievers, constantly tried to beat by achieving more. Now, considering the impressive level of dedication to her work and athletics, I was pretty sure that Lisa would breeze through her twenty minutes per day of self-empowerment assignments. But she didn't. Feeling overwhelmed already, she couldn't commit to one more obligation and gave up, proving to herself once again that she wasn't really good enough.

A closer look into Lisa's history revealed that her older sister, despite her multiple problems and misbehaviors, received all the love and attention from her parents, whereas Lisa felt seen and appreciated only when she earned straight A's or was the fastest on her track team. As an adult, Lisa continued to treat herself with the same conditional acceptance, but by that time her own expectations were so high that she could never reach them.

In one of our sessions, she shared with me that the only person she felt had truly loved her was her grandmother. "Grandma didn't have to tell me that she loved me," Lisa said. "I just knew. When I was at her house, she focused only on me. I was the most important part of her world. Of course, she had rules and expectations, but I didn't feel pressured, and it was easy to meet them. I loved her, because she was so kind to me and always showed with little gestures that she was thinking of me. She really made me feel that I mattered."

When I asked Lisa to imagine looking at herself through her grandmother's eyes, she started crying. Those tears weren't only for her long-gone nana; that moment during our session was the first time since her childhood that Lisa could see herself as a loveable and valuable being. I suggested to Lisa that she start her daily self-empowerment homework from the same place: viewing herself through the eyes of her loving grandmother. This made all the difference for her. She stopped thinking of working on herself as just another burden or opportunity to fail. Instead, Lisa treasured this time as "her daily pauses for self-love"—and for the love for her grandmother.

It's difficult to commit to your self-improvement practice if you consider it a chore or a sign that there's something wrong with you. However, if you approach your growth and empowerment commitments from a place of love and self-appreciation, you'll open your heart to yourself more and more and, thus, make this inner work the most precious gift you can give to yourself.

A SENSE OF COHERENCE: CONFIDENCE FOR LIFE

Medical sociologist Aaron Antonovsky became famous for his research on *salutogenesis,* which investigates the reasons why some people can stay healthy and well despite the most difficult circumstances. In the 1970s, Antonovsky studied the health of women who had survived concentration camps in Nazi Germany. He found that only 29 percent of the survivors had adjusted to life and attained mental and emotional stability. How were these women able to overcome the horrific experiences they went through and regain their health and wholeness? When Antonovsky interviewed these women, he noticed that they all approached their lives with great confidence or, as he called it, a "sense of coherence."[1]

Coherence is defined as a state where various parts integrate to a whole through logical and systematic connections. Antonovsky described a sense of coherence as the "extent to which one has a pervasive, enduring, though dynamic feeling of confidence that one's environment is predictable and that things will work out as well as can reasonably be expected." In other words, a sense of coherence is a sound mixture of confidence, control, and a positive, optimistic attitude. This sound combination provided the concentration-camp survivors with the foundation and the strength to heal the past and build a new, self-empowered life.

Remember when you used to feel overwhelmed with worry, doubt, and insecurity—when you believed you were powerless and not good enough to successfully deal with everyday challenges? At that time, you probably felt the opposite of coherence—disconnected, fragmented—and believed that your emotions and your life were beyond your control. By working through the various steps and processes in this book you've changed and grown; you now have the insights and tools to deal with future situations that could trigger fear and anxiety. But to achieve a solid sense of coherence in which your newfound confidence, inner congruency, and peace with yourself are deeply ingrained in the fabric of your being, you need to further integrate these positive changes and growth into your daily life. You may have already experienced coherence in different areas of your life, such as with your family, at your work, or in a fulfilling hobby. But imagine how it would feel if you could approach your entire life with such a strong sense of empowerment.

In his study, Antonovsky found that a sense of coherence consists of three basic components:

- **Comprehensibility,** which describes the belief that we can make sense out of our life and approach it in an orderly and structured fashion.
- **Manageability,** which is about believing that we have the resources, skills, and abilities to take care of ourselves and own our lives.

- **Meaningfulness,** which is characterized by finding purpose and value in what we pursue and commit to.

Antonovsky's theories resonate strongly with me because they reflect the essential message of this book: true confidence and empowerment require continuous conscious awareness of our ability to choose our thoughts, emotions, and actions (comprehensibility); trust in our potential and resources (manageability); and a deep appreciation of our own worthiness (meaningfulness). So I've designed the following forty-day commitment program to anchor the three building blocks of coherence in your conscious and subconscious minds.

The daily practice will provide you with a structured routine. By reinforcing patterns of self-reliance and empowerment, you'll fortify the belief that you can manage any challenges that come your way. And by approaching this program every day with love, care, and appreciation for yourself, you'll infuse it with deeper meaning.

Through your commitment to the following forty-day program, you will:

- Establish a structured self-empowering routine
- Solidify and expand on the results you've already accomplished so far
- Integrate your new identity into your daily life
- Practice self-love and appreciation
- Build a strong sense of coherence to pursue the journey of your life with unshakable confidence

Completing the forty days will leave you with a strong sense of coherence about how to manage fear and anxiety. But even more important, you'll have established a solid, self-empowering strategy for approaching life in general—with structure, confidence, and purpose.

And best of all, the program takes only twenty to thirty minutes per day, plus a bit of time for focusing on and attending to your daily intentions. Isn't this the best investment of time and energy you can make right now?

CARE (CENTER, ALIGN, REINFORCE, ENHANCE): A FORTY-DAY COMMITMENT TO SELF-EMPOWERMENT

Regardless of whether we're learning to play the piano or tennis, a foreign language or ballroom dancing, the three key ingredients to achieving excellence are *focus, repetition,* and *acknowledgement.* The mind, and in particular the subconscious, thrives and excels when it receives consistent guidance and, at the end of the day, some positive strokes. I've based the forty-day program, CARE (center, align, reinforce, and enhance), on this premise.

Since ancient times, a cycle of forty days has carried great significance. The Egyptians devoted forty days to embalming the deceased. Moses spent forty days on Mount Sinai, and Jesus wandered for forty days through the desert. In yoga teachings it is said that if you dedicate yourself to a specific focus for forty days, you can break and replace any old patterns and habits, which is exactly what you're aiming to do with this empowerment program.

The four parts of CARE, which should be done daily and in sequence, provide you with an easy-to-follow framework for forging your life with awareness, confidence, and self-worth. You begin this forty-day empowerment program every morning with the *centering* and the *alignment* steps. The centering step deepens your connection with your core essence. Through the alignment process you strengthen the new, empowering belief and identity you established in chapter 10 and install it in your cellular memory. Focusing on the *reinforcement* topic throughout the day gives you an opportunity to master the tools and skills you've acquired so far. And at the end of each day, you *enhance* your growth and empowerment through positive reinforcement and appreciation.

CENTER

I'm sure you know this feeling: You wake in the morning feeling discombobulated at the thought of all the obligations and errands that require your attention that day. You move through your morning routine on autopilot, barely noticing what you're doing as you take a shower, get dressed, and grab a cup of coffee on your way out the door. And it goes downhill from there. You only get more distracted as the day goes on.

Over the course of a day, we're pulled in many different directions. A client once said, "At some point during the day, I feel that my life pushes me aside and grabs the wheel—and I no longer have any say on where we're going." And at the end of our day we come home, feeling spent and spread so thin that vegging out is all we have energy for or want to do, even though there may be more obligations waiting for us.

Even at the gym—where running on a treadmill or striding on the elliptical machine should be all about being with and in our body—we often occupy our minds by reading or watching TV, and we avoid paying attention to anything happening inside ourselves. As we continue to live "outside" ourselves and lose touch with our core, we feel increasingly ungrounded, imbalanced, and out of control. As a result, we're much more susceptible to fear and anxiety. So it's very important to re-collect our mind and energy and bring the focus back inside—every day. For the forty-day self-empowerment program, I suggest using two methods to center yourself and stay connected with your core.

Long, deep breathing for ten minutes. This is the easiest way to regain your center and balance. "Take a deep breath"—we've all heard this friendly advice when we're overly excited or stressed and our breath becomes short and shallow. Deep breathing, as a way to relax and release internal pressure, is something we instinctively do right. While a racing mind speeds up breathing, consciously slowing our inhalation and exhalation has a calming effect on the entire nervous system. Just as the breath follows the mind, the mind can also follow the way we are breathing.

As the first daily step of your forty-day commitment, simply breathe long and deeply with your eyes closed. Make sure to engage your chest and your abdomen. On the inhale, fully expand your lungs by letting your belly rise; on the exhale, pull your abdomen slightly back toward your spine to push all the air out.

One-minute breathing. This kundalini yoga technique is one of the quickest and most powerful ways to clear and center your mind. The goal is to be able to inhale, hold your breath, and exhale for twenty seconds each, creating a one-minute breathing cycle. Sound daunting? Honestly, it took me several months to get to a full minute. So don't push yourself too hard.

Begin by making each part of the cycle between three to ten seconds long. Just make sure to inhale, hold, and exhale for the same amount of time. You can either mentally count the seconds—"one, two, three . . ."—or repeat an affirmation, such as "I am calm, centered, and at peace," for the amount of time you've chosen for each piece of the cycle.

This breathing pattern symbolizes life's fundamental cycle of receiving, maintaining, and letting go. Routinely, I ask my clients which part of the process they find most challenging: drawing the air in, keeping it in, or letting it out. It continues to fascinate me that their struggles with this technique often appear to reflect their challenges with receiving, maintaining, and letting go in life. See for yourself which part feels the most natural to you and which brings up resistance and takes more effort to accomplish.

After you've practiced this one-minute breathing exercise for a couple of weeks, you may want to challenge yourself a little bit. Just for five or ten breaths, extend the time of inhaling, holding in, and exhaling. Each time, allow yourself to approach the point where you feel the urge to quickly progress to the next part. When you notice an almost panicky feeling rising from deep inside, wait another second or two before you move on, instead of giving into this sensation. There is something extremely empowering about being able to witness the emotion without instantaneously responding to it. Instead, if you draw the breathing cycle out a few seconds longer, you show yourself that there was no reason to panic, that you've been safe and in control the entire time.

After ten minutes of either of these two breathing meditations, allow your breath to regulate itself. Keep your eyes closed and complete the centering step by visualizing and connecting to the brilliant core light of your essence for another minute or two.

I am sure you will soon agree with one of my meditation teachers, who said, "Our breath controls our mind, and our mind controls our lives. So by learning how to master your breathing, you learn how to master your life."

ALIGN

Now that you're centered and grounded within your core, you've opened the door to the abundance of resources and potential that resides within. However, no matter how great your innate potential may be, it becomes meaningful only if you can access it, bring it into form, and channel it for a purpose. By defining a new, empowering core belief and identity, you've already laid the groundwork for fully embracing and utilizing your potential. The following daily process, the empowerment accelerator, helps you to completely incorporate and align yourself with this new identity.

In the past, you may have tried to change the way you thought and felt about yourself through positive affirmations. And you may have found out that for some reason and despite all your efforts, those "mantras" didn't seem to stick. As I mentioned before, words alone don't have an intrinsic meaning for the subconscious mind and, therefore, need to be decoded and translated into images, feelings, and sensations. In other words, you need to transfer the affirmations from your mind to your heart, which you've already accomplished by working through the processes in chapter 10. However, to fully embody your new identity, it needs to be anchored in your cellular memory. The physical is memorable.

The empowerment accelerator links your new belief with your whole body, dramatically speeding up the process of integrating your new belief, so that it quickly becomes second nature for you. At the end of this six-step process, every fiber of your being will be aligned with your new, empowered identity, like iron filings aligning with the force field of a magnet.

EMPOWERMENT ACCELERATOR

1. **Focus.** Stand comfortably with your eyes closed and take several deep breaths to center yourself. To complete this and each of the following five steps, anchor the new empowering belief by stating it out loud or silently to yourself at least three times.

2. **Imagine.** See yourself, as you did in chapter 10, having fully incorporated this belief. Adjust the picture of the new you by changing its size, color, brightness, and distance until the image is the most attractive and desirable it can be to you.

3. **Feel.** Notice the positive emotions you associate with the empowered self. Do you feel confident, energized, excited, relaxed, or self-assured? Tap into these emotions to infuse your new identity with life. Hold this focus for one to two minutes. (Remember to breathe as you do.)

4. **Embody.** Bring this image into physical form by mirroring and adopting the posture and facial expression of the empowered self. Are your shoulders back? Is your chest open? Are your arms comfortably hanging down by your sides or your hands relaxed in the pockets of your pants? Do you notice a friendly smile or a twinkle in your eyes? Are your facial muscles calm and at ease? Take on the stance and the air of confidence that radiates through and from the empowered self.

5. **Boost.** Move into a new posture—a power posture—and express your new belief with even greater intensity for one or two minutes. For example, raise your arms triumphantly into the air and enjoy the breakthrough you've accomplished. Or open your arms wide, embracing yourself and all the opportunities that life has to offer. You could also march in place, vigorously engaging your legs and arms to demonstrate that you're confidently moving forward on your path. Or you may just want to break into an uninhibited victory dance, celebrating how you've gained the freedom to be yourself. Try out different forms of expression and find the one that makes the strongest statement of your empowerment—and is the most fun. By turning up the positive energy you've already created, you anchor the new belief even more deeply into your cellular memory.

6. Commit. Bring your hands to your heart, take a few deep breaths, and center yourself again. Set your intention to fully embody your empowered identity on this day by visualizing how you will move through your day as the new you. To end, once again repeat your new belief three times.

• • •

Although the empowerment accelerator takes only five to ten minutes, you'll feel that your entire physiology has shifted by the time you complete it. Like a tuning fork, your whole being will vibrate with the uplifting energy and emotions of your empowered self. Now you're fully charged, ready to own the day.

REINFORCE

The value of any personal change and growth is largely determined by how it will benefit us in our daily lives. As the philosopher and physicist Buckminster Fuller said, "The environment is stronger than willpower." In other words, the people and circumstances we live with don't necessarily conspire to bolster our confidence and self-worth. Every day, we come across countless situations that can trigger anxiety or drain us of our power—a disapproving frown from a colleague, an hour spent in a traffic jam, a shortened deadline, an unexpected bill. Our confidence can deflate as quickly as a popped balloon.

Yet our environment has only as much power as we give it. The choice of whether to turn over our power is ours, but it doesn't always feel that way. We often don't believe that we can actually stop and decide whether or not we want to head back to the familiar territory of anxiety and insecurity. Why? Because we either approach this place of choice so quickly and so unconsciously that there really doesn't seem to be much of a choice at all, or we find ourselves at that junction but don't know what to do to remain calm and keep our power.

By practicing the reinforcement steps of your forty-day commitment program, you'll develop the awareness and flexibility to master these common challenges in ways that further strengthen your confidence—and your sense of coherence.

THE MOST COMMON ANXIETY PITFALLS

Although there are myriad situations that can send us from feeling balanced and empowered to out of balance and powerless, a large number of them fall under one of two major themes: making assumptions or taking something personally.

In general, assumptions are a normal part of life. There are simply too many variables and possible outcomes to consider. If we didn't act and make decisions based on assumptions, we would become completely overwhelmed and paralyzed.

Yet negative assumptions can make us feel angry, hurt, ashamed, and especially fearful and insecure. There are three ways in which we commonly scare ourselves by conjuring unfavorable assumptions; we assume that:

- We will lose something we care about.
- We are the victims of our circumstances.
- We have to fit in to be accepted.

One of the fundamental problems with negative assumptions is that we often don't recognize them as such. For example, think about the "what if" game. Any thoughts starting with "what if" should give us a clue that we're about to venture off into a fictional reality. We can get lost thinking through the consequences of terrible disasters, painful rejections, or enormous failures without realizing that they're all based on one, frequently ludicrous "what if" assumption. Other more subtle indicators that we're about to enter fantasy land are phrases such as, "I know what he's thinking," or "It just won't work out," or "She is so much better off than me." You get the idea. We make generalizations, ignore certain facts, and misread and overinterpret others, all to concoct stories that are detrimental to our inner peace and well-being.

Naturally, from the perspective of our subconscious (which is their creative source) negative assumptions have a valid purpose: to prepare us for and protect us from danger, rejection, or pain. But despite these positive intentions, negative assumptions never make us feel safe. Instead, they tend to deplete our energy, undermine our confidence, and take control of us rather than giving us control.

Taking something personally is another common reason we lose our power and shift out of alignment with ourselves. The opinion and behavior of others become the determinants of how we view and feel about ourselves. Usually, we take personally somebody else's:

- judgment
- approval
- energy

Taking anything personally is also a subconscious, protective strategy for avoiding hurt, rejection, and abandonment. But whether we're making assumptions or taking things personally, we're displacing our power and focusing on somebody or something outside of us. Ultimately, we abandon ourselves, and our subconscious responds by generating more fear and anxiety.

DAILY REINFORCEMENT EXERCISES

The following exercises give you the opportunity every day of the week to focus specifically on these common anxiety pitfalls. By working through these exercises, you'll develop resourceful patterns for identifying and responding to these pitfalls with ease and proficiency.

Monday: Counterbalancing Negative Assumptions

For many people, Monday is the least favorite day of the week. After tasting the sweet joys of freedom and relaxation for a couple of days, we dread Mondays as the rude awakening to a reality filled with obligations and challenges—with ample opportunities to potentially fail, get hurt, or lose something of importance to us. So Monday is the perfect day to pay attention to and address the assumptions that something bad has happened or is about to happen.

Focus

Notice at least five negative assumptions you make during the course of the day. Become aware of the moment when you traverse from facts into fiction. For example:

- You get stuck in traffic on your way to work. You tell yourself, "I'll be late for the team meeting, and the others will think I'm a flake."
- You're calling your spouse or partner, but he or she doesn't pick up or answer your text messages. You wonder, "What if something bad has happened?"
- You bring your child to school and see that one of the other parents is driving a brand new car. Immediately you compare yourself: "These people are much more successful and happy than I am. I will never be able to afford what they can."

Empowerment Acts

Counterbalance. Address these negative assumptions with the counterbalancing exercise from chapter 6. Start each positive statement with "I trust." Make sure to communicate from your heart and imagine that you are connecting with the younger, subconscious protector who may still need some more reassurance. For example, to counterbalance the three assumptions above, you might try:

- "I trust in the value I bring to the team, regardless of whether I'm late or not."
- "I trust that my spouse/partner is perfectly fine. He/she is probably just busy and not paying attention to the phone. I've done the same thing many times."
- "I trust that I am in charge of my own success and happiness. Each person's life is unique and therefore can't be compared to another's."

Avoid micromanagement. Notice when assumptions tempt you to spring into frantic action to control the circumstances. For example:

- You are driving faster and taking more risks on the road.
- You are calling your spouse every two minutes to check on him/her.
- You are calling your bank to see if you could qualify for a car loan.

Instead, take a deep breath and ask yourself the following three questions:

- Am I giving my power to the assumption?
- Is acting on the assumption really the best use of my time and energy right now?
- How can I view and respond to this assumption from the perspective of my new, empowered self?

By practicing these empowerment patterns, you'll sharpen your awareness of how often you're tempted to raise negative assumptions, thereby abandoning the present and, with it, your sense of control. You'll increase your mental and emotional flexibility and, thus, your ability to quickly shift back into the now and to choose to think and act from a place of self-empowerment and inner peace.

Tuesday: Pleasing Yourself Instead of Others

During my residency in Germany, it was a common practice to present young doctors with short contracts and long lists of high expectations they needed to fulfill for an employment extension to be granted. Talk about maximizing people's willingness to go above and beyond the call of duty! As you have probably experienced, increased pressure can lead to a significant decrease in self-esteem. Not only did I work extremely hard, I also became a master of anticipating my professors' expectations. While I relished any little signs of their approval, I more frequently wrestled with self-doubt and disappointment when my efforts and diligence weren't acknowledged. Rather than appreciating myself and building more trust and confidence in my knowledge and skills, I allowed my self-worth to become dependent on the recognition of my superiors, which only augmented my already enormous stress and anxiety levels.

Pleasing others, no matter what the underlying motivation may be, never leads to a sense of inner peace and self-empowerment. We're hoping that others will fulfill our need to be accepted and approved of instead of learning how to appreciate and value ourselves. As time wears on, the need and emptiness in between those brief moments of feeling accepted become greater and start to consume any residue of our self-worth. The dilemma is similar to a coin. One side of the coin represents the approval, recognition, and acceptance of others; the other symbolizes their judgment, criticism, and pressure. The problem is that you can't just pick up one side of the coin. It's impossible to enjoy and cherish praise and acknowledgment without also becoming more susceptible to disapproval and dismissal.

Today, focus on putting this coin down by practicing self-reliance and independence from other people's approval.

Focus

Notice today how often your opinion of yourself depends on what other people are thinking of you. How often are you trying to please others, trying to make them like you, trying to meet their expectations? For example:

- Your sibling calls and complains that her computer is broken. You know she looks up to you, and you immediately volunteer to buy her a new computer, although you don't really have money for it.
- Your boss piles more work on your desk right before he leaves for the day. You decide to stay longer in the office to make sure he notices your impeccable work ethic.
- You're meeting friends for lunch. As usual, you listen and ask questions, but you don't share your own problems because you don't want to be a downer or appear needy.

Empowerment Act

Once you notice that you're trying to please somebody else, ask yourself whether doing so increases or diminishes your confidence and self-worth. If the latter is true, choose one or several of the following responses:

- **Create healthy boundaries as an expression of self-worth and self-care instead of overextending yourself.** As my wife likes to say, "*No* is a complete sentence." Practice saying no to somebody else's expectations and yes to taking care of your own needs.
- **Change the dynamic of your relationship by adopting the opposite of your habitual pleasing role.** Move from being the listener to the one who shares, from the giver to the receiver. Instead of being passive, try the active role. Instead of following, make a decision.
- **Please yourself by attending to your own needs.** For example, eat something healthful and nourishing, take a bath, book a massage, or go to bed earlier than usual. Do something that makes you feel good about yourself and increases your self-appreciation.
- **Ask yourself, "Is the person or organization I'm trying to please my true source of happiness, self-worth, and inner peace?"** This question has changed my perception dramatically. I only wish I knew about it when I was a young medical resident.

Being more self-reliant and independent from others' approval doesn't mean that you'll become antisocial, ignorant, or closed to their positive or negative feedback. Self-reliance simply means that *you* become your primary frame of reference for how you choose to relate to yourself. Not only does self-reliance lead to greater self-appreciation and confidence, it also leads to openness, equality, and fulfillment in your relationships with others.

Wednesday: Becoming the Master of Your Circumstances

There is no question that some unexpected circumstances—an unexpected death of a loved one, a serious health issue, an accident, a burglary in our home—can truly make us feel victimized. Although we have no say in these events, we always have a choice about how to respond. It continues to amaze me how the most challenging conditions tend to bring forth the best in human beings. People often seem more capable of dealing with unforeseeable large disasters than small, day-to-day troubles. One of the reasons for this conundrum is that we're overwhelmed on a daily basis.

In this day and age, being busy and having a lot on our plates becomes almost a justification for our existence. As the to-do lists get longer and the periods of unscheduled time shorter, a sense of uneasiness creeps in. No matter how hard we try, the mountain of unfinished tasks and obligations seems to grow only larger, increasingly overshadowing our lives. Our initial frustration, the result of not being able to make headway, inevitably turns into stress, anxiety, and a sense of being overwhelmed. Then everything becomes too much and too difficult to handle, and we don't know where to begin or what to do. From this point, we're just a hop, skip, and a jump away from feeling we're a victim of circumstances. We interpret small mishaps and incidences—spilling a glass of milk, misplacing a bill, being cut off in traffic—as personal attacks by life or the universe that push us over the edge into the abyss of despair and powerlessness.

To move from being victims to becoming the masters of our lives, we need to take responsibility for how we become overwhelmed in the first place and then commit to bold adjustments. So today, let's focus on addressing the preconditions that lead to feeling overwhelmed and victimized by life.

Focus

Become aware of the following habitual patterns that can set you up for feeling stressed and disempowered:

- Overextending yourself and taking on more than you can handle
- Cramming in a last-minute task or activity and thus always running late
- Not maintaining firm boundaries
- Taking responsibility for other people's obligations
- Not prioritizing, but instead viewing everything as equally important and urgent
- Neglecting to define an ending point for your work day

Empowerment Act

To overcome your feeling of being overwhelmed, use the following steps:

1. **Write a fresh list of all the tasks that need to be finished within the next few weeks.** Include only projects that have a start point and an end point. Avoid including daily duties such as getting the kids to school or walking the dog.

2. Condense this list by choosing the top five to ten focus items. Prioritize them according to:

- External conditions, such as the due date for a bill, the guidelines from work, or pressure from your family.
- What gives you the greatest leverage—meaning what makes the greatest difference for you and takes the most weight off your mind (for example, replacing the light bulb in the closet, writing an overdue thank-you card to the in-laws, or completing an unpleasant task at work).
- What is most gratifying and enjoyable for you (for example, getting a new coffee machine, scheduling a haircut, calling a good friend you haven't talked to in a while).

3. Give each project a specific date by which you want to have it completed. Be reasonable with your estimates. This process isn't about fostering your ambitions; it's about taking some pressure off your mind.

4. Determine how long each task will take to complete. Once again, approach this step with generosity, and assume that it will take longer than you can foresee right now.

5. Check your calendar to plan the dates you want to work on that task and how many hours you want to spend on it. Make sure that you don't fill up more than 50 percent of the time you have available. (For example, for an eight-hour work day, plan to spend no more than four hours on work-related tasks). If it turns out you have time to spare that day, you can choose to do more. The difference is that now you will feel ahead of schedule, not lagging behind.

There are multiple benefits to this process. By limiting the number of projects you focus on and by determining their end points and the amount of time they require to complete, you already gain a much greater sense of control over these tasks. When you allocate specific focus times in your calendar, the unfinished tasks no longer weigh heavily on your mind but are now appointments that can be kept and fulfilled easily. At the end of the day, you'll have a satisfying sense of being on top of everything.

Thursday: Freeing Yourself from Taking Anything Personally

At some point in our lives, we've all felt criticized, judged, avoided, rejected, or ignored. And more often than not, we take someone's impolite behavior personally rather than ignoring it. A client once told me that he felt extremely angry and disrespected when people didn't notice him walking on the sidewalk, bumped into him, or just obstructed his way. He also observed that waiters in restaurants deliberately ignored him when he tried to catch their attention. Then there were the selfish drivers who constantly cut him off or blocked him by double parking.

Another client noticed that people always attacked her. Whether she was at work or at the shopping mall, everybody seemed to be so rude and negative toward her that she began to wonder if there was something seriously wrong with her. The other day I even heard someone accusing his newly acquired goldfish of being rude and standoffish.

Carl Jung coined the concept of "perception is projection." Whatever we perceive in others is predominately a reflection of what is going on within ourselves. When we're in a splendid mood, the world appears a much friendlier place than when we're depressed or irritated. As you recall, it all has to do with the filters of our subconscious, which delete, distort, and generalize the input from our environment. It turns out that we're all in the same boat—meaning everybody projects onto everybody else. So theoretically, you can't take personally somebody else's opinion, good or bad, because that opinion says more about them than about you.

Instead of reacting to judgment or unfriendly behavior with self-doubt or hurt, imagine what might be the cause of the others' behavior. Is it possible that they are insecure themselves, that they feel ignored, rejected, or criticized? Maybe they're dealing with tremendous stress in their lives and aren't even fully aware of anything or anybody else. It could also be that they've just had a bad day and feel tired, frustrated, or lonely. Make sure that your story opens the way for more compassion for them and understanding about what may be at the root of their behavior. Although you may never find out what was really going on, you'll discover that your initial, self-deflating reactions quickly disappear.

Taking things personally can be an opportunity to gain greater insights about ourselves and what we may still have to work on. Let's say you're a professional race-car driver and a commuter on the interstate flips you off. Would you take that insult personally, or would you know with every fiber of your being that his reactions are completely unwarranted? I bet in this case it would be very easy for you to deflect this judgment about your driving abilities.

On the flip side, the things we take most to heart are often things we struggle hardest with. So whenever you're reacting with insecurity to something another person has done or said, check with yourself to see if there's a lingering, self-limiting belief deep inside that needs to be addressed. This way, you can see the person who prompted you to discover a residual limiting belief as a teacher and a catalyst for self-empowerment. And you can turn anger and anxiety into acceptance and appreciation.

Today, the focus is on shifting from taking something personally to staying in your power.

Focus

Be aware of when you're taking somebody's comments, opinions, or actions personally. Notice your thoughts, emotions, and energy. What do you think about this person—and yourself? Do you feel anxious and self-conscious? Or irritated and annoyed? Does your energy contract and shrink? Or do you feel shaky and ungrounded?

Empowerment Acts

Ask yourself clarifying questions. Considering the following questions will clarify the situation and interrupt the knee-jerk response of taking something personally:

- Does this person really know me or what's best for me?
- Does this person's behavior say more about me or him/her?
- How can I see the person differently, with more compassion and understanding?
- Am I giving my power to this person? And if so, is my power really in the best hands?
- What do I believe about myself when I choose to take this personally?
- What do I want to believe instead?

Modify your internal interpretation. When you take something personally, chances are that your subconscious holds a distorted view of the situation. That was the case with Jane, the woman I told you about in the previous chapter who didn't dare inform her husband that she wanted a divorce. Just as you can create a new identity (using the process I described in chapter 10), you can completely change how your subconscious perceives and thus feels about whatever you took personally. Here's how:

1. Close your eyes and observe the internal image of this situation.
2. Notice the color, size, and brightness of the picture, how far away from you it is, and the details that are depicted in it. For example, in this picture, are you smaller than the person whose behavior or comments you took personally? Does the person appear to be in the foreground or brighter than you?

3. Adjust those aspects in ways that signal to your subconscious mind that you're reclaiming your power.
4. Imagine that you can send the light energy of compassion and appreciation to the person whose projection you've taken on—and thus gradually dissolve his or her presence from this internal scenario.

After practicing these steps, you'll find that it will be much more difficult to take anything personally—and if you do take something personally, it will be much easier for you to reclaim your power.

Friday: Expressing Yourself and Living Up to Your Size

Ada never felt that her brothers and sisters really cared about her. In fact, whenever she expressed her views and opinions, she felt ridiculed and put down. As the odd one out, she dreaded family events because she felt she could never be herself. "To avoid being attacked," she told me, "I felt I had to hold my breath the entire time and become invisible."

On a day-to-day basis, our need to blend in or fit in outweighs the desire to express our authentic self. We often have a deep-seated fear of standing out, being criticized or rejected, or losing the connection to "the tribe." As a result, speaking up and expressing ourselves can be a major anxiety-triggering challenge. Even in relationships with the people we're closest to, we don't often allow ourselves to share our thoughts, feelings, and needs honestly. We don't clarify hurtful comments and misunderstandings because we don't want to create any conflict. We don't talk about our pains, concerns, and vulnerabilities because we're afraid we might appear needy or weak and, therefore, less attractive—and that's a risk we're unwilling to take.

So we hold ourselves back. We don't allow ourselves to buy the car of our dreams because the neighbors might think we're too flashy, materialistic, or suffering from a midlife crisis. We avoid holding hands with our spouse or partner when we're around our single friends. Or we dress more conservatively to avoid standing out, as did the young woman who once told me she didn't dare wear form-fitting clothes because she feared the other mothers at her daughter's school would judge her. We even downplay our gifts, strengths, and accomplishments because we don't want to make someone feel bad or envious.

Feeling only conditionally accepted, we lose our power and sense of self by believing that who we truly are needs to be hidden. As a result, either we dare to show only the side of us that appears confident, entertaining, and agreeable, or we simply withdraw into obscurity, isolation, and loneliness.

Denying ourselves our right to express our authenticity ties into the subconscious protective patterns of making assumptions and our tendencies to take others' opinions personally. Let's take Ada, for instance. Her assumption that she didn't matter to her family led her to microanalyze their responses to her and interpret the slightest whiff of disapproval as a major rejection. A series of chronic physical ailments led Ada to realize that her tendency to disappear in the presence of her family was rooted in her beliefs that she wasn't good enough or lovable. Although her family might have been the original cause of these beliefs, she admitted that it was now her—and not her family's—responsibility to change them.

"Now I have so much more understanding and compassion for my brothers and sisters," she said. "I can imagine that they felt my insecurity as something uncomfortable and threatening because it reminded them of their own unresolved issues."

By learning to love and appreciate her gifts and values, Ada became so self-empowered that she went on her own path of spiritual and metaphysical exploration. In the past, doing her own thing would have made her feel even more disconnected from her traditional Catholic family. Instead, by that point, she was convinced that her happiness and inner peace would be healing and beneficial for everyone. At the family's next Thanksgiving gathering, she openly shared her newfound spirituality and her more esoteric beliefs without worrying or assuming she'd be judged or rejected. To her delight, before dinner she was asked to offer the blessing. From that point on, various family members frequently consulted Ada for advice and support.

I know it takes courage and strength to openly and honestly show who you really are. But as it becomes more and more normal for you to share both your light and strength along with your needs and vulnerabilities, you'll solidify your foundation of self-acceptance. And once you accept yourself, you're free.

Focus today on breaking through the self-imposed restrictions that have prevented you from fully expressing yourself.

Focus

- **Pay attention to when you hold yourself back from speaking up.** Notice when you refrain from expressing your opinions, asking for what you want, or sharing something personal.

- **Notice when worries about others' judgments stop you from doing something you want.** For example, you might eat lunch at your desk as your colleagues do, even though you would rather eat outside on a park bench. Or perhaps you won't get the mail in your bathrobe because the neighbors might see you. Or maybe you keep your usual, conservative haircut rather than going for one that appears more fun and attractive to you.
- **Be aware of the times when you try to blend in or become invisible.** For example, you might walk down the street with your head down, not looking at anybody, or you might avoid wearing clothes with strong colors. Or, do you always sit in the last row of the theater or choose restaurant tables that are tucked away in a corner?

Empowerment Acts

Practice gestures of self-expression, like the following:

- **Give yourself a voice.** Voice an opinion about something you're interested in. Let yourself be heard when you disagree with someone or are bothered by something. Ask for something you need or would like help with.
- **Challenge yourself to be noticed.** Wear a bright-colored tie or shawl. Share a personal story with a colleague. Tell someone about an accomplishment or a special talent you have.
- **Reach out and connect.** Call a friend or family member you haven't talked to in a while. Strike up a conversation with a stranger at the coffee shop or the bus stop. Make eye contact with the people you meet.
- **Try any form of creative expression.** Sing in the car or shower. Draw. Write a poem, a letter, or a story. Cook a new dish. Get out your camera and take a picture.

By more freely shining the light of who you are into the world, you give yourself permission to expand into your fully actualized self, and you inspire many others to do the same.

Saturday: Clearing Your Energy

There are those days when, despite all your positive affirmations, intentions, and great self-empowering work, you may still feel small and vulnerable—days when just leaving your house makes you feel anxious and insecure, when all you really want is to hide under the blankets in bed. Taking refuge under the covers can be extremely comforting and self-nurturing. However, it's not a long-term solution, and most of the time it's not an option.

Perhaps you routinely feel overwhelmed and drained after a visit to the mall or a dinner party with friends. You watch the news and feel the suffering of the world weighing on your heart. A colleague having a bad day can leave you feeling deflated and depressed. You see yourself as oversensitive and incapable of interacting with the world in sustainable ways.

If you can relate to any of these examples, you're taking on other people's energy and emotions due to extreme empathy, a form of hypersensitivity that is another protective strategy of the subconscious mind. Lack of communication, confusion, and unpredictability in your childhood may have prompted your subconscious to develop a heightened awareness of the subtle cues in the environment. You needed to know what the people around you were thinking and feeling in order to be safe. The downside of this strategy is that, at some point, your internal radar becomes so tuned in to the external that you begin to absorb and take on the energy of others while losing the connection to yourself—the extreme version of taking others personally. The subconscious needs training to discern between the feelings and energies of those around you and your own. It needs to learn how to avoid sponging up input from the environment and to set up a healthy energetic boundary anchored in a solid core of self-awareness.

Another form of energetic cluttering of the subconscious is a continual attachment to the people and situations that have occupied our attention and time. Have you ever found yourself still thinking about work on Saturday morning or waking in the middle of the night because a difficult conversation from a few days ago was still weighing on you? You're experiencing something similar to the reaction you have after attending a rock concert. All is quiet in your bedroom, but your ears don't stop ringing from the noise. In the same way, our subconscious reverberates from the intensity of certain situations that had previously captured all of our energy. In order to provide our mind with the rest it needs to function at its best, it is important to be able to disconnect from outside stimulation and activities and to develop a practice of clearing our subconscious.

Today's focus is on your personal energy and cultivating a practice to detach and free yourself from external influences.

Focus

- **Pay attention to how your feelings shift over the course of the day.** When you notice such a change, ask yourself whether you're feeling your own emotions or whether what you're feeling is a result of tuning in to and picking up others' emotions.
- **When you're in a public place, tune in to yourself to sense whether or not your energy is fluctuating.** Do you feel hyper or drained, spacey or anxious, without any reason you can put your finger on?
- **Notice what people and circumstances stick in your mind, draw on your energy, or pull you out of the present moment.** Are you still thinking about your office colleague, an unfinished project, or a concern you can't do anything about at that moment?

Empowerment Acts

- **Clear your subconscious.** Practice the guided meditation from chapter 9, "Realign with Your Essence," by reading it or listening to the mp3 recording. This meditation helps clear your subconscious and your cellular memory from any energy you may have picked up from outside influences.
- **Detach and rejuvenate.** Using this guided meditation, you can, for the time being, consciously disconnect from the people and situations that may have occupied your thoughts and prevented you from recharging and enjoying your Saturday.
- **When you go out in public, sense and visualize the protective field of energy you've generated during the meditation.** Imagine how this energy keeps any outside influences from overwhelming you and provides you with a comfortable space for quiet, peace, and self-reliance.

The protective shield is a very effective tool for approaching the world from a safer and more empowered place. Rather than being pulled into other people's energy and emotions, you're creating a habit of keeping your subconscious clear and unattached to external influences, and you're staying centered and grounded in your core.

Sunday: Reinforcing the Growth and Learning from Your Week

Let's take one more look at assumptions. Most of our assumptions aren't actually negative but pertain to aspects in our lives that we simply take for granted, such as having a phone that works, a car that starts, a family we come home to, a healthy body that gets us out of bed in the morning. We assume these are normal, stable facts in our lives and don't think or feel much about them—until they're no longer there. Then we become upset and vow to pay the phone bill on time and to take better care of our car, our loved ones, or our health.

How much do you take *yourself* for granted? How often do you simply assume that it's normal to be a good parent, a reliable employee, a decent human being, and a caring friend without really appreciating the value of your efforts and contributions? Good questions, right?

We'll address this topic further in the enforcement step, the final part of CARE. The main question right now is this: *are you aware of how much you've learned and grown in the past week, or are you also just taking the results of your inner work for granted?*

Sunday is the day when you want to lean back, reflect, and enjoy the fruits of your hard work. Instead of doing a focus exercise and empowerment acts, I invite you to simply answer the following empowerment questions. By considering them, you hone the insights you've gained, amplify the progress you've made, and create momentum for further growth during the coming week.

1. What are the top three things that you appreciated or that pleased you this week?
2. In what situations did you express your new, empowered identity?
3. Which negative assumptions did you successfully counter-balance and avoid buying into? Did these assumptions turn out to be false?
4. How well did you take care of yourself this week?
5. What positive choices did you make to avoid feeling overwhelmed?
6. What happened this week that, in the past, you could have taken personally but in this case you didn't?
7. How specifically did you choose to express yourself in a more expansive manner?

• • •

As you move through all seven days' worth of reinforcement exercises, you may find that certain topics are currently more pertinent for your journey of self-empowerment than others. So you may choose to focus on these subjects more frequently. For example, if pleasing others is a major issue for you, you can replace other reinforcement exercises with the one you need, practicing the suggested steps several days of the week instead of just one day.

The reinforcement part of the forty-day program has one main objective: to form a habit of living from a place of intention and alignment with your authentic self. Every day that you focus on these tools and exercises, you're further integrating the empowering work you have done so far into the matrix of your life.

ENHANCE

It's a strange phenomenon. Although gratitude and appreciation are natural emotions, expressing them doesn't come naturally to us at all. As a child, when I was feverishly unwrapping the fabulous toys my aunts and uncles gave me for my birthday or for Christmas, saying thank you wasn't the first thing on my mind. Actually, it was somewhat of a buzz kill when my mom made me write thank-you cards or call up my relatives to express my thankfulness. But at the same time, I always enjoyed it when they expressed their appreciation for the cookies I baked or the little gifts I made for them.

Appreciation is not just a polite gesture, it's a reward or gift for what we have done for others. Imagine you work for someone who expects you to be available at all times but takes you for granted. Instead of appreciating you, your boss either criticizes your efforts or completely ignores you. Sounds like drudgery, right? But don't we often treat ourselves exactly like that?

As you already know, in many ways our subconscious acts as a faithful servant, always ready to follow our conscious guidance, eager to protect and please us. Naturally, the subconscious thrives with appreciative feedback, whereas constant criticism and negative input lead it to feel despondent and to distrust the authority of the conscious mind. Every animal trainer understands that positive reinforcement with a little treat is the best way to teach an animal a new skill.

Unfortunately, for most of us self-appreciation is a highly underdeveloped skill. Early in our lives, well-intended messages such as "Don't show off," "Don't feel too good about yourself," or "Pride goes before a fall" cause us to believe that praising ourselves only leads to arrogance and complacency and, consequently, rejection and failure. In general, we put more stock in the opinions of others than in our own opinions, so self-appreciation seems like a complete waste of time.

Case in point: I routinely ask my clients to write three reasons why they can feel good about themselves every day. Many of them forget that I gave them this assignment; others dutifully write down everything they appreciated about their days—except for themselves. Don't get me wrong—I'm a big believer in the power of routinely acknowledging all the gifts and blessings in our lives. But for the purpose of building confidence, self-trust, and self-love, you need to acknowledge the gifts and blessings that define *who you are.* Which brings me back to the subconscious mind and the enhancement step of CARE.

Every night, write in a special notebook at least three things you appreciated about yourself on that day. Here are three things to keep in mind as you do this:

- **Be specific.** Rather than affirming that you're smart or friendly, write down (at least the Cliffs Notes version) what particular incidents made you realize this today.
- **Make it mainly about "being" you.** I've seen people scribble pages of self-appreciation notes listing all the things they've done for their careers, their families, and their communities. Although this is a step in the right direction, if you value only your contributions and accomplishments, self-appreciation can easily turn into conditional approval, which obstructs your goal of unconditional acceptance of who you are. And your "doing" doesn't necessarily reveal your "being." Pay attention, for example, to the aspects of yourself that the light of your essence illuminates—the qualities that make you a unique and brilliant human being. Acknowledge your sense of humor, your creativity, or your capacity to love. Recognize when you are compassionate and kind or when you take the time to stop and enjoy the beauty of a moment.
- **Be open.** Reflect on your day with an open mind and appreciate both those qualities of yourself that you usually take for granted and those you weren't really aware of until you paid attention to them. Open your heart to truly feel and savor the gratitude for yourself because appreciation without feelings is like a gift that's never been unwrapped.

• • •

Every day you take CARE of yourself, you add another layer to your growing foundation of self-reliance and empowerment. By the way, feel free to commit to these steps beyond the forty days. Some of my clients have been continuously using this program as their mental and emotional framework for a life of excellence and inner peace. According to Yogi Bhajan, "It takes forty days

1	2	3	4	5	6	7	8	9	10
11	12	13	14	15	16	17	18	19	20
21	22	23	24	25	26	27	28	29	30
31	32	33	34	35	36	37	38	39	40

FIGURE 5 Forty days to a new habit

to establish a habit, ninety days to confirm it, and 120 days to master it—and everybody will know it." Isn't the *habit* of being your authentic self and thus inspiring others to discover, embrace, and express their own truth something you want to be known for?

CARE SUMMARY

Center yourself for ten minutes through either long, deep breathing or the one-minute breathing exercise.

Align your mind, heart, and body with your new, self-empowered identity using the six-step empowerment accelerator.

Reinforce the insights, tools, and growth you have created through a daily changing-empowerment focus.

- Monday: Counterbalancing negative assumptions
- Tuesday: Pleasing yourself instead of others
- Wednesday: Becoming the master of your circumstances
- Thursday: Freeing yourself from taking things personally
- Friday: Expressing yourself and living up to your size
- Saturday: Clearing your energy
- Sunday: Reinforcing the growth and learning from your week

Enhance your sense of confidence and self-reliance by writing down every night three specific aspects of yourself you appreciated that day.

At the end of each day, track your progress by checking off the box for that day in figure 5.

Final Words

MAKING PEACE WITH FEAR AND ANXIETY

IN THE MIDST of the United States' Great Depression, President Franklin Delano Roosevelt delivered his inaugural address, during which he said the famous words, "The only thing we have to fear is fear itself—nameless, unreasoning, and unjustified terror which paralyzes needed efforts to convert retreat into advance." He expressed a sentiment most people would agree with. Because of the disempowering qualities of fear and anxiety, these emotions feel as though they're our true enemies that must be fought and conquered.

I imagine that when you picked up this book you shared this perspective, hoping that you would eventually be able to rid yourself of fear and anxiety for good. Now that you've arrived at the end of the program, I'm sure you realize that you haven't lost your ability to create fear and anxiety—and as you now know, that's a good thing. However, what you *have* lost are the self-limiting ways in which you perceived and responded to these emotions.

Like a rock climber holding on to a blade of grass for dear life, you may still cling to old worries about the resurgence of overwhelming fear and anxiety and its potentially debilitating consequences. But at this point, it's safe for you to let go because, if you look down, you'll see that you're no more than two inches off the ground. You have all the necessary insights, resources, strategies, and tools at hand to address fear and anxiety in positive and empowering ways.

We fear what we don't understand, and we avoid what we're afraid of—a combination that isn't conducive to change. It takes courage to face our emotions, patience to listen to their messages, and wisdom to embrace their deeper meanings. All of these virtues have helped you break through the fear of fear itself and develop a new and deeper understanding of its true purpose. Fear and anxiety no longer hold the same meaning for you. Whereas in the past their intensity fueled your desire to control and suppress these feelings, you've since learned to appreciate that your subconscious has your best interest in mind. It makes these feelings so intense and undeniable because they fulfill important functions—functions that I like to refer to as "the healing powers of fear and anxiety."

As you've moved through the processes in this book, you've experienced first-hand that these emotions were the catalysts for the healing of your past. They prodded you to go inside, take an inventory, and address and resolve the deeper root causes of your self-limiting beliefs. By delving more deeply into your fear and anxiety, you've discovered and reintegrated the fragmented parts of your subconscious; released old thoughts, feelings, self-limiting patterns; and reinstated your wholeness. Fear and anxiety were the bridge that led you to your heart so that you could recognize and embrace the light of your true essence. And these emotions were ultimately the impetus for the creation of your new, self-empowered identity, one that allows you to harness your true potential.

You may wonder: what could be the use of fear and anxiety in the future? The other day, a friend of mine told me about her meditation teacher, who said, "In view of the challenges we're facing individually and globally at this time, anxiety is a luxury we no longer can afford." Apart from the fact that most people wouldn't consider being anxious as a self-indulgent hobby, at first glance it certainly appears to be sound advice to dedicate our precious time and focus on more important matters than combating our own fears and worries—unless fear and anxiety have a much more significant purpose than just distracting us and draining our energy. You know by now that is the case.

Looking back, you probably agree that it's easy to take our fears and anxieties too personally by letting them become our reality—or even our identity. Like a galactic black hole, fear and anxiety can seem to swallow all our powers and aspirations, leaving us feeling small and helpless. However, as the processes in this book show, fear and anxiety neither demand our power nor aim to shrink us into insignificance. In many ways, we diminish ourselves by misinterpreting the message these feelings are trying to communicate.

By working with your negative self-talk—the "inner, younger protector" and other aspects of your subconscious mind—your relationship to and communication with fear and anxiety have already significantly changed and improved. The key to making peace with fear and anxiety is to avoid getting caught in their emotional charge and to instead decipher correctly the valuable information they have to convey. Then, ideally, you can make the appropriate adjustments.

I would like to leave you with my fear and anxiety checklist, which contains the most common fear and anxiety triggers and which allows you to accurately pinpoint the reasons you're feeling anxious or worried. By turning to the checklist's questions the minute you start to notice that you're getting anxious or worried, you're already shifting from passively enduring to proactively engaging with your emotions. Then by addressing their underlying causes—for example, through the tools you've masterfully practiced during the forty-day CARE program—you will quickly move beyond them. Even more important, you'll take full advantage of the growth and balance-promoting leverage fear and anxiety offer you.

THE FEAR AND ANXIETY CHECKLIST

Approach this process with the intention of gaining more information about why and what your subconscious is communicating to you through fear and anxiety. Ask yourself the following questions when you begin to feel uneasy, stressed, or self-doubting. Don't overthink the answers. Instead get an intuitive sense for which of the following topics resonates with you the most and appears the most important to address.

1. Did I give my power away by:

- Taking something or someone personally?
- Identifying my self-worth with an external goal or an agenda?
- Trying to please others or meet their expectations?
- Making myself smaller and holding myself back so I wouldn't be judged or rejected?

2. Did I not take care of myself by:

- Neglecting my physical needs or abusing my body?
- Not allowing myself to get enough rest?
- Overwhelming or putting too much pressure on myself?
- Taking on other people's energy, feelings, or problems?
- Dishonoring my personal boundaries?

3. Did I leave my center by:

- Making assumptions and living in a "what if" reality?
- Battling an inner conflict without coming to a resolution?
- Acting against my better knowledge, values, and beliefs?
- Forcing something to happen rather than allowing it to unfold?
- Underappreciating myself and the gifts in my life?

This list has plenty of room to grow and for you to add to it. I can imagine that you're already thinking of personal messages fear and anxiety have been sending you that are not tabulated here. Although you may not always like these memos from your subconscious—who wants to be reminded, for example, that once again you've handed over your power to someone else?—you can be certain that responding to them will serve you in countless ways.

Having come this far in your healing and breakthrough journey, facing your fears no longer means mustering the courage to stare them down and then act in spite of them. For you, the face of fear and anxiety has changed. You no longer see them as debilitating enemies but as friends and guides that are right there to help you claim your power and to be, express, and love who you truly are. Therefore, I believe that ignoring anxiety is a luxury we can no longer afford. Or to expand on President Roosevelt's famous words: the only thing we have to fear is *the fear of* fear itself.

Notes

INTRODUCTION

1. J. C. Reed, "Dysregulation of Apoptosis in Cancer," *Journal of Clinical Oncology* 17, no. 9 (1999): 2941–2953.
2. Friedemann J. Schaub et al., "Fas/FADD-Mediated Activation of a Specific Program of Inflammatory Gene Expression in Vascular Smooth Muscle Cells," *Nature Medicine* 6, no. 7 (2000): 790–796.
3. Y. Barak, "The Immune System and Happiness," *Autoimmunity Reviews* 5, no. 8 (2006): 523–527.
4. T. Hayashi and K. Murakami, "The Effects of Laughter on Post-Prandial Glucose Levels and Gene Expression in Type 2 Diabetic Patients," *Life Sciences* 85, no. 56 (2009): 185–187.
5. Sherita Hill Golden et al., "Examining a Bidirectional Association Between Depressive Symptoms and Diabetes," *Journal of the American Medical Association* 299, no. 23 (2008): 2751–2759.
6. Biing-Jiun Shen et al., "Anxiety Characteristics Independently and Prospectively Predict Myocardial Infarction in Men," *Journal of the American College of Cardiology* 51, no. 2 (2008): 113–119.

CHAPTER 1

1. R. C. Kessler et al., "Prevalence, Severity, and Comorbidity of Twelve-Month DSM-IV Disorders in the National Comorbidity Survey Replication (NCS-R)," *Archives of General Psychiatry* 62, no. 6 (2005): 617–627.

2. Matthew Herper, "America's Most Popular Drugs," *Forbes,* August 14, 2009.
3. Jeff Donn, Martha Mendoza, and Justin Pritchard, "Drugs Found in Drinking Water," *USA Today,* September 12, 2008.

CHAPTER 3

1. J. S. Deloache and V. Lobue, "The Narrow Fellow in the Grass: Human Infants Associate Snakes and Fear," *Developmental Science* 12, no. 1 (2009): 201–207. J. S. Deloache and V. Lobue, "Detecting the Snake in the Grass: Attention to Fear-Relevant Stimuli by Adults and Young Children," *Psychological Science* 19, no. 3 (2008): 284–289. A. Ohman, "Of Snakes and Faces: An Evolutionary Perspective on the Psychology of Fear," *Scandinavian Journal of Psychology* 50, no. 6 (2009): 543–552.
2. Vladin Starcevic, "Review: Worldwide Lifetime Prevalence of Anxiety Disorders Is 16.6%, with Considerable Heterogeneity between Studies," *Evidence-Based Mental Health* 9, no. 115 (2006): 100–113.
3. Jeffrey Brewer, "Snakes Top List of Americans' Fears," *Gallup,* March 19, 2001.
4. J. B. Rosen and J. Schulkin, "From Normal Fear to Pathological Anxiety," *Psychological Review* 105, no. 2 (1998): 325–350.
5. M. Olfson and S. C. Marcus, "National Patterns in Antidepressant Medication Treatment," *Archives of General Psychiatry* 66, no. 8 (2009): 848–856.
6. I. Kirsch and G. Sapirstein, "Listening to Prozac but Hearing Placebo: A Meta-Analysis of Antidepressant Medication," *Prevention and Treatment* 1, no. 2 (1998): article 0002a.

CHAPTER 4

1. K. C. Klemenhagen et al., "Individual Differences in Trait Anxiety Predict the Response of the Basolateral Amygdala to Unconsciously Processed Fearful Faces," *Neuron* 44, no. 6 (2004): 1043–1055.

CHAPTER 5

1. T. Koyama et al., "The Subjective Experience of Pain: Where Expectations Become Reality," *Proceedings of the National Academy of Sciences* 102, no. 36 (2005): 12950–12955.

CHAPTER 7

1. To stream an abbreviated version of the Parts Reintegration Process, visit SoundsTrue.com/bonus/FearSolution.

CHAPTER 8

1. Tad James and Wyatt Woodsmall, *Time Line Therapy and the Basis of Personality* (Capitola, CA: Meta, 1988).
2. S. W. Askay, D. R. Patterson, and S. R. Sharar, "Virtual Reality Hypnosis," *Contemporary Hypnosis* 26, no. 1 (2009): 40–47.
3. Søren Kierkegaard, *The Concept of Anxiety: A Simple Psychologically Orienting Deliberation on the Dogmatic Issue of Hereditary Sin* (Princeton, NJ: Princeton University Press, 1981).
4. Rollo May, *The Meaning of Anxiety* (New York: Norton, 1996), 355.
5. Rollo May, *The Courage to Create* (New York: Norton, 1994), 58.
6. Kierkegaard, 61.
7. To listen to a recording of the Pattern Resolution Process, stream it online at SoundsTrue.com/bonus/FearSolution.

CHAPTER 9

1. Attilio D'Alberto, "Zangfu Theory and Cellular Memory," article on the Chinese Herb Academy website, accessed June 15, 2011, chineseherbacademy.org/articles/cellmem.shtml. Huang Di, *The Yellow Emperor's Classic of Chinese Medicine,* trans. Maoshing Ni (Boston: Shambhala, 1995).
2. G. E. Miller et al., "A Functional Genomic Fingerprint of Chronic Stress in Humans: Blunted Glucocorticoid and Increased NF- B Signaling," *Biological Psychiatry* 64, no. 4 (2008) 266–272.
3. Paul Pearsall, *The Heart's Code* (New York: Broadway Books, 1998).
4. Claire Sylvia and William Novak, *A Change of Heart* (New York: Little, Brown, 1997).
5. Bruce Lipton, *The Biology of Belief: Unleashing the Power of Consciousness, Matter and Miracles* (Carlsbad, CA: Hay House, 2008).
6. R. Khanfer et al., "Altered Human Neutrophil Function in Response to Acute Psychological Stress," *Psychosomatic Medicine* 72, no. 7 (2010): 636–640.

7. J. Bouayed, H. Rameal, and R. Soulimani, "Oxidative Stress and Anxiety: Relationship and Cellular Pathways," *Oxidative Medicine and Cellular Longevity* 2, no. 2 (2009): 63–67.
8. Elissa S. Epel et al., "Accelerated Telomere Shortening in Response to Life Stress," *Proceedings of the National Academy of Sciences* 101, no. 29 (2004): 17312–17315.
9. A. H. Goldfarb and A. Z. Jamurtas, "Beta-Endorphin Response to Exercise: An Update," *Sports Medicine* 24, no. 1 (1997): 8–16.
10. Richard J. Davidson et al., "Alterations in Brain and Immune Function Produced by Mindfulness Meditation," *Psychosomatic Medicine* 65 (2003): 564–570. S. I. Nidich et al., "A Randomized Controlled Trial on Effects of the Transcendental Meditation Program on Blood Pressure, Psychological Distress, and Coping in Young Adults," *American Journal for Hypertension* 22, no. 12 (2009): 1326–1331. J. Kabat-Zinn, L. Lipworth, and R. Burney, "The Clinical Use of Mindfulness Meditation for the Self-Regulation of Chronic Pain," *Journal of Behavioral Medicine* 8, no. 2 (1985): 163–190.
11. R. Manocha et al., "A Randomized, Controlled Trial of Meditation for Work Stress, Anxiety and Depressed Mood in Full-Time Workers," *Evidence-Based Complementary and Alternative Medicine* 2011 (2011). J. Vøllestad, B. Sivertsen, and G. H. Nielsen, "Mindfulness-Based Stress Reduction for Patients with Anxiety Disorders: Evaluation in a Randomized Controlled Trial," *Behaviour Research and Therapy* 49, no. 4 (2011): 281–288.
12. B. W. Smith et al., "A Pilot Study Comparing the Effects of Mindfulness-Based and Cognitive-Behavioral Stress Reduction," *Journal of Alternative and Complementary Medicine* 14, no. 3 (2008): 251–258.
13. To stream this guided meditation, "Realign with Your Essence," visit SoundsTrue.com/bonus/FearSolution and the author's website, thefearandanxietysolution.com.

CHAPTER 10

1. S. M. Friedman et al., "Falls and Fear of Falling: Which Comes First? A Longitudinal Prediction Model Suggests Strategies for Primary and Secondary Prevention," *Journal of the American Geriatrics Society* 50, no. 8 (2002) 1329–1335.

2. A. Dijksterhuis et al., "On Making the Right Choice: The Deliberation-Without-Attention Effect," *Science* 311, no. 5763 (2006): 1005–1007.

CHAPTER 11

1. Aaron Antonovsky, *Health, Stress, and Coping* (San Francisco: Jossey-Bass, 1979).

Acknowledgments

MY INTENTION FOR this book is to provide people who suffer from fear and anxiety with a step-by-step process to overcome these emotions and to learn and grow from them. The work described here is based upon my experiences with the many clients I have had the privilege to support during their healing journey. I am very grateful for their trust and confidence in my work and for their courage, openness, and commitment to breaking through these emotional challenges. Their changes and breakthroughs are truly inspirational and demonstrate that by consciously working with our subconscious mind, we all have access to unlimited healing potential within.

I am thankful for the founders of Neuro-Linguistic Programming, Richard Bandler and John Grinder, and for Dr. Tad James, the founder of Time Line Therapy. The outstanding work of these pioneers in healing with the subconscious mind has greatly influenced my practice and the program described in this book.

Having studied with Dr. Tad James and his wife, Adriana James, for several years, I greatly appreciate all their teachings and wisdom, which have transformed my life on a personal and professional level.

I want to thank Michelle Sherman of the Vast Institute, who encouraged and coached me to venture off the path of allopathic medicine and pursue my own healing work.

My gratitude goes to my personal editor, the very gifted Kelly Malone, for her extremely valuable suggestions, deletions, and comments—which gave the book much greater clarity and structure—and for her patience and uncanny ability to uplift me with her great sense of humor.

Thanks to Andrea Rouleau's creativity and artistry for the original designs of the figures.

I also would like to give thanks to my fabulous agent, Stephanie Tade, for believing in this book and ushering it to the perfect publisher.

I am deeply appreciative for the wonderful people at Sounds True, especially Tami Simon and Jennifer Y. Brown, for saying yes to publishing this book—and to everyone else who makes Sounds True a joy to work with.

My heartfelt gratitude goes to my editor, Amy Rost, for her enthusiastic support and thoughtful attention to detail during the final "midwifing" of the book, and to copyeditor Laurel Kallenbach and production editor Jennifer Holder, who skillfully provided this work with its final polish.

Words can't describe my appreciation for my beloved wife, Danielle. I thank you for your love, your friendship, and your unshakable belief in me and my mission; for your gentle and persistent nudges to complete the first manuscript; for all your editorial guidance; and for grounding me and reminding me to continue to take care of myself. You are and always will be the greatest blessing in my life.

Index

Note: Italicized page numbers indicate figures.

About the Author

FRIEDEMANN SCHAUB, MD, PhD, received his medical degree from the University of Munich and pursued a career in cardiology at the Munich University Hospital before moving to Seattle where he received a doctorate in molecular biology from the University of Washington. His research has been published and featured in national and international medical and science journals.

After more than fifteen years in the medical field, Dr. Schaub became increasingly fascinated by the powerful influence of our thoughts, emotions, and beliefs on health and disease. He recognized that our abundant self-healing abilities can function effectively only when mind, body, and spirit are in alignment, and that the mind-body-spirit connection—in particular the subconscious mind—holds the keys to accelerated healing, well-being, and success. Realizing this enormous potential, he extensively studied mind-activating modalities and became a certified master practitioner in Neuro-Linguistic Programming (NLP) and Time Line Therapy. He is also an American Board of Hypnotherapy (ABH)–certified trainer of clinical hypnotherapy.

Based on this wealth of knowledge and experience, Dr. Schaub created a personal breakthrough and empowerment program specifically designed to eliminate emotional and mental blocks and limitations that prevent us from fully activating our potential to heal, change, and succeed. He has helped thousands of people all over the world overcome fear and anxiety to lead confident, authentic, and successful lives.

Dr. Schaub lives with his wife, Danielle, in Seattle. For more details about his work, please visit his website, cellularwisdom.com.

About Sounds True

Sounds True is a multimedia publisher whose mission is to inspire and support personal transformation and spiritual awakening. Founded in 1985 and located in Boulder, Colorado, we work with many of the leading spiritual teachers, thinkers, healers, and visionary artists of our time. We strive with every title to preserve the essential "living wisdom" of the author or artist. It is our goal to create products that not only provide information to a reader or listener, but that also embody the quality of a wisdom transmission.

For those seeking genuine transformation, Sounds True is your trusted partner. At SoundsTrue.com you will find a wealth of free resources to support your journey, including exclusive weekly audio interviews, free downloads, interactive learning tools, and other special savings on all our titles.

To listen to a podcast interview with Sounds True publisher Tami Simon and author Friedemann Schaub, please visit SoundsTrue.com/bonus/FearSolution.